Growing Up with Vampires

Growing Up with Vampires

Essays on the Undead in Children's Media

Edited by Simon Bacon *and* Katarzyna Bronk

McFarland & Company, Inc., Publishers
Jefferson, North Carolina

ALSO OF INTEREST

To Boldly Go: Essays on Gender and Identity in the Star Trek *Universe,* edited by Nadine Farghaly and Simon Bacon (McFarland, 2017)

LIBRARY OF CONGRESS CATALOGUING-IN-PUBLICATION DATA

Names: Bacon, Simon, 1965– editor. | Bronk, Katarzyna, editor.
Title: Growing up with vampires : essays on the undead in children's media / edited by Simon Bacon and Katarzyna Bronk.
Description: Jefferson, North Carolina : McFarland & Company, Inc., Publishers, 2018. | Includes bibliographical references and index.
Identifiers: LCCN 2018023797 | ISBN 9781476675527 (softcover : acid free paper) ∞
Subjects: LCSH: Vampires in mass media. | Children's mass media.
Classification: LCC P96.V35 G76 2018 | DDC 809/.93375—dc23
LC record available at https://lccn.loc.gov/2018023797

BRITISH LIBRARY CATALOGUING DATA ARE AVAILABLE

ISBN (print) 978-1-4766-7552-7
ISBN (ebook) 978-1-4766-3387-9

© 2018 Simon Bacon and Katarzyna Bronk. All rights reserved

No part of this book may be reproduced or transmitted in any form or by any means, electronic or mechanical, including photocopying or recording, or by any information storage and retrieval system, without permission in writing from the publisher.

Front cover image © 2018 MorozVyacheslav/iStock

Printed in the United States of America

McFarland & Company, Inc., Publishers
 Box 611, Jefferson, North Carolina 28640
 www.mcfarlandpub.com

For Elbie B-B and Majki

Table of Contents

Introduction
    Simon Bacon *and* Katarzyna Bronk   1

Section One: Children's Media— Chronologies and Mediums

Children of the Night: Mainstreaming Vampires Through Children's Media
    Andrew M. Boylan   17

An Invitation to a Beheading (and Another to a Birthday Bash): Encountering Dracula in Contemporary Gothic Metamorphoses Books
    Jen Baker   29

The Drawn Daughters of Dracula: Vampire Girlhood in British Comics of the 1970s and 1980s
    Jack Fennell   47

Section Two: Negotiating Femininity and Identity

Jeepers Creepers: The American Vampirization of the Female Immigrant Teacher in *Vampires Don't Wear Polka Dots*
    Sharon Pajka   63

Under Her Batwings: Jung's Shadow Aspect as Depicted in *Monster High* and *My Little Pony* Vampires
    Jacquelyn E. Bent   82

Metamorphosis of the Blood: Vampiric Femininity in Contemporary Children's Fiction
    Chloé Germaine Buckley   95

Problematic Parenting: Tweens and Vampire Fiction
    LESLIE J. ORMANDY   112

Section Three: Symbolism, Meanings and Interpretations

Dick and Jane and Vampires: The Interstitial Bridge Between Social Imaginary and Spirituality
    PHIL FITZSIMMONS   131

The Dhampir Gets His Fangs: Miscegenation and Exogamy in the Hotel Transylvania Film Franchise
    MARK CHEKARES   150

Food for Thought: Vegetarian Vampires in Children's Reading Diets
    JANE M. KUBIESA   166

Every Generation Gets the Vampire It Needs: What Can Vampire Narratives in Children's Films Tell Us About Childhood in the Twenty-First Century?
    ALLISON MOORE   183

Looking Back and Seeing the Future: Adult Nostalgia and Negotiating the Future in Children's Books and Films Featuring Vampires
    SIMON BACON AND KATARZYNA BRONK   200

About the Contributors   217

Index   219

Introduction

SIMON BACON *and* KATARZYNA BRONK

While previously somewhat overlooked, horror and gothic texts intended for children—particularly for children 12 years old and younger—is a growing area of research. Studies focusing solely on the figure of the vampire in the context of narratives aimed at children are even more rare, making this volume an important addition to the field. As such, it functions as an opening foray into the possible uses, meanings and symbolism of the vampire in western culture across various media and historical periods.

The figure of the vampire is so prevalent in Western 21st-century culture, both for adults and children, it is almost difficult to think of a time when the undead would not have been viewed as acceptable for younger audiences. The familiarity of Count Dracula's widow's peak, silk-lined cloak, impenetrable Eastern European accent and (plastic) fangs[1] makes him not only a regular for Halloween "trick or treating" and costume parties, but also an integral part of popular culture in the new millennium. And yet, there was a period when this stagey-looking vampire was considered so shocking that nurses were on hand for fainting audience members in the theaters where the film *Dracula* (Browning 1931) was being shown.[2] In fact it was not until almost the 1950s that the vampire on film was given a rating that meant older children would be allowed to watch it in cinemas. This change was mainly due to the then highly successful comedy duo of Abbott and Costello who spoofed the classic Universal monsters (Dracula, the Wolf Man, the Mummy and Frankenstein's Monster) in a series of comedy horror films labeled "Meet the Monsters" (see Miller), with *Bud Abbott and Lou Costello Meet Frankenstein* (Barton 1948) being the most important of these, at least in terms of the figure of the vampire, which is played by Bela Lugosi.[3] Lugosi plays the role of Count Dracula quite seriously but the tomfoolery of the comedians around him highlights the way in which even he is acting like himself playing Dracula, creating a level of parody and self-spoofing. As noted by Kamilla Elliot, "recast and typecast as Dracula in subsequent films, he [Lugosi] was already a parody of himself as original" (28).[4] This has the effect of diffusing the anxiety around the figure of the vampire count, as Catherine Spooner states, the notion of copying and parody opens up an area of gothic humor or campness that proposes a "comic version of the world" (132) which subsequently allows for the creation of increasingly child-friendly versions of the undead.

This idea of parody certainly informs the increasingly family-friendly versions of vampires that began to appear in the 1960s, such as Grandpa in *The Munsters* (Burns and Hayward 1964–1966) and Morticia in *The Addams Family* (Levy 1964–1966), and most famously in the figure of Count Von Count in *Sesame Street* from 1972. All of these films referenced and spoofed culturally well-known vampire characteristics, with Grandpa and Count Von Count playing on signifiers taken from Lugosi's portrayal of Dracula, while Morticia drew from earlier female vampires such as Countess Zeleska (*Dracula's Daughter*, Lambert 1936), Luna (*Mark of the Vampire*, Browning 1935)[5] and Vampira from the series of the same name.[6] The 1970s were something of a watershed decade for the vampire, seeing it more completely change from a monstrous other into a misunderstood, often romantic, hero that might be more suitable for children. Of course, in retrospect, literary characters such as Heathcliff from Emily Brontë's *Wuthering Heights* (1847) are now also recast as vampires or vampire-like, but it was the '70s that really changed the relationship between the undead and popular culture. The main thing that facilitated this change was that the vampire was allowed to speak for itself.

Speaking for Oneself

Count Dracula's absolute otherness and monstrosity are maintained in Stoker's novel as his words and thoughts are only ever described or explained by others, ostensibly those that are trying to kill him—the same is true of the Hammer Dracula films where it is usually the vampire slayers that interpret the intentions of the undead. This situation, arguably, remained in place up until Anne Rice published *Interview with the Vampire* in 1976. The plot of the novel sees a vampire, Louis de Pointe du Lac, telling his life story to a reporter, and while much of what he relates is monstrous, his motivations, angst and remorse make him a compelling, almost tragic figure, or antihero, that the audience/reader can relate to. It was a fundamental shift in the portrayal of the vampire across all mediums and one that was soon to make its way into narratives meant for children.

It was also seen in films from the period, many of which featured vampire children or teenagers, such as George Romero's *Martin* (1978).[7] It was possibly one of the most mundane, domestic, down-to-earth vampire films made until that point in time. The protagonist, the eponymously named Martin, might be a young boy having some kind of mental breakdown *or* an ages-old vampire. By the end of the film even he does not seem to know which. At one point, he dons fake fangs and a cape to scare his cousin, Tata Cuda, parodying both the genre and the expectations of the world around him—the latter embodied in his aged relative, a would-be vampire killer. But by wearing the stereotypical "props" of the vampire, or by parodying it, he only seems to fracture his personality more. Stacey Abbott interestingly reads the film as also being about disaffected youth—Martin is potentially in his late teens—which sees much of his internal conflict reflecting the one occurring in the real world between the younger and older generation. The vampire youth expresses not so much the child that cannot grow up but, as Abbott notes, the one who "is trapped in a seemingly hopeless world created by the adults who surround him" (94).

This idea is seen even more clearly in the figure of Claudia from *Interview with the Vampire*, who is made into a vampire when she is five years old. On being turned she does not just become immortal but, through the will of her sire/maker, is forced to look like a perfect little girl. As Claudia herself says "Do you want me to be a doll forever?" (Jordan 1994). Nina Auerbach explains this further "she [Claudia] is a visual icon of arrested development … who will always look like a doll, vampirism is no release from patriarchy, but a perpetuation of it until the end of time" (154).

Martin and *Interview with the Vampire* are both narratives meant for an adult audience, but their themes of the child being trapped in a world not of their own making is a useful one to take forward. It begins to delineate one of the many reasons why vampires work so well in narratives meant for children—they equally embody the notion of being trapped in a world they have no control over and yet are not of that world; something that children trying to find their own place in the world can often experience. As with the discussion of parody, something of a gap opens up between the world the child is born into and the one the vampire allows them to enter/escape into. This forms one of the core themes of essays in this volume, where the "twixt" nature of vampire, and many of the narratives featuring them, permits this "gap" of agency to open up in their stories allowing for individual and unique identity positions for the characters involved, and by inference, for readers/audience as well.

Difference and Agency

In very broad terms, texts produced for younger children represent such forms of agency as some kind of acceptance of difference, where the vampires' innate otherness is no longer configured as monstrous, threatening, and therefore scary, but special, idiosyncratic, and in need of understanding. The exact form of this otherness is worthy of closer examination because it is not just centered on how the vampire differs from humans in the 21st century, but also on the historical "baggage," or what Judith Halberstam calls "traces," that they bring with them. Halberstam constructs her argument around the seminal gothic "monsters," Mary Shelley's Frankenstein's Monster, Robert Louis Stevenson's Mr. Hyde and, of course, Stoker's Count Dracula—though one could equally include Sheridan Le Fanu's female vampire, Carmilla—which were created in the 19th century. As such, they embody all that respectable—more often than not Victorian—society viewed as monstrous; they are quite literally constructed from all the things, sexual, racial, etc., that society finds threatening and/or hates. Halberstam speaks of Gothic economies—with the Victorian period being viewed as the driving impetuous of future capitalistic intent—and notes anti–Semitism and deviant sexual practice (anything non-heteronormative) as being "written upon the body" (349) of said monsters. Count Dracula in particular is a product of these gothic technologies that reproduce his traces of anti–Semitism and homophobia over time with each new incarnation and on into the future.[8] This would seem a far stretch from contemporary children's stories and yet the vampires that appear in them carry this "baggage" with them.

Monsters, even in narratives for children, are meant to be monstrous. They are created specifically by cultures to give shape to their deepest fears and anxieties as well as to warn and socialize its members to obey the rules and regulations of society. Fairytales are an obvious example of how this is done in regard to the socialization of children, as observed by A. Levorato: "it has been proved that fairy tales help children to discover their place in society, influencing to a great to a great extent how they apprehend the world surrounding them" (149). Though as Jack Zipes notes, certain texts and/or intertextualizations both reflect and create "possibilities for a different socialization process from the standard children's books" (60). The overlaying, or intertextuality of gothic texts with children's stories can often be seen to enact this "different process" or produce the gaps where alternate readings can be made.

Alternate readings themselves are also highly dependent on the historical and cultural context that a text is being read in. So, for example, a text such as *Gruesome and Bloodsocks* (Holiday), meant for early readers, shows a teenage vampire leave her bloodthirsty family to go and live in council housing where she makes friends with her neighbors by saving their cars from kidnappers. The gothic overlaying of Gruesome's story sees her as a vampire denying her father's authority, referencing *Dracula's Daughter* (Hilliard), the first text to show such a rebellious undead daughter. As such,

Gruesome inevitably carries the traces of undesirable femininity and lesbianism that constructed the figure of the monstrous female vampire in pre–World War II America. In contrast, in 1980s Britain, being a rebellious woman was not quite so bad, and even less so if it meant that she was spurning her outsider family to be integrated into mainstream society. The UK at this time was experiencing many race riots due to lack of ethnic integration and multicultural recognition, and so Gruesome, as the ultimate outsider, a vampire, represents a positive move toward acculturation. However, looking back from the early 21st century, Gruesome can be seen as a victim on two counts: first, she is vilified because of her unusual dietary habits—she likes to eat unusual combinations of foods, as she is allergic to blood—marking her as culturally different and undesirable; second, to be accepted, she has to deny her true historical/cultural background. As such, her act of resistance to gain individual agency can now be read as leading to a loss of her true identity.

Undead Negotiations

Texts meant for children that contain gothic elements then multiply the amount of layering involved, which might be better described as an intersectional arrangement that has no fixed meaning but which opens up an area within which all the forces involved can interact and be negotiated with in an ongoing process of meaning making. The idea of a text never having a totally fixed meaning is important then, as it suggests the ambivalence, or "gap" that Spooner spoke about earlier, and that what a child can take away from a text is constantly open to revision and renegotiation. Meaning then is made not just through the layering of texts in the work itself, but also through its interaction with the reader/audience and their own historical and cultural contexts.

A Thoroughly Modern Vampire

Within this it is worth mentioning the nature and positioning of the vampire itself, for while it is obviously part of the Gothic "fictional" tradition, it has manifested itself in very particular ways that can been seen to give it an extra dimension and importance within 21st-century culture. As such, there are two characteristics or aspects of the contemporary vampire that are important to mention in relation to children's narratives.

The first is the ubiquity of the vampire across multiple mediums and platforms—television, films, advertisements, gaming, comics, books, costumes, etc.—seeing it create a world of its own, that on some level intersects with our everyday existence. Henry Jenkins describes this process as convergence culture, which he sees particularly in terms of the multi-media promotion and consumption of films, where transmedia narratives—he particularly cites *The Matrix* (The Wachowski Brothers 1999) as its narrative was disseminated across many different mediums and platforms—create a believable and intersectional universe around the characters, narratives, and meanings (93–130). The vampire here is not restricted to one storyline but many, often with contradictory details and outcomes, yet they all combine to produce an overarching impression of some form of reality.[9]

Secondly is the depiction of vampires in popular culture. This is not just about them becoming more family friendly, or vegetarian, or wearing fashionable clothes but what vampires or vampirism is able to offer to those that embrace it. If seminal texts in the vampire genre, such as Polidori's *The Vampyre* (1819), or Le Fanu's *Carmilla* (1872), show that it is extremely dangerous to accept the attentions of the undead, narratives in the late 20th and early 21st century like the Twilight Saga (Meyer 2005–2008), *The Little Vampire* (Edel 2000), and *Let the Right One In* (Alfredson 2008) are examples of a very different result where the young human associate of the undead gains happiness and individual agency. Victoria Nelson observes that young fans of the Twilight Saga do not want be like Bella Swan but to actually be her (262), not unlike the way children used to want to be Cinderella or Snow White. The vampire is no longer a threat but a chance at gaining control over one's life and a world that is often confusing, threatening, and violent.

This level of cultural recognition and acceptance helps to make the vampire a believable enough character for it to be able to convey and/or embody the child's own feelings of otherness, outsidership, and/or desire for personal agency. What is of particular note here—and some of the essays in this volume focus on this aspect—is the way in which the vampire's otherness is rarely represented as being a simple case of being different—in the way that someone from another cultural or ethnic background is—but carries a power and agency that the human characters do not. In fact, even pretending to be a vampire can be enough to gain its power[10]—see Mona in *Mona the Vampire* (Holleyman), Robin in *Young Dracula* (Robins and Tetsell), and Resus Negative in *Scream Street* (Donbavand). The powers bestowed by the vampire hark back to its supernatural gothic roots and its effects change overtime, for Mona it provides impetuous for her own gifts, for Robin it makes him feel special, and for Resus it allows him to blend in as "normal." As such, any reading of a text meant for a young audience needs to negotiate both the cultural expectations and needs of that audience as well as the ghosts of history that linger around any of the gothic characters or narratives used within those texts.

Subsequently, this volume is about exploring the areas of ambivalence arising at the many intersections between the layering of children's and gothic texts, the forms of intertextual referencing and parody being applied, as well as the nature of the mediums utilized and audience/reader interaction, while positioning them in relation to their historical and cultural contexts to exemplify some of the possible readings.

Chronologies, Readings and Possible Meanings

The book itself is divided into three sections that explore themes around the topics of chronologies and mediums, femininities and identity, and symbolism, meanings and interpretation, respectively. The first part is "Children's Media—Chronologies and Mediums," which works as something of an introduction to vampires in texts meant for children as well as opening discussions on the types of media used, all of which would come under the general heading of popular culture. It begins with Andrew M. Boylan's "Children of the Night: Mainstreaming Vampires Through Children's Media." The essay offers a selected introductory overview of novels, films, and television programs featuring vampires that were intended for children, while also touching upon some selected intersections with adult media that features vampiric children. Beginning in the 19th century, Boylan traces the evolution of the child vampire until it, and its adult counterparts, were deemed acceptable for children. Picking out texts of importance, the author notes the inevitable entrenchment of vampires in narratives for the under twelves where now it can, arguably, represent all things to all readers. This is largely due to its malleability and cultural recontextualization, as Boylan notes, "This also allows the vampire to be symbolic of youth culture, positively as the hero, negatively as the villain and rebelliously as the anti-hero." Boylan's essay provides a useful starting point and broad introduction to the topic and texts, allowing later studies to hone in and focus on more specific areas of interest.

Jen Baker widens this theme of possible platforms for the interaction of vampires and children in her examination of "metamorphosis" or "pop-up" books in "An Invitation to a Beheading (and Another to a Birthday Bash): Encountering Dracula in Contemporary Gothic Metamorphoses Books." These books extend the more usual flat-page picture books for children into something more wholly interactive, as the author notes they can feature "mechanical movable elements ... pullable tabs, pop-ups, liftable flaps ... pull-out documents and three dimensional buildings, or interactive components such as sounds created by pushing buttons, or puzzles, textured pages, and figurines." She further enhances the more mechanical side of such stories to include the idea of gothic layering mentioned previously, or what she calls here gothic metamorphoses books, "which draw from the history of the gothic spectacle and the theatrical devices of horror, and fuse them with a familiar literary source." The vampire here is not always the friendly type, and interestingly the use of the anxiety or fear produced by the more traditional undead plays a large part in the meaning making process. If the films, television series and, arguably less so, books cited in the first article can be seen to wash over its child audience, the medium of pop-ups demands interaction and participation from its readers—one almost has to enter the three dimensional "world" of the metamorphosis book. This highlights the importance of the audience in any act of meaning making, particularly in a medium that is as performative and theatrically centered as the ones mentioned in Baker's essay.

The comics discussed in Jack Fennell's essay, "The Drawn Daughters of Dracula: Vampire Girlhood in British Comics of the 1970s and 1980s," continues to open up the ways in which a medium allows for different forms of "reader" engagement. The layout of the page in comic books, as Benjamin Smith notes, allows for the audience to control their own speed of engagement with the narrative (19–20), which is combined with the deferred pleasures of the weekly installment that typified so many childhoods in the 1970s and '80s, as mentioned in Fennell's study. Unlike the previous two essays, "Drawn Daughters" focuses on narratives meant for girls, though as the author points out, such distinctions were not so important for female readers and "that girls were just as interested as boys in comics, and if the newspaper strip figures are reliable, children at the time did not seem to care which gender the comic was intended for." That said, comics such as *Tammy* and *Misty* created stories aimed at a female readership, featuring vampires where the heroines were represented as "curious and courageous," offering an independence of thought and action that the real world often seemed to discourage. Other comics, meant for slightly younger children, like *Monster Fun* and *Buster*, contained main female characters that were actually vampires themselves. One such was Draculass, who typified much of what the vampire can bring to children's texts, and as Fennell comments, "it is not difficult to see how Draculass might have appealed to girls who felt like they did not fit in (or did not want to); like other vampires, she demonstrated an alternative, powerful femininity." The closing essay in this section then begins to delineate the ways in which the intersection of the figure of the vampire with narrative, medium and audience engagement allows for both identification opening up spaces for individual agency and identity positions. This leads into the second portion of the volume, which deals more explicitly with how the vampire in children's texts allows for gaps of ambivalence to open up and individual readings to be made.

Femininity and Identity

The next section, "Negotiating Femininity and Identity," starts with Sharon Pajka and her essay "Jeepers Creepers: The American Vampirization of the Female Immigrant Teacher in *Vampires Don't Wear Polka Dots*." Unlike many of the essays here, this one does not show the vampire as a potential figure of child agency, but instead as an examination of how wider society views outsiders. As Pajka explains, the female, foreign schoolteacher, Mrs. Jeepers, who might or might not be undead, "becomes a model for analyzing the construction of gender, the representation of teachers in children's books, and the American response to immigrants." The interjection of the vampire into the tale of the ordinarily sedate Bailey City school causes much anxiety for the school children and, potentially, the readers especially, as the story follows many of the gothic tropes of the genre with mysterious boxes, unexplained appearances and disappearances, and the strange power the female teacher seems to have over her pupils. While many children's books feature school teachers as characters, the intersection of vampire imagery brings to the fore ideas about gender and ethnic difference and cultural anxieties around the figure of the immigrant—a topic that is even more prescient now than it was back in the 1990s when *Vampires Don't Wear Polka Dots* was published. The teacher is eventually accepted by her charges and her foreignness becomes something that makes her memorable and special rather than untrustworthy, even if the air of vampiric mystery is never dispelled—though arguably this is what makes her a "different kind of woman" and a "role model" for young girls.

If Mrs. Jeepers shows that embracing otherness can be a good thing, then Jacquelyn E. Bent's essay argues that it is vitally important to becoming a whole, and arguably, better person. In her essay, "Under Her Batwings: Jung's Shadow Aspect as Depicted in *Monster High* and *My Little Pony* Vampires," Bent looks at two highly popular contemporary franchises that are specifically aimed at young girls.[11] Both franchises feature characters that are either vampires, or at certain points take on vampiric traits. *Monster High* in particular receives much negative criticism for its unrealistic body types, not unlike Barbie (both franchises are owned by Mattel) and explicitly shows its gothic influences, as the main characters are all daughters of the classic movie monsters—Dracula, Frankenstein's Monster, the Mummy, etc. In contrast, *My Little Pony* features talking ponies that are "kind yet flawed creatures that extol the magic of friendship" but its gothic layering is often more hidden. It largely reveals them through its heavy referencing of myth and legend, not always wholly Western, as characters and plot lines that seem to push their way up into the consciousness of the viewer (the study concentrates on the TV shows that serve as a central focus for both franchises), which invites the kind of Jungian interpretation given by Bent. Each series sees characters expressing and often embracing their dark sides, which often reveal themselves as the more traditional vampire traits of aggression, threatening behavior, and "baring ones fangs." Unfortunately, as the author notes, often the shows are not allowed to go as far as they might due to industry regulations, but they still manage to encourage young girls to a level of self-acceptance of their good and bad sides.

Chloé Germaine Buckley continues the study of feminine identity in children's literature. In "Metamorphosis of the Blood: Vampiric Femininity in Contemporary Children's Fiction," the author examines late 20th/early 21st-century Gothic texts meant for children, or tweens,[12] in the light of 19th-century vampires. Traditionally, female vampires in particular, as Germaine Buckley observes, are described through a pathologizing lens that sees the vampirized female body as diseased, contagious, and ultimately needing to be cured to be reintegrated into patriarchal society. As the author notes, "The vampiric feminine of nineteenth-century Gothic is composed of ambiguities and anxieties about 'normative' femininity," and the traces of these are brought forward into more recent children's narratives featuring female vampires. Subsequently, Germaine Buckley utilizes texts that go against such readings, often seeing vampirism as a positive condition, and observes, "children's novels explicitly rewrite elements of their source texts, paving the way for a more determined overturning of a pathologized femininity (as weakness, voicelessness, confinement) in twenty-first-century children's Gothic." Female agency then becomes an ongoing negotiation that the child makes with the expectations of the adult world around her.

Leslie J. Ormandy continues on the thread of literature meant for older, tween children in her essay, "Problematic Parenting: Tweens and Vampire Fiction." Here, though, the role of the vampire changes, returning to something like that seen in Sharon Pajka's essay, where it becomes a cypher for real-world situations, or more specifically in this piece, entering into the world of adults. Ormandy's study focuses on "the wide variety of parents and parental stand-ins, such as teachers or authoritative adults who are both like, and unlike their own, [that] allows the 'tween a distanced and less emotionally traumatic experience concerning growing up and eventually leaving home." In the texts examined, the absent parent, for whatever reason, is often replaced by the figure of the vampire—this makes an interesting contrast to the many teen vampire films of the 1980s where absent parents often allowed entrance to the monstrous vampire whose eventual destruction signaled the teenage boys' entry into manhood.[13] The vampire in these more contemporary written texts becomes a catalyst for negotiating with the otherness of a new dimension, one without the constantly available/dependable parent. The challenge of this "entirely new world" is, as Ormandy notes, that it is one "in which they usually acquire full agency," that can allow them to "reach for new opportunities" even while they have to "comply to new rules." However, as the essay suggests, one's transition into adulthood, or finding oneself, is possible "with a little help from a vampire."

The final section of this volume continues to explore how the intersection of the Gothic often subverts contemporary texts, but less in terms of identity positions and more in what the meaning of said text might be in the context of the 21st century.

Symbolism, Meanings and Interpretations

This final part of the book opens with "*Dick and Jane and Vampires*: The Interstitial Bridge Between Social Imaginary and Spirituality" by Phil Fitzsimmons. The essay is a close reading of a recent addition to a series of children's books that were once a stalwart of the American education system, the Dick and Jane books. The story examined here sees the interjection of the figure of the vampire into what were traditionally everyday adventures to help young children learn to read. This imposter from the gothic past is only the first of the many intersections that occur in Fitzsimmons' analysis that considers the traces not only of an American past—as represented in the dress worn by the books characters—but its reception and engagement with an Australian audience, being where the author is based, but also the ways in which pictorial cues and mismatches often contradict the message that is conveyed by the text. The unraveling of pictorial meaning making is central to the author's study, and to what is understood by the book's intended audience, as the author observes, "Visual elements are sublimated by children at both the conscious and unconscious levels ... and are the pictorial spaces where intuition and ideas interact ... and that the representation so created constitutes the world we [they] operate in." What follows is an in-depth picking apart of the narrative's visual meaning so that what superficially appears to be a whimsical, parodic text integrated into the schematics of a children's book becomes a call for subversion and new identity positions beyond that from which the world is currently constructed. As Fitzsimmons observes in regard to the continually changing figure of the undead and its affect on the ideologically "safe" text, "the constant morphing of the vampire images speaks to the possibility of a new mindset in an emerging generation that in actuality is suspended between multiple forms and identities, and threatens to shatter all cultural distinctions."

The idea that the presence of the vampire subverts the intended meaning of a text, largely due to its cultural "baggage," or scars from the past, is continued by Mark Chekares in his essay, "The Dhampir Gets His Fangs:

Miscegenation and Exogamy in the Hotel Transylvania Film Franchise." *Hotel Transylvania* (Tartakovsky 2012) and its sequels—number three in the series is due out in 2018[14]—are highly successful animated films meant for children that attempt to bring the "classic" monsters into the 21st century. Chekares observes that although the films "are heavy on monster puns, cartoon slapstick, and toilet humor," they equally contain "a convoluted racial and cultural coding" demarcating "that monsters and humans are of different cultures." The author describes the ongoing anxiety caused throughout the film, and indeed the series, of possible miscegenation and racial hybridity. In fact, the contemporary narrative largely ignores the historical gothic baggage of the vampire subverting the supposedly "family friendly" atmosphere of the story into one that is rife with anti–Semitism, homophobia, xenophobia and sexism. The films themselves seem to constantly alter their positioning on who the "monster" really is and what constitutes "monstrosity," making any definitive readings, as the author notes, "complicated."

Hidden cultural codings are also the focus of the next essay, "Food for Thought: Vegetarian Vampires in Children's Reading Diets" by Jane M. Kubiesa. Vegetarian vampires were brought into the spotlight of popular culture by the Twilight Saga, even though the vampires there were anything but. However, the non–blood drinking undead were already a staple of children's stories, consuming everything from vegetable juices to washing liquid. Curiously though, as Kubiesa points out, while the Twilight vampires are culturally constructed as acceptable, even aspirational, the vegetarian diets of other undead characters sees them being "villainized" and/or othered. The author goes on to examine the nature of the descriptions of vegetarian diets of vampires in children's narratives seeing them predominantly reflect "real-world eating trends for the under 12s." Consequently, as Western culture has changed its approach to the consumption of meat, so too has the nature of the vegetable-eating vampire, as Kubiesa comments, "As the embodiment of modern social eating practices and a vehicle for the discussion of the problematization of food for children, the vegetarian vampire covers the gamut of issues and has successfully negotiated and challenged each new discourse."

If diets find representation in the figure of the vampire in stories for children, then, as Allison Moore, the author of the next study, argues, the kinds of vampires shown in contemporary films for the under twelves might tell us something about childhood in the 21st century. Her essay, "Every Generation Gets the Vampire It Needs: What Can Vampire Narratives in Children's Films Tell Us About Childhood in the Twenty-First Century?" does this through focusing on the "overlapping and interacting" cultural "worlds of adults and children." Moore looks at six films to examine the influence in them of the adult cultural world and how they might be constructed around ideas of what heteronormativity deems as "appropriate." The author then considers ways in which human and/or vampire children within the same movies resist adult control and create spaces within which their own cultural worlds might take sway. Somewhat perplexingly, while vampires in adult narratives configure multiple gender and sexual positions within those meant for children, heteronormativity is by far the most dominant. Fortunately though, as the author concludes, both children and vampires "have ways to circumvent these demands."

This intersection, or tensionality, between the worlds of adults and children is one that informs the final essay in the book, "Looking Back and Seeing the Future: Adult Nostalgia and Negotiating the Future in Children's Books and Films Featuring Vampires" by Simon Bacon and Katarzyna Bronk. Here, the notion of nostalgia is tantamount both as an adult construct of an idealized and idealizing past, and as cultural recognition and remembrance for the child. The figure of the vampire is crucial in this configuration, as it is an easily recognizable cultural symbol but one whose significance is rapidly changing. As the authors note, the vampire and nostalgia rely on intertextuality, a constant negotiation between the past and its movement into the future. Bacon and Bronk further argue that the child is not a passive recipient in these negotiations, and as their cultural sophistication expands, they are able to resist and adapt the narratives they engage with, so that "the direction of nostalgia, or idealized remembrance" no longer sees "the past shaped by the longings of the present but a present being potentialized by aspirations for the future."

While the present volume ends here, it is one that, hopefully, provides potential for future studies. As Erik Butler observes, "more than any other mythic entity, the vampire has the necessary quickness to reincarnate itself in order to meet—and master—new social and historical realities" (193), and as times change, so will its representation within children's texts. This will bring with it new ways in which the undead can be read against their past and in relation to the child's future. Future interpretations will find new directions in how to subvert the authors' original intentions, allowing the traces of the past to bleed through into the 21st century and beyond. Alongside this, it will also produce new possibilities for children to become authors and actors in their own stories, seeing the vampire not as a creature veiled in a past of prejudice and ostracization, but instead as an agent in the recognition and embracing of difference and individual agency.

NOTES

1. The popular image of Count Dracula comes from Tod Browning's 1931 version and Bela Lugosi's seminal performance; however, he never actually revealed his fangs during the film. The first time Dracula's/vampire fangs were seen was in *El Vampiro* by Fernando Méndez from 1957.

2. This was first done for early showings of Browning's Dracula in the early 1930s,

largely as a promotional device and was copied from the theatrical versions in England when the play of Stoker's novel, by Hamilton Dean, was first shown in 1924.

    3. This was only the second time on screen that Legosi played Dracula and in fact the last time he would play the real vampire Count rather than an imitation or copy.

    4. The later Universal Studio's monster movies featuring John Carradine as Dracula rather than Lugosi, *House of Frankenstein* (Kenton: 1944) and *House of Dracula* (Kenton: 1945) resist the same levels of campness or parody due to a far more restrained dramatization of the role, something equally true of Christopher Lee who played the role multiple times in the Hammer Dracula films.

    5. Luna, played by Carroll Borland was not strictly a vampire, as she and her father were only pretending to be to help catch a killer, but her distinctive make-up and waist length long hair influenced both the look of Morticia Addams and Lily Munster.

    6. The show *Vampira* ran from 1954–1955 but the eponymously named female host actually took her look from the cartoons of Charles Addams (1912–1988), some of whose most popular characters came together as the Addams Family.

    7. There was something of a vampire rejuvenation in the 1970s, seeing a host of important films being released: *The Vampire Lovers.*, directed by Roy Ward Baker. Hammer Film Productions, 1970; an influential adaptation of Le Fanu's novella *Carmilla—Daughters of Darkness.* Directed by Harry Kümel. Showking Films, 1971, a reinterpretation of the story of Erzebet Bathory highlighting sisterhood against the violence of men; *Rabid*, directed by David Cronenberg. New World Pictures, 1977, showing the medicalization of the vampire and forerunner of "running" zombie narratives such as *28 Days Later* (Boyle: 2002); *Dracula*. Directed by John Badham, Universal, 1979, with an unabashedly romantic Count; and *Love at First Bite*. Stan Dragotti, Universal, 1979, a direct spoof of Dracula films.

    8. This forms a somewhat contradictory version of parody of copying where the power of the original is not diffused by humor but hidden behind layers of external detail.

    9. See Bacon, 2014.

    10. This would provide a very interesting reading of Romero's *Martin*.

    11. Curiously, *My Little Pony* also had a large middle-aged male following known as "Bronies" (see Angel: 2012).

    12. Tween is a term identifying children that are on the cusp of becoming teenagers.

    13. *Buffy the Vampire Slayer* (Kuzui: 1992) provided rather an ironic death knell to the male fueled fantasies of the 1980s as was seen in movies such as *Once Bitten* (Storm: 1985), *Fright Night* (Holland: 1985), and *The Lost Boys* (Schumacher: 1987).

    14. There was also a video game released in 2012 and a television series of the same name began in 2017.

Works Cited

Abbott, Stacey. *Celluloid Vampires: Life After a Death in the Modern World*. Austin: University of Texas, 2007.

Angel, Rebecca. "Adult Male My Little Pony Fans? Bronies Are True Rebels." *The Guardian*, 1 October 2012. https://www.theguardian.com/commentisfree/2012/oct/01/my-little-pony-bronies-rebels. accessed 10 August 2017.

Auerbach, Nina. *Our Vampires, Ourselves*. Chicago: University of Chicago Press, 1996.

Bacon, Simon. "The Transmedia Vampire: From Bram Stoker's *Dracula* to HBO's *True Blood*," edited by Tawnya Ravy and Eric Forcier. *Words, World's and Narratives*. Oxford: Inter-Disciplinary Press, 2014. 55–78.

Browning, Tod. *Dracula*. Universal Studios, 1931.

Butler, Erik. *Metamorphosis of the Vampire in Literature and Film: Cultural Transformations in Europe, 1732–1933*. Rochester: Camden House, 2010.

Elliot, Kamilla. "Gothic—Film—Parody." *Adaption*. 1, 1 (March 2008), 24–43.

Halberstam, Judith. "Technologies of Monstrosity: Bram Stoker's *Dracula*," *Victorian Studies* 36/ 3 Victorian Sexualities (1993), 333–352.

Holiday, Jane. *Gruesome and Bloodsocks*. London: Young Lions, 1984.

Jenkins, Henry. *Convergence Culture: Where Old and New Media Collide*. New York: New York University Press, 2006.
Jordan, Neil, director. *Interview with the Vampire*. Warner Brothers Pictures, 1994.
Levorato, Alessandro. *Language and Gender in the Fairy Tale Tradition: A Linguistic Analysis of Old and New Story-Telling*. London: Palgrave Macmillan, 2003.
Miller, Jeffrey S. *The Horror Spoofs of Abbott and Costello: A Critical Assessment of the Comedy Team's Monster Films*. Jefferson, NC: McFarland, 2000.
Nelson, Victoria. *Gothicka: Vampire Heroes, Human Gods, and the New Supernatural*. Cambridge: Harvard University Press, 2013.
Romero, George, director. *Martin*. Libra Films International, 1978.
Smith, Benjamin. "Spandex Cinema: Three Approaches to Comic Book Film Adaptation." Master's degree thesis, University of Central Oklahoma, 2009.
Spooner, Catherine. *Post-Millennial Gothic: Comedy, Romance and the Rise of Happy Gothic*. London: Bloomsbury Academic, 2017.
Zipes, Jack. *Happily Ever After: Fairy Tales, Children, and the Culture Industry*. London: Routledge, 1997.

Section One: Children's Media—Chronologies and Mediums

Children of the Night

Mainstreaming Vampires Through Children's Media

ANDREW M. BOYLAN

While looking at vampire fandom, Milly Williamson suggested that the 1987 film *The Lost Boys* (Schumacher) was "one of the first of a series of vampire films that addresses rebelliousness and youth culture" (67). *The Lost Boys* was not, of course, a children's film –children here being loosely termed as 12 years old or younger. It received a classification rating of 15 in the UK[1] and the rebellious youth were teens rather than pre-teens.[2] Indeed, the association of vampires with rebellious youth goes back much further and one might cite such drive-in fair as the 1957 film *Blood of Dracula* (Strock). However, the mainstreaming of vampires into children's media had been occurring for some time and the inclusion of vampires within children's shows, films and books—sometimes as heroes, sometimes as villains—opened the door for the vampire to become a mainstay of young-adult material and Williamson's symbol of youth culture. Williamson's comments were made in regard to media generated in or for Western Europe and North America, and so this essay will do the same.

As this essay explores the vampire's place in children's media it will become apparent that it was, very much, a journey. With a notable early exception, the nineteenth-century vampire material placed the child as a victim, if a child appeared at all, and the material was adult orientated. The early comic books may have contained vampires but they, too, were designed for adult consumption, which is evidenced by the fact that there was a movement to protect children from them. However, children did read comic books; and, as TV developed, vampires moved into programs designed for family viewing. This led to a softening of the depiction of vampires—notably through programs like *Sesame Street*—and embedded the archetype in children's story telling. The vampire, being generally malleable as an archetype and symbol, soon stretched its wings to become representative of multiple stereotypes of children's media, and imposed itself as a mainstay of those media.

First Associations: The Nineteenth Century

The vampire has had an association with children from its earliest appearance in prose literature. In what is probably the second English-language prose vampire story, *The Black Vampyre: A Legend of Saint Domingo*, attributed to Uriah Derick D'Arcy and published in 1819 which saw the vampire of the piece kidnapping a plantation owner's infant son, with evidence left behind that the child was killed, and returning years later with a European page boy named Zembo, who was the missing son and who was by then a vampire in his own right.[3] But, even if Zembo was a vampire, most children appearing in nineteenth-century literature were victims. The 1824 novel *La Vampire ou la Vierge de Hongrie*,[4] has the female vampire Alinska prey on infants: "She places her fetid mouth on the pure mouth of the child, and seems to drink long draughts of blood, which she aspires from the unfortunate victim's lungs" (134). Likewise, the victims in the 1850 story, "The Mysterious Lodger" by Sheridan Le Fanu, are exclusively children, one being harrowingly subjected to premature burial. In Bram Stoker's *Dracula*, the three vampire women in the Count's castle are given a sack that may contain an infant, while the vampirized Lucy preys on children, and is given the name "Bloofer Lady" by her young victims. However, the children are, with the exception of Zembo, victims and all the works are intended for adults.

Comic Books and Family Viewing

The vampire genre was once designed for the mature reader and J.G. Melton suggests that this would hold true until the 1940s, when the advent of Horror Comics opened the idea of vampires in juvenile literature (391). In fact, Batman faced a vampire known as "the Monk" as early as 1939.[5] The Comics Code in America, however, sought to remove such influences from children. Doctor Frederic Wertham was an outspoken critic of comic books and of the negative impact that they were supposed to have on children. He publicly spoke out against comics in an interview in 1948 and by 1954 he had published the book *Seduction of the Innocent* specifically about the dangers of horror comics. This influential book ignored the fact that the target audience was actually adult (see Coville). As a response to Wertham's rhetoric, the comic book industry created the Comics Code to voluntarily censor their own output. Vampires were a direct casualty, as General Standards Part B (5) of the code stated, "Scenes dealing with, or instruments associated with walking dead, torture, vampires and vampirism, ghouls, cannibalism, and werewolfism are prohibited" (Gabilliet 315).

Whether there was a corrupting influence is highly debatable, but the self-censorship did marry up to an event across the Atlantic Ocean in Scotland. On 23 September 1954 a constable was dispatched to a disturbance at Glasgow's Southern Necropolis and found hundreds of children, reportedly between the age of 4 and 14, armed with sharp sticks and knives, who were hunting for the Gorbals Vampire—a 7-foot vampire with iron teeth who had already eaten two children, they claimed. The blame for this was placed on American horror comics (see Nicolson). The story of the Gorbals Vampire would seem to have been the basis for the 1979 TV program "Play for Today: Vampires"—though the trigger in that was the film *Dracula: Prince of Darkness* rather than comic books. Melton suggests that the self-imposed ban on vampires in comics started to be lifted in the late 1960s with the emergence of a *Dark Shadows* comic and *Vampirella* (391). The *Dark Shadows* comic began publication in 1969 but the television series *Dark Shadows*, which inspired the comic, was a U.S. TV soap opera that first aired in 1966 and soon introduced a vampire character named Barnabas Collins, played by Jonathan Frid. It should be noted that *Dark Shadows* was not designed for children but children will have watched the show, airing as it did at 4PM Eastern. This is something that should be remembered—not all children's viewing consists of shows designed for children. In the early 1970s, the UK had just three TV channels and a show such as *Doctor Who* might be watched by very young children. A show like *The Munsters*, which ran from 1964 to 1966, was family viewing and featured Universal's core monster triumvirate (the Wolf Man, the vampire and Frankenstein's monster) in the guise of a suburban family. Both Al Lewis' character Grandpa and the mother of the family Lily, played by Yvonne De Carlo, were vampires. Indeed, Grandpa was Dracula—though his name became the much more Western sounding Sam Dracula. These were the stars of the show and, by making them the primary focus, the program helped rehabilitate the monsters, with many of the gags being based on ordinary folk being wrongly scared of the monsters when their actions were purely innocent, perhaps even naïve.

Children Claim the Vampires: The 1970s

As the 70s dawned, the stage was set for vampires to emerge as a mainstay of children's programming, though their presence had not necessarily been entirely missing. Loony Tunes, for instance, had Bugs Bunny meet a vampire in the cartoon *Transylvania 6500* as far back as 1963. *Scooby-Doo Where Are You!* had a vampire (albeit not a real one) appear in the cartoon "A Gaggle of Galloping Ghosts" in 1969. If Scooby-Doo did not contain real monsters[6] then this was matched in literature by the Hardy Boys, whose 1971 adventure *Danger on Vampire Trail* contained no hint of an actual vampire—though it did have a brief appearance of a vampire bat (Dixon 128). Disney got in on the act too, and their 1973 film *Mystery in Dracula's Castle* not only failed to have a vampire, but there was no castle either. What is interesting, regarding *Mystery in Dracula's Castle*, is that the film starts with three young children watching a vampire film in a movie theatre. Though the youngest child, Leonard (Scott C. Kolden), is scared by the film, his brother Alfie (Johnny Whitaker) is inspired. As they talk about the film on the way home—with the conversation between the older boys identifying a need for more blood in the film—they stumble across the robbery of a jewelry store. The fact that the three children attend a movie theatre where they watch a vampire film, and Alfie wants to make a vampire movie, indicates that Disney recognized that vampires were popular amongst the young. Although Alfie wants to make his film (utilizing a hand held camera he owns), he, Leonard and their mother are going away for summer and so he has to convince Leonard to be in the film. This then sees Leonard in cape and sporting fake fangs as his brother films him. Soon they come across a lighthouse, which Alfie wants to shoot as the castle—unbeknown to them the very same where the crooks that have robbed the jewelry store in their home town are hiding out.

If vampires were being referenced in some programming they were actually appearing in others. In the U.S., family viewing such as *Gilligan's Island* had featured a vampire episode in 1966 and teen pop sensations the Monkees had a monster mash episode with vampires in 1968. Similarly the cartoon series the *Groovie Goolies*, which was a 1970 spin-off of *Sabrina the Teenage Witch*, featured the triumvirate of Frankenstein's monster, the Wolf Man and the vampire.[7] In Canada the 1971 TV series *The Hilarious House of Frightenstein* was a sketch comedy show with a monster theme and centered on Billy Van's Count Frightenstein, the thirteenth son of Count Dracula. The show featured horror icon Vincent Price, who agreed to do the show as he wanted to do something for children (Perkins).

Another comedy variety show that featured a vampire was *The Electric Company*, which ran from 1971 until 1977 and featured Morgan Freeman as Vincent the Vegetable Vampire, a vampire who preyed on vegetables—this vegetable stalking variety of vampire would become a stock character in children's vampire-themed shows. *The Electric Company* was from the same stable as the better known *Sesame Street*, which first aired in 1969 and added the vampire character Count von Count in 1972. Based on Bela Lugosi's performance of Dracula, the Count taught simple numeracy through his obsessional need to count. This is possibly based on the idea of Arithmomania, which is a trait that some traditional folklore bestows upon vampires and leads to vampire deterrents such as casting grain over a vampire's grave as they will have to count the grains before seeking their prey (Hawkes 80). *Sesame Street* is a worldwide phenomenon, which attained its 46th season in 2016 and there can be little doubt that Count von Count has had a huge impact on the mainstreaming of the vampire character into children's entertainment. The character was softened as time went on; in the early days of the Count he had a hypnotic power and could use it to freeze a person who interrupted his counting. This was removed as it was thought the power might be too scary for the pre-school audience. Likewise, his original manic laughter at the end of the counting was replaced by a laugh that was more triumphant. It might be argued that Count von Count was, and is, a primary factor in maintaining the stereotype of the vampire appearing and sounding in the Bela Lugosi mold.

This softening—be it removal of the hypnotic powers in *Sesame Street* or being a vegetable eating vampire in the *Electric Company*—certainly helped to mainstream the vampire. Coupled with this there was also the idea that the vampire would be the hero of the show. The U.S. series the *Monster Squad* (1976) was a show in which such rehabilitation occurred. This used the core monster triumvirate again but on this occasion they were waxworks brought to life at night. The voice over at the head of each episode, narrated by Fred Grandy, is worth reproducing in full:

> My name is Walt. I work as night watchman here at Fred's Wax Museum to put myself through Criminology College. It used to be lonely until recently when I plugged in my crime computer, suddenly oscillating vibrations brought to life three legendary monsters ... Dracula, the Werewolf and Frankenstein. Creatures hated and feared for centuries, now determined to make up for their past misbehavings by fighting crime wherever they find it. Together, we're the ... Monster Squad! [*Monster Squad* 1976]

The language openly refers to rehabilitating the monsters' less than illustrious pasts—despite their being waxworks brought to life—and the show itself followed a superhero pattern. A similar premise of the monsters as crime fighters would be used a few years later in the 1980 cartoon the *Drak Pack*. Not all juvenile-orientated depictions of vampires through the 70s had them rehabilitated, however. Marvel re-introduced vampires as the comic code relaxed in the form of Morbius the Living Vampire, who first appeared in October 1971[8] and was at least a sympathetic anti-hero, if not a full-fledged hero, but followed this with the *Tomb of Dracula*, in 1972, in which Dracula was most definitely the villain.

In 1979, two book series had a strong impact on juvenile vampire literature. In the U.S., James and Deborah Howe published *Bunnicula* about a vampire rabbit. Interestingly, in the book, the rabbit is found at a movie theatre when the family go to see *Dracula* and the youngest attendee is Toby, who is eight years old—again young children are shown attending vampire films. Bunnicula feeds on vegetables, which carries on the trope of vegetarian vampires. Unfortunately, Deborah Howe died prior to the publication of the first book, but James Howe continued the series, which led to a 1982 animated special entitled *Bunnicula: The Vampire Rabbit* and to a 2016 cartoon series entitled simply *Bunnicula*. Also in 1979, German author Angela Sommer-Bodenburg published *Der Kleine Vampir*.[9] This featured a nine-year-old boy named Anton who was fascinated with vampires and then befriended a vampire boy called Rüdiger. Moving on from just watching vampire movies, here the child protagonist was fascinated by vampires—a sign of recognition of fandom in younger children. The book became the first in a long-running series and spawned a German/Canadian 1986 TV series called *The Little Vampire*, a 1993–94 German TV series entitled *Der Kleine Vampir—Neue Abenteuer*[10] and an English-language feature film entitled *The Little Vampire* (2000). The feature film changed the protagonist's name from Anton to Tony, played by Jonathan Lipnicki, who actively acted as a vampire and again had a fan's fixation on vampires despite his parents' better judgment. By depicting the children as fans of the genre in the post–*Sesame Street* years, the vampire was well and truly mainstreamed.

Of course the vampire was still making its way into shows that were classed as family entertainment, often as a villain. It was, and still is, commonplace for shows to include a vampire-related episode—these may have an actual vampire, someone pretending to be a vampire or the show can be deliberately vague as to whether the vampire is real or not. Examples include the *BJ and the Bear* episode "Coffin with a View" (1979) and the *Buck Rogers in the 25th Century* episode "Space Vampire" (1980). The former featured horror veteran John Carradine as guest star and obfuscated the reality of the vampire, and the latter featured an alien vampire, but both vehicles placed the vampire, and their own take on vampire lore, at the heart of family TV viewing. It is interesting to note that TV allowed the Hardy Boys to confront a (possible) vampire in the 1979 episode "Hardy Boys and Nancy Drew Meet Dracula" while their earlier novel did not.

Consolidating the Vampire: The 1980s and 90s

The 1980s not only saw the adaptations of *Der Kleine Vampir* and *Bunnicula* but it also marked the decade of one of the most successful UK vampire characters for children—Count Duckula. The character started off as a villain (albeit an inept one) in the cartoon series *Danger Mouse* and first appeared in the 1982 episode the "Four Tasks of Danger Mouse" (Cosgrove). The character would appear in just four episodes in all, but in 1988 the character would be rehabilitated and given his own series. *Count Duckula* ran for four seasons of varying lengths and the rehabilitation process played with the trope of vampiric resurrection. In the series the Count could be resurrected from death in a ritual, but an accidental use of tomato ketchup rather than blood led to this incarnation as a vegetarian. This was, of course, another example of a vegetarian vampire and this breed of vampire would resurface in the form of the cartoon series the *Ketchup Vampires* from 1992. The U.S. release of this series split the cartoon series into two ninety-minute features and included voice work by Cassandra Peterson narrating in her Elvira persona. By the nineties it was clear that vampires could run the gamut between hero and villain and so the 1990 Canadian production *Dracula: The Series* had the vampires as villains hunted by the kids and their vampire-hunting Uncle. Likewise, while Frankenstein's Monster and the Wolfman character are both heroes in the 1994 cartoon series *Monster Force*, it would eschew the idea of the vampire being allowed to be the hero, by making Dracula the primary villain.

Other children's shows played on a space between the two extremes. *Goosebumps* had an episode entitled "Vampire Breath" (1996) in which vampires seem to be after the kids until it turns out that the kids are vampires themselves, but they just do not know it yet.[11] *Goosebumps* was based on the R. L. Stein book series of the same name and Stein has made a career out of writing horror books for children—these include several vampire titles. Likewise, the *Shadow Zone* book series were a short-lived series of children's horror books penned by various authors under the nom de plume J. R. Black. One of these was filmed under the name *Shadow Zone: The Undead Express* (1996) and the vampires are definitely villainous. A similar children's series, "*Are You Afraid of the Dark?*" (1990–2000), produced several vampire episodes through the nineties in which the vampires were villains to be foiled rather than the heroes of the piece. An unusual vampire type is the machine vampire and it appears occasionally in both children's and adult's media. Keeping with the vampire-as-villain theme, the 1997 series *Van-pires*, which was a mixture of live action and CGI animation, had anthropomorphic vampire motor vehicles out to drain cars of gasoline. The Van-pires were created by a meteor that crashed in a junkyard but it also melded four human teens in with vehicles, who were the good guys known as Motor Vators. However, by the end of the first episode the Motor Vators realized they were much like the Van-pires in that they needed gasoline (and had to avoid the sun) but they were distinct by the fact that they paid their way, buying gasoline rather than stealing it. As such the show had both hero and villain vampires, while offering a consumerist-based morality aspect to the internal lore.

On the other end of the scale the cartoon show *Mona the Vampire* was based on a series of books and featured a young girl named Mona who pretends she is a vampire and each episode, with her friends, imagines overcoming a supernatural foe or solving a mystery. In this the vampire has again become the hero, something for the child to aspire to be. Looking towards teen-orientated material for a moment, the series *Buffy the Vampire Slayer* (1997–2003) also played with this dualistic view of the vampire, and while most vampires in the series are depicted as evil there were those—mainly David Boreanaz's Angel and later James Marsters' Spike—who were depicted as heroes. The series would prove not only popular but also had a substantial influence on the subsequent genre as a whole, and yet this duality had been developed within media aimed at a younger audience already.

The Millennial Vampire: Into the Twenty-First Century

As the millennium turned, the vampire seemed to become more and more popular in media designed for every age group. Disney returned to vampires in their feature *Mom's Got a Date with a Vampire* (2000) in which the villain was a vampire and the Mom had to be rescued by her kids. Disney would also include vampires in the family series *Wizards of Waverly Place* but their most interesting use of the vampire was perhaps in the 2000 cartoon series *Buzz Lightyear of Star Command*. The episode Nos-4-A2 introduced the vampire, which would recur in four more episodes and was a robotic vampire. As such it had fangs but would bite other robots, draining them of their energy and making them its slaves. Highlighting the fact that vampires would crop up in long running shows, the children's series *Power Rangers* released a season entitled "Mystic Force" (2006) in which the enemies were undead and one was a vampire queen. In two specific episodes the pink ranger was turned into a vampire. While one of her fellow rangers turns out to be a vampire hunting expert, at its core the story demanded that the pink ranger had to show her fortitude and fight the curse she was put under. Her ability to rise above the vampirism and aid her fellow rangers was the factor that saved the day in those particular episodes.

The BBC skirted across the idea of vampires being both the hero and villain in their series *Young Dracula* (2006–present) and carried forward several of the tropes identified as the genre developed. In the first series Vlad, played by Gerran Howell, was the son of Dracula and hated the idea of becoming a vampire as he matured. When the Dracula family moves to the UK (to escape marauding peasants) he meets his new best friend, the human Robin (Craig Roberts), who is obsessed with vampires and wants to be one (again, a child depicted as a fan of the genre). In the first series especially, the role of villain was blurred. Partly, it was Dracula, who was played with gusto by Keith-Lee Castle; however, he developed into almost an anti-hero. Partly, it was Van Helsing (Terence Maynard) as he wanted to kill the vampires living in the town's castle, which includes the primary hero of the show. As the series progressed, things grew darker. There was actually a four-year gap between the second and third season. This gap allowed the series to be pitched at an older demographic in its later seasons and add a much darker hue to the series, as Vlad tries to control the world's vampires and broker a peace with the slayers. The show's themes also matured, as Vlad's character developed, and a premise of the vampire as romantic lead was also touched upon, a strand of the genre more young-adult orientated than perhaps would be found in juvenile media.

Vampires would continue to be depicted as the hero (or anti-hero), so in the cartoon series *Adventure Time* the character Marceline the Vampire Queen started life as an occasional antagonist, though perhaps her archetype would be better described as a trickster, who became so popular as a character that she became the protagonist of a mini-series during season 7, called "Stakes." Marceline does not drink blood; rather she drains the color red. Similarly, Fang from the film *Vampire Dog* (2012) eats jelly, preferably of a red color. While *Adventure Time* plays with themes in a very mature way the reasoning, ultimately, must be that stopping the vampire from drinking blood sanitizes it for an audience of children, much as making the vampire a vegetarian did in the past. The fact that Fang eats jelly because of the gelatin (and is therefore not a vegetarian vampire) is not explored in depth. Similarly, the big-screen outing *Hotel Transylvania* (2012) sidestepped the touchy subject of blood drinking by suggesting that Dracula now used a blood substitute.

Conclusion

Vampires are now as deeply embedded as a facet of children's media as they are in the media for any other demographic. The filmmakers who grew up with *Sesame Street* bringing Count von Count into their living rooms are, in their turn, bringing vampires to the small screen and the big screen, and know that the vampire is malleable enough as an archetype to be the villain, the hero and something in between, while being suitable fare for the younger demographics. This also allows the vampire to be symbolic of youth culture, positively as the hero, negatively as the villain and rebelliously as the anti-hero. Recognizing that the figure of the vampire is popular with the children demographic and that the vampire is malleable enough as an archetype to allow it to be tamed for a younger audience, we should see it as a stepping stone between juvenile and teen media and from there into adult media.

NOTES

1. See "The Lost Boys," British Board of Film Classification.
2. Whilst the vampire character Laddie is recognizably pre-teen, he is less a rounded character and more the embodiment of a narrative point.
3. It is a curious tale which contains a possible cure for vampirism in the form of a potion created through the Obeah mysteries and one of its main protagonists, Zembo, is likely the first child vampire in English prose. Uriah Derick D'Arcy was a pseudonym (and an anagram) of Richard Varick Dey (1801–1837). Katie Bray, in a recent essay ("A Climate ... More Prolific ... in Sorcery," American Literature 87.1 [March 2015]: 1–21), argues convincingly that the story belongs to Dey, not to Robert Charles Sands (1799–1832), as suggested in 1845 in the *Knickerbocker* and accepted by Andrew Barger, the editor mentioned here in the Works Cited section.
4. The first edition by Cardinal is dated 1825, although its publication was acknowledged by French journals as early as November 1824. The English edition is titled *The Virgin Vampire*.
5. In *Detective Comics* #31.
6. Scooby-Doo is famous for the monster being a man in a mask; however, various incarnations of Scooby-Doo have also featured "real" monsters.
7. Whilst this chapter concentrates on Western media, the vampire was appearing across international media, some of which were children orientated. In Japan, the 1971 kaiju adventure series *Kaettekita Urutoraman* (*The Return of Ultraman*) showed footage of a vampire film in one episode, watched by characters from the series, which the English subtitles suggested was called "Blood-sucking Dude Ranch" and later had an episode that featured a vampire kaiju called Draculas, from the planet Carmilla, which possesses the corpse of a young woman.
8. *The Amazing Spider-Man* #101.
9. Published in English as *The Little Vampire*.
10. That is, *The Little Vampire—New Adventures*.
11. The two children are twins and it is the night before their thirteenth birthday, the age at which they are to discover their vampire heritage.

WORKS CITED

Anonymous. "The Lost Boys." *British Board of Film Classification*. http://www.bbfc.co.uk/releases/lost-boys-1970-1. Accessed 20 October 2016.
Coville, Jamie. "Seduction of the Innocents and the Attack on Comic Books." *Integrative Arts 10. American Comic Books*. Penn State University, 19 February 2000. http://www.psu.edu/dept/inart10_110/inart10/cmbk4cca.html. Accessed 1 July 2016.
D'Arcy, Uriah Derick. "The Black Vampyre: A Legend of Saint Domingo" [1819]. *The Best Vampire Stories 1800–1849: A Classic Vampire Anthology*. Ed. Andrew Barger. U.S.: Bottletree Books, 2012. 133–162.
Dixon, Franklin W. *The Hardy Boys Mystery Stories: Danger on Vampire Trail*. New York: Grosset & Dunlap, 1971.
Gabilliet, Jean-Paul. "Code of the Comics Magazine Association of America" [26 October 1954]. *Of Comics and Men: A Cultural History of American Comic Books*. Trans. Bart Beaty and Nick Nguyen. Jackson: University Press of Mississippi, 2010.
Hawkes, Lesley. "Staking and Restaking the Vampire: Generational Ownership of the Vampire." *Popular Appeal: Books and Films in Contemporary Youth Culture*. Ed. Sharyn Pearce, Vivienne Muller, and Lesley Hawkes. Newcastle upon Tyne: Cambridge Scholars Publishing, 2013. 79–110.

Howe, Deborah, and James Howe. *Bunnicula: A Rabbit-Tale of Mystery*. New York: Atheneum Books for Young Readers, 1979.
Lamothe-Langon, Étienne-Léon. *The Virgin Vampire* [1824]. Trans. Brian Stableford. Tarzana, CA: Black Coat Press, 2011.
LeFanu, Joseph Sheridan. "The Mysterious Lodger" [1850]. *J.S. Le Fanu's Ghostly Tales, Volume 4*. Project Gutenberg, 2004. http://livros01.livrosgratis.com.br/gu012647.pdf. Accessed 1 July 2016.
Melton, J. Gordon. *The Vampire Book: The Encyclopedia of the Undead*. 3rd ed. Canton, MI: Visible Ink Press, 2011.
Nicolson, Stuart. "Child Vampire Hunters Sparked Comic Crackdown." *BBC News* 22 March 2010. http://news.bbc.co.uk/2/hi/uk_news/scotland/8574484.stm. Accessed 14 May 2016.
Perkins, Will. "How Horror Legend Vincent Price Helped a Tiny Canadian TV Show Become a Cult Classic." *Yahoo Movies* 24 October 2013. https://ca.movies.yahoo.com/blogs/widescreen/horror-legend-vincent-price-helped-tiny-canadian-tv-141830527.html. Accessed 14 May 2016.
Stoker, Bram. *The New Annotated Dracula*. Ed. Leslie S. Klinger. New York: W.W. Norton, 2008.
Williamson, Milly. *The Lure of the Vampire: Gender, Fiction and Fandom from Bram Stoker to Buffy*. London: Wallflower Press, 2005.

Filmography

Adventure Time. Dir. Various. Warner Brothers Television, 2010–present.
Are You Afraid of the Dark? Dir. Various. Nickelodeon Productions, 1990–2000.
BJ and the Bear: A Coffin with a View. Dir. Ray Austin. Universal Television, 1979.
Blood of Dracula. Dir. Herbert L Strock. American International Film, 1957.
Buck Rogers in the 25th Century: Space Vampire. Dir. Larry Stewart. NBC Universal Television, 1980.
Buffy the Vampire Slayer. Dir. various. 20th Television, 1997–2003.
Bunnicula. Dir. Various. Warner Brothers Television, 2016.
Bunnicula: The Vampire Rabbit. Dir. Charles A. Nichols. ABC, 1982.
Buzz Lightyear of Star Command: Nos-4-A2. Dir. Nicholas Filippi. Buena Vista Television, 2000.
Count Duckula. Dir. Various. Thames Television, 1988–1993.
Danger Mouse: The Four Tasks of Danger Mouse. Dir. Brian Cosgrove. Thames Television, 1982.
Dark Shadows. Dir. Various. Dan Curtis Productions 1966–1971.
Doctor Who: State of Decay. Dir. Peter Moffatt. BBC, 1980.
Doctor Who: The Seeds of Doom. Dir. Douglas Camfield. BBC, 1976.
Dracula: Prince of Darkness. Dir. Terrence Fisher. Hammer Film Productions, 1966.
Dracula: The Series. Dir. Various. RHI Entertainment, 1990.
Drak Pack. Dir. Chris Cuddington. Warner Brothers Television, 1980.
The Electric Company. Dir. Various. Sesame Television, 1971–1977.
Gilligan's Island: Up at Bat. Dir. Jerry Hopper. United Artists Television, 1966.
Goosebumps: Vampire Breath. Dir. Ron Oliver. 20th Television, 1996.
The Groovy Goolies. Dir. Hal Sutherland. Filmation, 1970.
Hardy Boys and Nancy Drew Meet Dracula. Dir. Joseph Pevney. Universal Television, 1979.
The Hilarious House of Frightenstein. Dir. Various. CHCH-TV, 1971.
Hotel Transylvania. Dir. Genndy Tartakovsky. Columbia Pictures, 2012.
Kaettekita Urutoraman. Dir. Various. Tokyo Broadcasting System, 1971–1972.
Ketchup Vampires. Dir. Alexander Zapletal. Kidpix, 1992.
Der kleine Vampir—Neue Abenteuer. Dir. Christian Görlitz. Polyphon, 1993–1994.
The Little Vampire. Dir. René Bonnière. Polyphon, 1986.
The Little Vampire. Dir. Uli Edel. New Line Cinema, 2000.
The Lost Boys. Dir. Joel Schumacher. Warner Brothers, 1987.
Mom's Got a Date with a Vampire. Dir. Steve Boyum. Disney Channel, 2000.

Mona the Vampire. Dir. Various. YTV, 1999–2003.
The Monkees: Monstrous Monkee Mash. Dir. James Frawley. Columbia Pictures Television, 1968.
Monster Force. Dir. Chris Schouten. Universal/MCA TV, 1994.
Monster Squad. Dir. Various. NBC, 1976.
The Munsters. Dir. Various. Universal Television, 1964–66.
Mystery in Dracula's Castle. Dir. Robert Totten. Disney Channel, 1973.
Play for Today: Vampires. Dir. John Goldschmidt. BBC, 1979.
Power Rangers: Mystic Force. Dir. Various. MarVista Entertainment, 2006. TV Series.
Scooby-Doo Where Are You! A Gaggle of Galloping Ghosts. Dir. William Hannah and Joseph Barbera. Warner Brothers Television, 1969.
Sesame Street. Dir. Various. Children's Television Workshop, 1969–present.
Shadow Zone: The Undead Express. Dir. Stephen Williams. Full Moon, 1996.
Transylvania 6-5000. Dir. Chuck Jones. Warner Brothers, 1963.
Vampire Dog. Dir. Geoff Anderson. Joker Films, 2012.
Van-pires. Dir. Joey Elardy. Fox, 1997.
Wizards of Waverly Place. Dir. Various. Disney Channel, 2007–2012.
Young Dracula. Dir. Various. BBC Cymru Wales, 2006–2014.

An Invitation to a Beheading (and Another to a Birthday Bash)

Encountering Dracula in Contemporary Gothic Metamorphoses Books

Jen Baker

"Are you ready for a hair-raising adventure? Are you brave enough to stare evil in the face? Then join Professor Van Helsing and his team of Vampire hunters as they track down the terrifying COUNT DRACULA" (Robson n.p.). This tantalizing invitation, scrawled in red dripping lettering on the back cover of Eddie Robson's textually and visually interactive retelling of Bram Stoker's Classic, is indicative of a trend in various Gothic picture books for children of approximately 12 years old or younger. Such texts directly challenge or provoke the reader into a demonstration of courage, by posing provocative questions such as "Dare you Peek through the Pop-Up Windows?," or warning that you open the book "at your peril!," even when it ensues that the monster is not a threat. Not all such invitations are as explicit as Robson's, nor is their narratorial purpose so grim. Across different examples the reader may embark on a quest to various strange lands or into unfamiliar lairs; will sometimes be given the tools to detect clues and encouraged to find, communicate with or help kill the monster; and the more successful pieces provide the reader with a valuable platform for empowerment. This is particularly enhanced by the addition of interactive elements that are found in what I call Gothic metamorphoses books, which draw from the history of the Gothic spectacle and the theatrical devices of horror, and fuse them with a familiar literary source (or at least its cultural codes) to provide a multimodal experience for the child reader. This not only develops cognitive skills, but has the potential to be distinctly empowering by providing them with, what Victoria Carrington identifies as, "the resources for ongoing identity construction" and the provision of "skill sets and attitudes that allow the young to construct coherent resilient bespoke identities using multiple forms of text as a key resource" (305).

The metamorphoses book is characterized and classified by its mechanical movable elements such as pullable tabs, pop-ups, liftable flaps, or extendable elements such as pull-out documents and three-dimensional buildings, or interactive components such as sounds created by pushing buttons, or puzzles, textured pages, and figurines. Some examples have no narrative text at all, but the majority—and the ones that concern this essay—demonstrate a multi-faceted relationship between text, image, and mechanical feature. Within the form, there is a distinct (and vastly under-researched) genre characterized by "Gothic" tropes such as ghosts, monsters, haunted houses, and themed in some way around traditional Gothic plots such as visiting a terrifying location, or uncanny and bizarre encounters with the spooky or the macabre.[1] Such texts are exemplars of what Fred Botting identifies as the Gothic genre's propensity for diffusion and hybridity (9). In their contemporary format, mechanical devices in Gothic literary texts work in conjunction with the accompanying narrative in an attempt to emulate the theatrical effects associated with the genre; such as the monster leaping out at you from behind the door or under the bed, or paintings of people whose eyes follow you around the room. The narrative and illustrations attempt to convey a sense of anticipation and dread by leading the reader through the labyrinthine passageways of a vampire's castle, or through the close confines of a spooky forest with the intention of provoking those psycho-somatic effects of dread—such as a tight chest, chills, numbness—and those physiological externalized projections of horror such as jumping, gasping, and screaming with both delight and fright. As such, they can be considered an integral medium in the young reader/viewer's initiation into the Gothic and its codes. While some examples may appear simplistic (in the minimal lift-the-flap book for the early reader, for instance), they work toward developing the same "cognitively complex emotions" that Xavier Aldana Reyes has suggested are at play in the horror film, and many of those for slightly older readers are sophisticated feats of engineering and of suspense (85).

Although the "hunting" of the monster is a varied trope in the metamorphoses book, the vampire, and Dracula in particular, is the most staple and consistent presence; superseding ghosts, Things, mummies, skeletons, werewolves. It is surpassed as a popular choice perhaps only by the monstrous form of the Haunted House, which embodies and encases such menageries of horror. Perhaps in part this is because, as Nina Auerbach famously posited, "every generation creates and embraces its own vampires" and so the Vampire is reinvented and maintains its popularity—although the constant return of many children's works to "classic" forms is also telling (vii). This essay will analyze how a small selection of Gothic metamorphoses books marketed for children re-appropriate either the *Dracula* story, or the character of Dracula, and how the use of picture books and interactive elements in the staging of the vampire encounter can potentially empower the young reader or, owing to particular creative choices, potentially disempower them. The texts chosen either engage the reader in an "active role" in the hunting of the vampire, or involve an unexpected meeting with the vampire. I will be discussing how these examples, which are laden with intertextual references, draw from the original formation of the character and his setting, and the popularized tropes created from other adaptations, in a manner that ultimately conforms to the more traditional literary-vampire canon.

Predominantly, I hope to demonstrate how these works (the more successful pieces in particular) are key contributions to the Gothic genre, the vampire tradition, and to the field of movable, mechanical books more widely. The effectiveness and quality of plot, illustration, type of mechanical feature, and character involvement are varied in the examples chosen, but I hope to demonstrate why certain examples are (un)successful as innovative and creative stimuli, and educational tools. Furthermore, how, as examples of Gothic literature, they continue to push and subvert the boundaries of tradition and convention through the utilization of the monstrous hybrid form, with many engaging in a sophisticated play of comic exaggeration and parody that has been "at the heart of Gothic since its inception," as a tool for facing fear and potentially discovering the pleasure in terror (Jackson, Coats, and McGillis 4).

A Comedy of Terrors: Transformations of Dracula

The plot of Keith Faulkner's *Dracula: A Spooky Lift-the-Flap Book* (1993), illustrated by Jonathan Lambert and marketed for readers aged 3–7, concerns someone who has been invited to a birthday party (a terrifying prospect for anyone) for his neighbor Count Dracula. The text denotes the comic–Gothic through simple vocabulary and alternate rhyme, and the luminous colors and cartoonish contours of Gothic textual symbols and tropes of creaking doors, a "strange and musty smell," a "long, dark path" (Faulkner n.p.),[2] bats, grotesque statues, and the staple component of the castle. The child (or even the adult) may not have read *Dracula* in its original form, or perhaps even read or seen an adaptation, but Jackson, Coats, and McGillis suggest an awareness that can be attributed to the wider exposure of the child-reader to cultural depictions of the Gothic which allows them to read the codes of monstrosity in new settings (1–14).

The first-person narrator of Faulkner's text (identified only at one point in the text as "a child") is unseen by the reader for the page is occularized through the narrator. However, the narrative and visual alignment through the homodiegetic narrator (that is, the first-person narrator who also participates in the story) allows the reader to also assume the role of protagonist. As the narrator stands at the doorstep having rung the bell, they ask questions that are at once rhetorical and a means of direct engagement with the reader, by inviting their participation: "'Come in, my child,' croaks the butler, / As he beckons me inside. / Should I walk straight in and risk my skin, Or run away and hide?" As the narrator walks in, so too does the reader, (if, that is, they are brave enough to turn the page), and the narrator/reader encounters various "monsters," whose status as threat is questionable. A double-address to both child and adult reader, each monster undertakes ordinary birthday party activities, but with a parodic twist. For instance, in the kitchen a cake is being baked that is made of ingredients which, as can be detected from the movable packaging, are deliberately and comically disgusting and ridiculous: The intraiconic text tells us that the cakes are, with a wink to the more experienced reader, "Just like mummy makes." As the reader lifts down the flap comprising the cake-mix box, a cheerfully smiling "figure wrapped in bandages [...] Appears with a birthday cake" and offers some to the narrator and, as suggested by eye contact, the reader. The various other creatures encountered from behind the flaps of the book—a skeleton who offers "beetle sauce" for your ice-cream sundae, or a ghost wrapping gifts—are not actively threatening but inviting and merry.

On the penultimate page, intensifying the sense of strangeness, but also playing with the setting of a birthday party, the narrator observes of the sleeping Dracula that, "You'd never know to look at him / He's almost a thousand years old." The child and company get ready to sing, and turning to the final double-page the reader encounters the only actual pop-up of the text, and the comic and the terrifying converge: the text jovially reads "Wake up! Wake up! Count Dracula / And have a HAPPY BIRTHDAY!" (n.p.) but the reader is simultaneously confronted by a large, imposing, fanged Dracula whose menace is enhanced by the breaking of the fourth wall as he stares directly at the reader. Yet the terror is slightly neutralized by his bright attire and luminous cartoonish features, his blue and yellow spotty neckerchief and his unkempt and bushy grey and white hair. And it is with this comic-grotesque vision that the text concludes. Faulkner's text is not particularly sophisticated—there are just four flaps and one pop-up—and standard, simple, and familiar forms of poetry are used. Although the text is placed under the flaps as well as on the left-hand page, the reader does not need to physically turn the book in different directions or work hard to progress with the poem. The visual confrontation with Dracula at the end utilizes the basic principles of scare tactics—of invading the experiential space of the reader to force a physical proximity and thus imply potential physical harm. Yet the text on a whole is not overtly dark or enticing in its foray into the Gothic—it uses a few monsters whose intentions are ambivalent and actions are strange but which, ultimately, are undeveloped props used to lead the reader to the main event: they contribute to a limited and basic form of suspense by forestalling the inevitable fright that the narrator pre-warns the reader of.

The ending also provokes further questions—some of which are answered by paratextual information. From the use of the past tense in the rhyme on the back cover, for instance, the discerning reader might surmise that the narrator lived to tell the tale, but there is nevertheless the suggestion that, in recounting the story to the reader, the fright the narrator received will be imparted. However, it is not made clear exactly what happened after Dracula popped up—did they all eat the cake and open the gifts and play games? Did the narrator become a vampire? Although the inner-narrative is in the past tense, as a story being recounted, the paratextual rhyme is less clear: the declaration "it's sure to be a smash" is seemingly proleptic. And although the narrator starts the rhyme self-referentially, the final couplet refers to *you* meeting Count Dracula and suggests *you will* really get a fright, which the narrator could not know, but predicts. The ending is unresolved, it is open, and relies on the comic elements to allay the sense of threat, but also to distract from these issues of incongruity. Furthermore, to return to the wider context of the story, the child narrator is, conspicuously on its own; having received an invitation from a neighbor whom he does not know, but has attended without any adult company, and with no indication of "permission" to do so. Yet, it is this element that has the greatest potential to empower. Like Max in Maurice Sendak's well-known narrative picture book *Where the Wild Things Are* (1963), without adult supervision the child can wreak havoc and break the rules, embark on fantastical excursions and can test the boundaries—but also, without anyone else as potential protector, the child may learn essential skills more quickly. The absent parent in fiction has long been a staple trope that allows, suggests Virginia Walters, for "a voyage of self-discovery in which the children learn the follies of regression and denial and discover the empowerment of self-reliance and independence" (205). However, as Max's desire to return home also suggests, the unaided encounter with the monster is simultaneously a metaphor for fears of abandonment and despair that requires resolution and comfort. The ambiguous ending of Faulkner's text that denies the reader a definite chance to fight or to party with the monster, creates an uncertainty that could be seen as debilitating.

Similar issues are present in *Dracula's Tomb* (1998), written and illustrated by Colin McNaughton and marketed for ages 5–9 years. This also has only one pop-up, and has no other mechanical elements, but attempts to create diversity of form through an irregular hexagonal (tomb-shaped) book, with the cover's design emulating a tombstone. The text is devised—in an ironic twist on the epistolary devices of Stoker's novel—as the vampire's secret journals. The first inner-page designed as an old leather journal, or a school-book, and the inscription reads "KEEP OUT! The Journals of Count Dracula. PRIVATE" (n.p.). Despite this warning, when the page is turned, the text contradicts the suggestion of a private and introspective narrative, and directly addresses the reader: under the heading "Drac-Facts," it reads, "Welcome—Count Dracula's the name and drinking blood's the game." Like many "handbooks" to vampires published in recent years for adults, such as Scott Bowen's, *The Vampire Survival Guide: How to Fight, and Win, Against the Undead* (2008), and Roger Ma's, *The Vampire Combat Manual: A Guide to Fighting the Bloodthirsty Undead* (2012), the intertextual mode that draws together tropes and impressions from the wider vampire canon has both educational (even where parodic) as well as entertainment value in providing such a close and intimate encounter with the vampire.

In McNaughton's text, Dracula presents his baby-pictures, tells the reader about where he lives and his lineage, he describes his transformative potential, and what can kill or harm him. The initial illustration of him does not suggest he is a child-vampire at the time of writing. Yet the journal contains intimate childhood items: a school report by Doctor Frankenstein with scribbles and graffiti around the edge with jokes and proclamations like "Werewolf is normal" underneath the drawing of a human child which is captioned "A monster"; letters Dracula wrote to his parents from school—in one of which he tells of meeting a "real-life author called Mister Bram Stoker" who "said he was going to write a book" about Dracula's family; a list of his pets; a reproduction of the contents of his fridge; pictures of what he wears and owns, and a "night in the life of Count Dracula" which sketches his exploits on a typical evening.

Julie Cross asserts that, as well as "farce-like" and "gross" humor, comic Gothic texts for both older and younger readers often rely "on a sophisticated understanding of irony, parody, genre convention, and 'higher' order cognitive forms of humour, such as the perception of, and ultimate enjoyment and even acceptance of, incongruity" (58). *Dracula's Tomb* features numerous examples of humorous intertextual word play, such as Drac in the bath singing "Fangs for the Memories," the "dead tasty" "tombatoes" in his fridge, and visual puns such as his coffin-shaped suitcase, or the blank photograph of his friend the Invisible Man in the snow. Furthermore, any incongruous and seemingly absurd objects owned, or activities undertaken, by Dracula are not necessarily unfamiliar to its original literary incarnation. For, as Royce MacGillivray suggests, elements such as Dracula cooking for Jonathan himself and later his wearing of a straw hat, which Van Helsing suggests suited neither him, nor the time, can be read as a "gentle form of self-parody, or of a mockery at tales of the supernatural," but might also be seen as Stoker's commentary on the "ironies, contradictions, and wild absurdities" of everyday life (520).

Although there are allusions to his deadly activities, the jovial, informative manner in which the reader of the lift-the-flap book is Dracula's confidant—privy to the aspects that form his identity—constructs a barrier between potential threat and reader for the majority of the text. Furthermore, it speaks to the very aspect that makes picture books in general transgressive, for, suggest Victor Watson and Morag Styles, "[t]he voices of picturebooks are intimate and the sharing of them tends towards the conspiratorial" (1). However, the final page of the journal is followed by what can be recognized as the top part of a wooden coffin with insects crawling over it and a plaque reading "Do Not Disturb. Within this casket lie the remains of Count Dracula. Do Not Open (You'll Regret It)." The rebellious reader does, of course, turn the page, and a large pop-up Dracula rises to greet the reader. This version is far more detailed and terrifying than the previous example. Rather than the block colors of Lambert's Dracula for Faulkner's the *Spooky Lift-the-Flap Book*, Dracula's features are here exaggerated and contoured: his sharp nose protrudes owing to the extra folds in the pop-up, his sclera are not white but red and his pupils appear white with a thin black iris conveying a piercing manic effect, his ears are sharply pointed, as are his fingernails, which emanate toward the reader, and his hair is black and slicked and streaked with grey at the sides. His mouth is wide open, so much so that his tonsils are visible, and all his teeth are bared. His suit is dark and caped, with a very high black and red collar, and covered in spiders and worms and bats escaping from the coffin and beneath the suit. The only comic relief, aside from the goofy expressions of the insects, is Dracula's bat-shaped bow tie. The various features are an amalgamation of both textual and visual depictions of Dracula across the decades, such as the strong aquiline face, huge eyebrows, "peculiarly sharp white teeth" which protrude "over the lips," pointed ears, and the sharp, long, fine nails of Stoker's original vision (Stoker 17).

The pop-up itself, in which Dracula comes towards the reader, is, on a basic level, the simple scare tactic of the monster leaping out and perhaps has deeper folkloric roots in what Lafcadio Hearn pinpoints as the innate dread of being touched by the supernatural (237). Further connections with the movement of Dracula in Stoker's novel are ascertainable through the kinetic movement of the mechanism: following the description of the vampire's features in Stoker's novel, Harker's journal observes that "[a]s the Count leaned over me and his hands touched me, I could not repress a shudder," and when Seward and company plan to ambush Dracula, Seward recounts that "[s]uddenly with a single bound he leaped into the room [...] There was something so panther-like in the movement some-thing so unhuman, that it seemed to sober us all from the shock of his coming" (Stoker 284–285). The power of this final pop-up and its terror lies in the disarmament of the reader through the conviviality with Dracula in the preceding narrative. Despite the warnings on the front of the journal, the reader has bravely (if rudely—after all, they are reading someone's diary) embarked on the narrative journey and has not encountered any clear signs of direct threat to themselves, and so are lulled into a false sense of security that makes the final pop-up somewhat, though not completely, surprising. Yet, as with Faulkner's text, there are no resolutions, no sense of what "happens next," and this is potentially all the more threatening and disempowering. On the other hand, the creative license of this open ending means that, for instance, an adult reader could ask the child to draw upon what they have learnt about the vampire and his weaknesses and describe how they would defeat Dracula (something hindered by the minimalism of Faulkner's), but there is no such cue from the text.

Perhaps one of the most successful comedic metamorphoses of the Dracula character in this medium is found in Michael Ratnett's *Dracula Steps Out: A Pop-Up Book* (1998) illustrated by June Goulding which is recommended for readers aged 6–8. Following a rhyme about Dracula's nightly prowl for food, the blurb reads:

> Close your windows! Lock your doors! Dracula is on the prowl, ready for his supper. But is he as dangerous as he seems? Open the pages of this fiendishly funny book to find out—if you dare! [n.p.].

The text uses pop-ups, secret doors, sliding panels and jokes to collectively and more progressively subvert any expectations the reader may have had of Dracula, or at least of vampires. Despite his grey-streaked hair, it is notable that this Dracula has a much more youthful stature and appearance than in the aforementioned texts. While the illustrations are cartoonish, they are contemporary and detailed, and the mechanical features are particularly sophisticated. Around the main narrative—which is comprised of simplistic rhyming couplets that are repeated and extended on each page—each double spread is filled with additional elements such as various creatures telling jokes that are revealed by lifting flaps, smiling moons become fanged when the dial is turned, and with elements which complement the narrative such as tabs that turn Dracula's eyes red to reveal his "X-ray sight" and another tab which then reveals the skeletons of some humans passing by.

A sense of dread is created by playing on those familiar visual tropes of Gothic and of vampire media—deadly or creepy creatures, anthropomorphic gargoyles with glowing red eyes—and through the repetitive narrative strain of the insatiably hungry vampire. On the fourth double spread, Dracula leers out of an alleyway toward a little boy holding a teddy bear, while his mother and sister look on in terror. The monstration—the narrative level of the image—corresponds with the implications of the text that the "tasty little mite" Dracula spies is the boy. Yet this is deliberately misleading, for on turning the page Dracula looks adoringly at the teddy because the boy has discerned that Dracula longs for cuddly toys and will sacrifice his teddy because the vampire looks, "so very sad and lonely." It seems that Dracula was going to take the toy by force, but by sharing, by seeing that someone else's need is greater than his own, the boy has delighted Dracula. On the final page the tabs reveal that Dracula's coffin-bed is full of different teddies "Because, despite his pointy teeth, he's a great big softy underneath!" The message, though simplistic, seems to suggest that should you dare to engage with the monster, you may find he is not so terrifying after all. Sympathy with the monster—a tactic often found in children's books—does not imply that there are no monsters; rather it invites the reader to reevaluate their initial prejudice and imbues them with the power to relate to those who are different and ostracized.

Mechanical Manifestations: Adapting Dracula

As with many other mediums, a number of metamorphoses books have identified Stoker's original text as a popular source for adaptation. As I wish to concentrate on the (inter)active participation of the reader and the potential for education and empowerment, the two examples I discuss ahead have adapted the narrative in a manner that poses an invitation to the reader (either explicitly or implicitly) to join the hunt for the vampire, with different degrees of success.

Gallery Books' 1990 classic pop-ups adaptation of *Dracula,* described (perhaps rather over-optimistically) in the blurb as "an exciting introduction" for young readers who will be "spellbound" and "enthralled by this chilling, fast-paced tale" (n.p.), heavily expurgates and summarizes the story to just six double-page scenes. There are tremendous gaps in the plot and often contradictions between the images (over-ambitiously described as "pop-ups") and the text. Some of the key reasons this adaptation fails to engage the reader is evidenced by the choice to avoid any of the epistolary elements characteristic to the novel and use only an omniscient narrator. Although, to some extent, this may be a reflection of the expected abilities of the younger reader, its heavy abridgment diminishes the nuances used by the original text to implicate threat and fails to provide the tools for reader sympathy. For instance, in its depiction of the archetypal villain, the text relies on simple but not strong visual signifiers—Dracula is overly pale, seemingly a bat, the sisters have red eyes and sharp teeth, they all sleep in coffins. It depends too heavily on a familiar reader to make the connections based on cultural codes of monstrosity perceived from wider popular media, rather than engaging with the role Stoker's novel played in establishing these codes. The reader cannot identify with the monster—for there is no attention to the charm and intelligence of the Count (and, owing the reading age, his desirability)—and so the blurring of the monster/human boundary of the original, and thus fears of contagion and the degraded body, are absent.

Neither is there opportunity for identification with any of the human characters because there is no character development or any development of suspense and fear that might draw the reader in. For instance, on the first two pages, the text is set over an illustration of a stagecoach being led along a path that, although framed by forest, is neither claustrophobic nor darkly colored. On the same page of the pop-up, the reader is told that when Jonathan tells the people in the coach that he is heading toward Castle Dracula, the response is rather sterile: "Frightened, they said, 'Do not go! You will be in danger.' 'But I must!' answered Jonathan as he stepped off the coach into the black night." While there is a hint of foreboding in their unexplained fear, it is weak and unsupported by any other portents, textual or visual, as the narrative unfolds. Fundamental tropes such as crying wolves, the howling wind, strange light, and the Count's pale skin and cold touch, are used to mimic a Gothic register, but the narrative lacks the logic necessary for a young reader to understand why these elements might be threatening.

The six double-spread illustrations depict a stage-coach in a forest area; meeting Dracula at the door to the Castle; Jonathan looking out of a window and seeing Dracula fly; three vampire-women attacking Jonathan; Lucy and Mina looking at a ship being wrecked, and two men standing over a box in the snow with a raised stake and the castle in the background. None of the illustrations pop-out to the extent at which they intrude on the experiential space of the reader; rather, simple cuts allow for a slight movement and three-dimensional aspect of certain features such as the terrified horses, the intimidating bat, and, in an attempt to offer perspective, to the women looking on the ship. They do not, however, enhance the text itself, and add little to the Gothic effect as other examples of vampire metamorphoses books do. The tale is, as it claims, "fast-paced," in that it is unwittingly isochronical—compressing the time-span of the novel into an incongruously swift movement from Transylvania to England and back to Transylvania as if the turning of the pages itself denotes the implausible travel. There is no explicit indication of periodization—there are no dates, no clear historical clues for the young reader. Confusion is also caused by the character's clothing and the style of the drawings, which, though imitative of a nineteenth-century setting, jar against the modern colloquial and at times anachronistic dialogue:

> "Mina! What's the matter?" said Lucy.
> "I'm worried about Jonathan," sighed Mina.
> "Maybe Arthur can help." Arthur was Lucy's boyfriend.

While neo–Victorian fictions for children can often be very successful in helping the child reconcile and recognize seemingly incongruous and anachronistic elements, they do so through a playfulness, as Lara Rutherford suggests in her article on Alan Moore's *The League of Extraordinary Gentleman* series (125)—an element absent in the Gallery Books adaptation. Like most of the characters, Lucy and Mina's role is minimal, relinquishing any opportunity for the reader (and predominantly the female reader) to engage with Mina's important role as transcriber of events in the original text. Furthermore, it does not even clearly affirm the heteronormative by bringing "the assertive heroine back into a conventional patriarchal relationship" at the story's close, as William Hughes notes is typical of Stoker's writings (6). In contrast, Jonathan's role in the Gallery version is the subject of four of the illustrations, and, as such, becomes the "hero"—with minimal room for the bravery, dedication and knowledge Stoker attributes to Van Helsing, Arthur Holmwood, John Seward, and Quincey Morris (the latter two entirely absent from the adaptation except as "the men" who pursue Dracula).[3] Despite the enticement of the blurb, the limited narrative does not actively invite the reader to participate in any form. Yet it does at least resolve the story by ending on the line "Dracula was gone"—an aspect Ann Trousdale has suggested to be essential for allaying the fears of younger child readers in scary stories with defined monsters: "Is it possible that when the wolf is allowed to survive and roam free, children are left with the sense that, indeed, he may certainly come back at any time?" (70). It is dubious whether such a resolution in this adaptation, however, makes it empowering.

In stark contrast, Eddie Robson's version (2009), elaborately illustrated by Nicola Robinson, and marketed eight years and up, is a detailed and multifaceted opportunity for the reader to engage with the *Dracula* legacy. Ten large double spreads are completely covered in illustration, text, multiple panels and icons, leaving no negative space, even across the paratext. It is not a straight adaptation, nor is it a complete transformation of Stoker's original. Visually, Robinson emulates the Victorian Gothic chronotrope, but does so through a neo–Victorian Gothic framework. For instance, the cover displays a dark, Gothic landscape—an imposing castle toward which a stagecoach rushes, pursued by wolves with glowing eyes and overlooked by bats shadowed against the moon, while along the right hand edge a vertical strip shows half of Dracula's heavily contoured features against his pale skin, his piercing red eyes, blood red lips framing a wide open mouth which reveal sharp blood-stained teeth: the monster stares at the reader, both threatening and daring. Yet, while the drawings are sophisticated and alluring the cartoonish quality deliberately avoids any easy mimetic representation of Stoker's original setting. In terms of the content, Robson's piece relies heavily on the characters, plot line, and settings of its textual sire—but it plays with and augments the themes of the original such as the weather, travel, epistolary forms, and with its structure by manipulating the dialogue and sequence of narration. It also elaborates on the contextual features of medical advancements and vampire lore by employing pseudo-original newspaper clippings and articles from periodicals.

The burdened text of Stoker's form is abridged, and the dialogue repurposed to make best use of the intraiconic text inserted on images of journals, newspaper clippings, and inscriptions on tombs. Robson's book re-focalizes the story through the homodiegetic narration of Van Helsing who participates both intradiegetically in his diary entries and conversations recorded by other characters, and extradiegetically through direct addresses to the reader: "I am Abraham Van Helsing and my hand trembles at the horrors I have just seen. But to begin at the beginning.... Recently, one of my former pupils, Dr John Seward, asked for my help" (n.p.). This, the opening statement to the main narrative, is, as with subsequent addresses, placed within a white, framed panel in the top left-hand corner of each double spread. Utilizing techniques found in the comic or graphic novel, as well as in contemporary filmic media, this style and placement signals to the reader that this dialogue is separate from the main narrative. This is not achieved simply through the visualization but works in conjunction with the text; for, like Jonathan Harker's note at the end of Stoker's novel, this is not a diary entry or letter to another character, but a deliberate introduction for and engagement with the reader. It is told from a time not long after the real-time events have finished, as indicated by the reference "recently," and so transports the reader into its particular chronotope.

There is much more to be said about the techniques employed and effects achieved by this intricate re-appropriation, but here I will focus on how the structural and textual choices and the use of interactive movable elements, engages, educates, and attempts to empower its reader. As previously mentioned, the paratext offers a direct invitation to join the team in the hunt for Dracula, with the front cover offering that enticing warning; "Beware! Blood-curdling Surprises Inside!" The paratext alludes to a collective experience that the reader will be a part of, and sets the text up as exciting and enticing. On the inside cover, the staged Gothic chronotope continues with a double spread map of Britain overlaid with callouts such as small scrolls describing the significance of the key locations of Whitby, Exeter, London, and Carfax, and the key dramatis personae are depicted in Gothic picture frames (although Quincey Morris is notably absent), accompanied by a short description based on the character's situation at the time this narrative begins; thus reframing the textual hunt as a theatrical performance. The scroll heading the page asks, "Do you believe in vampires—the undead who feast on the blood of the living? Meet the fearless cast who must confront Count Dracula, the Prince of Darkness, in an epic battle of good against evil." The question invites the reader into its narratorial confidence, ignites readerly agency through direct introductions, and asks not only whether you do believe, but suggests you *should* believe. Furthermore, it classifies all the cast—male and female alike—as fearless warriors in an epic battle.

Although the skirmish with the undead does occupy Stoker's text, the sequencing of the diary entries does not frame the plot in this way from the beginning—Robson's structure thus appeals to an impulse to do battle with monsters and to solve the problems of how to save ourselves and others, that many child psychologists have suggested are integral to children's fantasy stories (Bettelheim 111). So, rather than beginning with Harker's journal, the main tale is directed by Van Helsing, and with his arrival in Whitby in order to stress the sense of urgency and continuous movement. Furthermore, the events of the vampire killings are manipulated so that, when Van Helsing faces the three weird vampire sisters, he does not do it alone, as he does in the novel. Although it is still Van Helsing that performs the final deed, Mina is not confined to the protective circle that he encases her in as she is in the novel, but is by his side and playing an active part in the demise of the monsters. So too, when Dracula is killed, Robson fuses Stoker's ending with that of F.W. Murnau's *Nosferatu* (1922) by exaggerating the inhibiting qualities of sunlight on Dracula, who runs after Mina, having been provoked by her in order that she may protect the others, but as "He reached out a clawed hand to snatch her to him [...] he was struck by light from the rising sun! With a piercing scream from hell, he slumped to the ground." This then gives Van Helsing the opportunity to stake him—rather than the beheading by Harker and knife staking by Quincey Morris of the novel. Also in the novel, the final "battle" with Dracula, is not, in fact a fight at all. Although there is an exchange of violence in Carfax, at the end of Stoker's novel, the group has tracked down Dracula's final coffin and lift the lid and dispose of the Count while he lies immobilized. Robson's adaptation affords the monster a fighting chance, but also allows Mina to, once again, actively participate in the demise of the main evil—a decisive move to empower the female reader.

Rather than being didactic, the pedagogical elements of the text are the means by which the reader is immersed in the mythopoeia of *Dracula* and the folklore of the vampire, further providing historical context—something enhanced by the movable elements. For instance, attached to the frontispiece—which reiterates the title and the key publication information—is an intriguing interactive feature that amalgamates factual elements derived from Harker's journey to Transylvania and the wider Victorian context: a small, twelve-page booklet in neo-Victorian Gothic design and entitled *Land of the Vampires: A Bite-Sized Travel Guide to Transylvania, Home of Count Dracula*, mimics and parodies the original text's preoccupation with tourism for, as Arata observes, "Stoker maps his story not simply onto the Gothic but also onto a second, equally popular late–Victorian genre, the travel narrative" (626). Maps and travel are an integral theme of this adaptation, with two double spreads (one of Britain, one of Europe), one map of Dracula's castle as apparently sketched by Harker from memory and which is a separate document inserted into a slit in a page, and finally a reproduction of the inside of the castle which will be discussed further on. The use of these visual aids might be seen to correspond with the educational idea that maps help develop "spatial cognition and cognitive mapping" (Wiegand 2). Yet they are also key to the development of imaginative qualities by playing on the aesthetic appeal of the cartographic drawing, or what Patrick Wiegand calls the "romantic myth" of maps, that ignites a sense of adventure and purpose in the reader (1).

The booklet also functions as an informative tool and an opportunity to once again challenge the reader. The opening line asks, "Are you ready for a very different type of holiday—one you can really sink your teeth into?" The booklet informs through a repetitive humorous technique that is not integral to the original text but prevalent in the wider vampire-canon. Punning on the vampiric feature of biting, there are faux menus that emphasize garlic as a protective herb in folklore, but the narrative also quips, "We advise you to take a strong mouthwash if you are on honeymoon," the implications of which may be unclear to the emergent reader, but contribute to a growing comedic awareness. Coupons for crucifixes and mirror sets and vampire tours, and advertisements for neck protectors and "Eau de Garlic," a "new fragrance for women," are followed by a list of vampire facts, safety and survival tips, and the description of a Vampire Survival Course. Information in the pamphlet, such as the tour including meals and trips to the cemetery, and the recommendation of insurance, blurs the contextual boundaries of the hunt for Dracula—it is not the counter-cultural, secret mission of Stoker's text, but an interactive, consumerist activity familiar to the twenty-first-century reader, but one nevertheless present in late–Victorian culture.

In regard to the more obvious movable elements of the book—its pop-ups and pull-the-tabs—the function is far less pedagogical and much more visceral. The large protruding swarm of large red-eyed rats that seem to race directly toward and threaten to engulf the reader as they do Van Helsing and company when they enter Dracula's house at Carfax, plays on simple techniques of terror associated with the physical threat of an unpopular animal. So too, the tab that turns the portrait of Lucy from a beautiful young woman to a snarling evil vampire uses a classic Gothic trope of the haunted painting, while the tab that opens and lowers Dracula's long, sharp-toothed mouth to Mina's neck plays on the basic fear of the vampire's bite.

However, there is one final interactive element in this edition that directly engages the reader in the battle. The double spread on the inside of the back cover is a board game that complements but works outside of the main narrative. Perhaps the most successful version would have required the reader to use the knowledge learned from the booklet and text to complete the board game; however such pedagogical applications are familiar to children's picture books and stories in the guise of puzzles, clues to collect and mysteries to solve, and are evidence of the flexibility of such texts and their ability to appeal to different cognitive activities. The panel in the top left corner reads, "ESCAPE FROM DRACULA! You're trapped in Dracula's castle! Your only escape is to reach the cellar to destroy the evil count!" Inserted into the booklet at the beginning were four detachable cards presenting different players, along with a spinning form of die. Perhaps unusually, considering both the original text and the chronological narrative choices by Robson, the players are Lucy, Dr. Seward, Mina, and Arthur. This in itself defies the parameters of the text, transgressing the borders of plausibility (but I suspect attempting to bridge the deficit in female heroines in the novel). The players must navigate the spaces of Dracula's castle and its threats such as bats, tripping on a coffin, being distracted by reading a book in the library, or forgetting the holy water. The desired destination is the cellar, where the player must collect the stake and hammer, and then "spin a six to destroy Dracula and escape."

Conclusion

These various examples of encounters with vampires do not necessarily offer the transgressive experience that many contemporary picture books have done by playing with gender or utilizing the child vampire for a better sense of identification. For instance, Richard Egielski's *The Sleepless Little Vampire* (2011), in which Rebecca A. Brown suggests the child as vampire "physically and behaviourally subverts normative constructions of masculinity and femininity" (98), and other metamorphoses books such as *The Mystery of the Vampire Boy* (2014), written by Dereen Taylor and illustrated by Mike Spoor, where one of the children dressed as a vampire at a Halloween fancy dress party seems "all too realistic" (98). Nevertheless, their participatory invitations to the reader employ the allure of the Gothic to face the monster and allows them to do so—itself a demonstration of courage—but not all provide a successful scenario for defeating or befriending Dracula.

It is pertinent to note that, as the most recent example, Robson's adaptation appears in the clearly defined era from which media such as *Buffy the Vampire Slayer* and the *Twilight* series have explored these encounters and which are increasingly preoccupied with the relationship between the young human and the vampire. His version not only corresponds with this changing generational use of the vampire, but is concerned with preserving as well as playing with the folkloric and intertextual parameters outlined by Stoker, which may explain why it offers a far more useful, as well as aesthetically pleasing foray into the Gothic. Through the fusion with the comedic, as in Faulkner and McNaughton's texts, basic tools are provided to a younger reader to achieve what Avril Horner and Sue Zlosnik suggest the comic-Gothic can do for the adult reader: "[t]he comic Gothic turn self-consciously uses Gothic's propensity to bare the device in order to allay the reader's learnt response of fear, horror, and anxiety when encountering certain plots and tropes" (323). The young reader will not necessarily possess the "learnt response" to use the comic as a means of diffusing terror, and so may require the cue of the adult to follow expressions of fear with a laughter that signifies a realization (or perhaps a hope) that the object of terror is nothing but a farce or a trick. So too, like the adult reader and viewer, the child reader may find pleasure in the anticipation and in the experience of being scared. Horner and Zlosnik re-evaluate the comic elements in Gothic as part of a "spectrum that, at one end, produces horror writing containing moments of comic hysteria or relief and, at the other, works in which there are clear signals that nothing is to be taken seriously" (323), and texts like Faulkner's reside ambiguously somewhere between.

In all of the examples, the interactive elements have the potential to enhance the terror of the text, thus exacerbating the sense of achievement for the child who is courageous enough to continue reading. So too do they contribute to the hybridity of form and genre that defines the Gothic. For if, in the average picture book, "contributions of the visual and verbal [...] result in a 'great efficiency in communicating meaning ... high semantic or semiotic capacity'" (Golden and Gerber 204), then the addition of interactive elements can only enhance skills further. Margaret Higonnet, speaking of the picture book and its physical components more widely, suggests that "[a]lready evident in those physical features of children's literature is the deliberate seduction through play of the reader" (48), and again, with the infusion of Gothic in the examples above, that seduction of transgression is intensified. Uses of intraiconic text, such as the writing on product packaging, or across tombstones, and the more complex shifts between different panels, different narrators, and different scenarios, enable the reader to recognize cultural codes, gain pleasure from solving mysteries and even from being terrified, and enhances their cognitive abilities. The empowerment the child can receive through the juxtaposition of text/image/mechanical element and the integral genre of the Gothic is therefore intriguingly multifaceted.

NOTES

1. Perhaps surprisingly, despite the nineteenth-century fashion for mechanical books for children, and, separately, for theatrical and sensationalised spectaculars, the Gothic metamorphoses as a distinct and recognisable form does not appear until the late 1970s, and its contribution to the fields of both movable books and, particularly, the Gothic genre, is a distinctly under-researched medium.
2. A large amount of pop-up/metamorphosis books are often unpaginated as they are frequently comprised of a small amount of pages.
3. Astle notes in his Freudian reading that while Jonathan is "the hero of the heroic myth," Van Helsing is the "the 'head' of the corporate hero" who is assigned the role of leader (Astle 1979). However, in Gallery books' adaptation his name is mentioned only three times, with his knowledge limited to telling the others that Lucy has been turned and must be staked (not beheaded as is consistently discussed in the text).

WORKS CITED

Aldana Rayes, Xavier. *Horror Film and Affect: Towards a Corporeal Model of Viewership.* London: Routledge, 2016.
Arata, Stephen D. "The Occidental Tourist: 'Dracula' and the Anxiety of Reverse Colonization." *Victorian Studies* 33.4 (1990): 621–645.
Astle, Richard. "Dracula as Totemic Monster: Lacan, Freud, Oedipus and History." *SubStance*, 8.4, Issue 25 (1979). 98–105.
Auerbach, Nina. *Our Vampires, Ourselves.* Chicago: University of Chicago Press, 1995.
Bettelheim, Bruno. *The Uses of Enchantment: The Meaning and Importance of Fairy Tales.* New York: Random House, 1976.
Botting, Fred. *Gothic: A New Critical Idiom.* London: Routledge, 1996.
Brown, Rebecca A. "From Aggressive Wolf to Heteronormative Zombie: Performing Monstrosity and Masculinity in the Narrative Picturebook." *Reading in the Dark: Horror in Children's Literature and Culture.* Ed. Jessica McCort. University Press of Mississippi, 2016. 90–120.
Carrington, Victoria. "The Contemporary Gothic: Literacy and Childhood in Unsettled Times." *Journal of Early Childhood Literacy* 12.3 (2011): 293–310.
Cross, Julie. "Frightening and Funny: Humour in Children's Gothic Fiction." *The Gothic in Children's Literature: Haunting the Borders.* Ed. Anna Jackson, Karen Coats, and Roderick McGillis. London: Routledge, 2008. 57–76.
Faulkner, Keith. *Dracula: A Spooky Lift-the-Flap Book.* Basingstoke: HarperFestival, 1993.
Golden, Joanne M., and Annyce Gerber. "A Semiotic Perspective of Text: The Picture Story Book Event." *Journal of Reading Behavior* 22.3 (1990): 203–219.
Hearn, Lafcadio. "The Nightmare-Touch." *Shadowings.* Boston: Little, Brown, 1919. 235–248.
Higonnet, Margaret R. "The Playground and the Peritext." *Children's Literature Association Quarterly* 15.2 (1990): 47–49.
Horner, Avril, and Sue Zlosnick. "Comic Gothic." *A New Companion to the Gothic.* Ed. David Punter. Chichester: Wiley-Blackwell, 2012. 321–334.
Hughes, William. *Bram Stoker's Dracula: A Reader's Guide.* London: Continuum, 2009.
Jackson, Anna, Karen Coats, and Roderick McGillis. "Introduction." *The Gothic in Children's Literature: Haunting the Borders.* Ed. Anna Jackson, Karen Coats, and Roderick McGillis. London: Routledge, 2008. 1–14.
MacGillivray, Royce. "'Dracula': Bram Stoker's Spoiled Masterpiece." *Queen's Quarterly* 79.4 (1972): 518–527.
Ratnett, Michael. *Dracula Steps Out.* New York: Orchard Books, 1998.

Robson, Eddie. *Bram Stoker's Dracula: The Greatest Vampire*. London: Carlton Books, 2009.
Rutherford, Lara. "Victorian Genres at Play: Juvenile Fiction and *The League of Extraordinary Gentlemen*." *Neo-Victorian Studies* 5.1 (2012): 125–151.
Stoker, Bram. *Dracula*. New York: Grosset and Dunlap, 1897.
_____. *Dracula: Classic Pop-Ups*. New York: Gallery Books, 1990.
Trousdale, Ann. "Who's Afraid of the Big, Bad Wolf?" *Children's Literature in Education* 20.2 (1989): 69–79.
Walters, Virginia A. "Hansel and Gretel as Abandoned Children: Timeless Images for a Postmodern Age." *Children's Literature in Education* 23.4 (1992): 203–214.
Watson, Victor, and Morag Styles. "Introduction." *Talking Pictures: Pictorial Texts and Young Readers*. Ed. Victor Watson and Morag Styles. Hodder and Stoughton, 1996. 1–4.
Wiegand, Patrick. *Learning and Teaching with Maps*. London: Routledge, 2006.

The Drawn Daughters of Dracula
Vampire Girlhood in British Comics of the 1970s and 1980s

Jack Fennell

This essay will look at the depiction of vampires in comic books aimed particularly at girls, and vampire characters in general-audience comics that held particular appeal for girls. In much of the media in which they appear, vampires are often gleefully unrestrained, reveling in their supernatural ability to cause havoc, and, at first blush, their appeal would seem to be as straightforward wish-fulfillment fantasies: vampire characters do what they like, whenever they like, and it is not hard to see how this freedom would appeal to children and adolescents. As a medium, the comic book is ideally suited to this kind of escapism, and the form has developed its own visual vocabularies and storytelling strategies to enhance it.

Discussions of escapism and power are especially significant in the case of female vampire characters. Historically, girls have been much more closely monitored than boys, and been expected to adhere more stringently to cultural standards of decorum and propriety. The vampire girls and women of comic books, however, for the most part have freedom to misbehave. This study examines British comic books featuring vampire characters, and traces their impact on the female readers who may have identified with them.

The Horror Comics Hullaballoo

Between 1949 and 1955, inspired by the moral crusade against comics in the USA, a campaign began in the United Kingdom against American horror comics, which had first arrived in the country with the American GIs who had been stationed there during World War II. Part of the later negative reaction to the comics was due to the fact that the GIs who brought them were uncouth working-class youths, rather than sophisticated tourists (Barker 26). By 1954, the British small publishers had abandoned bulk importation and, having acquired the necessary matrices ("mats"), were instead re-printing American horror comics locally. Titles such as *Haunt of Fear* and *Tales from the Crypt* were re-printed with runs of up to 50,000 copies, triggering a public uproar (8–9).

In October of that year, the issue was raised in Parliament. Mister J. Rankin, Labour MP for Tradeston, expressed his concern that these imported comics "had a demoralizing effect on the minds of children, because they helped to spread illiteracy and encourage sadistic practices," and asked the Home Secretary, Major Gwilym Lloyd George, to "take steps to prevent their circulation among children." When Dr. Stross, the Labour member for Stoke-on-Trent Central, said that some newsagents did not even want to handle these comics, the Home Secretary drolly replied, "If they feel that they do not want to handle the material, I should have thought that the best thing was for them not to handle it." Lloyd George deflected the concerns of other MPs with vague promises to consider the matter further, and in response to a separate question said that he would "look into" amending the laws on obscenity in literature ("Medical Notes in Parliament" 1055).

Despite the Home Secretary's apparent lack of personal interest in the matter, late in 1954 legislation was introduced, based substantially on a draft bill produced by the Comics Campaign Committee (Barker 14); this bill would become the Children and Young Persons (Harmful Publications) Act. It received royal assent on May 6th 1955, and came into force a month later.[1] The influence of U.S. moral campaigns against comics seems clear: the campaign quoted psychiatrist Dr. Fredric Wertham's work as it suited them (Barker 30),[2] and the CCC's *British Comics—An Appraisal* (1954), published after the passing of the Act, used a rating system for comic books originally devised by the Cincinnati Parents' Council (37).

The efficacy of the Act, which is still in effect, is open to debate. On the one hand, it does nothing to impact the importation, sale and domestic production of adult-oriented crime and horror comics in the UK today, and prosecutions based on it are infrequent. In a written response to a question in the House of Commons from William "Bill" Hamling (Labour MP for Woolwich West) in 1974, Dr. Catherine Summerskill (Labour MP for Halifax; Secretary of State for the Home Department) established that the first prosecutions under this Act both took place in 1970, sixteen years after it was enacted ("Children's Publications (Prosecutions)"). On the other hand, however, it did more or less halt the production of such material until the 1970s—

and it was thanks to publications aimed specifically at girls that horror comics were able to make a comeback.

Comics for Girls

In 1950, amid the furor over imported American horror comics, Hulton Press hired Market Information Services Limited to conduct market research on boys aged between eight and fifteen, to determine whether they would be interested in their planned publication, *Eagle*.[3] The research was very thorough and comprehensive, covering not just the kinds of comics that these boys were interested in, but also their favorite "items," radio programs, newspapers, and hobbies and interests in general (Henry 373). Once *Eagle* was up and running, Market Information Services decided to pursue an ongoing, weekly survey of readers' interest levels. To mitigate the exorbitant cost of fieldwork, they decided to utilize the *Eagle* fan club as a sampling frame instead, which eventually gave them access to around 100,000 children. At this point, they were acting on the assumption that club members were broadly representative of the general readership (374). It was discovered that the respondents were quite discerning, as individual features' popularity could be correlated to previous ratings: children's responses were influenced by their memory of the previous week's installment (377).

A full-scale readership survey carried out in August 1950 determined that 29 percent of *Eagle* readers generally, but only 10 percent of club members, were girls. The reader responses for this group, stratified by age, returned the same statistical results as the majority boys' group (378). While MIS disregarded these figures (*Eagle* was a comic intended for boys, after all), it seems clear that girls who were inclined to read the comic enjoyed it to the same degree as the boys. Jacqueline Danziger-Russell argues that since "some human interests are universal," it is more than reasonable to assume that girls and women have always enjoyed material aimed at a specifically male readership, including the majority of comic books (10–11). There are, in fact, a number of American studies from the twentieth century that bear this out. A 1938 survey of 256 children aged nine to twelve in two Philadelphia schools concluded that boys were drawn to strips featuring "action, adventure, fighting, feats of strength and daring, fantastic tales of life in other lands and planets, [and] thrilling escapades in the field of aviation"; girls also "showed a marked interest in these things," with the addition of other elements such as romance and family life, and were much more interested than the boys in strips that told "familiar fairy tales" (Hill and Trent 35). In his seminal work *The Comics* (1947), Coulton Waugh (drawing on "the most reliable available figures") revealed that, between the ages of six and eleven, 95 percent of boys and 91 percent of girls purchased comics regularly; between the ages of twelve and seventeen, 87 percent of boys and 81 percent of girls continued to do so (334). Past the age of eighteen, the decline in interest in comic books seems to have been more pronounced among female readers than male ones, but the fact remains that throughout childhood and adolescence, the figures were almost the same. Clearly, neither the form nor the content of comics deterred girls from reading them.

Three years later, a similar survey was conducted on children in the same age bracket in a number of schools in Illinois. Focusing on the data from schools in Evanston, Paul Witty describes some interesting results: an all-grades results table shows that girls gave higher scores than boys to *Batman*, *Action*, *Flash*, *Detective* and *True Comics*. Furthermore, while children of both sexes reported roughly equal enthusiasm for newspaper comic strips (102), *Brenda Starr*, a strip about the investigations and romantic adventures of a glamorous investigative reporter, was by far the most popular strip among the surveyed boys, who gave it an average rank of 39.5, compared to the average rank of 4.0 given to it by girls of the same age (this is all the more remarkable for the fact that it was not included in the survey by the investigators, but added by the respondents themselves in the space provided). Among the children surveyed, equal percentages of boys and girls reported that they enjoyed making their own original comics (103). Once again, we have proof that girls were just as interested as boys in comics, and if the newspaper strip figures are reliable, children at the time did not seem to care which gender the comic was intended for.

With a 29 percent female readership for their boys-only title, it was perhaps inevitable that Hulton Press would launch a sister-title specifically for girls in November 1951 (Henry 378–379). By 1953, this title, *Girl*, was read by 50 percent of girls between the ages of eight and fifteen in the UK (380). The massive increase in readership figures indicates that girls responded favorably to comics specifically meant for them, but it would take another two decades before a comic publisher actually asked them what they wanted.

Tammy (1971–1984), published first by Fleetway Publications and later by IPC Magazines, was the first British girls' comic for which the publisher commissioned market research into the tastes of its intended audience (8- to 13-year-olds); this research revealed that a surprising number of respondents professed to enjoy stories that made them cry, which editor Pat Mills interpreted as a preference for "stories of emotional suffering and psychological cruelty" (Chapman 120). This became one of the guiding principles behind *Tammy*: as James Chapman puts it, "The narrative strategy of *Tammy* is to confront its (usually working-class) heroines with circumstances so extreme that there seems no hope of salvation" (120), with stories of enforced criminality, exploitation and economic hardship. Rich characters are snobby and dishonest, the upwardly mobile abandon their home communities, and the wealthy and privileged abuse their status to get what they want. This was a complete about-turn from the "consensual politics" of earlier girls' comics, and it proved extremely popular with readers, granting *Tammy* a regular circulation of almost 300,000 copies in the early 1970s. This shift was so pronounced that other publishers felt obliged to follow suit, with DC Thompson introducing similar kinds of conflict into their own girls' comics, *Bunty* and *Judy* (122).

Here Come the Ghouls

As part of the editorial preference for darker and more disturbing stories, *Tammy* was the first British girls' comic to include horror stories, usually one-off strips telling a self-contained tale. These proved very popular with readers, which suggested a new market to Thompson and IPC; *Spellbound* (1976–1977) and *Misty* (1978–1980) became the first British horror comics since the 1950s, and both were specifically targeted at girls (Chapman 122–23).

What makes the existence of *Spellbound* and *Misty* all the more remarkable is that there does not seem to have been any comparable publications in the U.S. Amid the furor over the evils of horror comics in the 1950s, gendered assumptions about children's reading habits had come into play. American publishers increasingly invested energy in romance comics and other titles targeted specifically at girls, apparently in the belief that these were "safe" genres to which moral guardians could not possibly object (Danziger-Russell 19). This paid off spectacularly, producing what Michelle Nolan refers to as the "Love Glut" of 1950: in the first half of 1949, 42 new romance titles appeared; in the second six month period, an additional 256 romance comics came into existence (Nolan 62). By the end of 1950 the glut was over and the number of new romance titles had declined (63), but the romance market remained stable until around 1956, thanks to post–War prosperity and a new culture of self-fulfillment (100–101). While romance comics lost their market position to superhero titles during the 1960s, this business decision on the part of comic book publishers had more or less established a dichotomy between girls' comics and horror that seems to have endured to the present day, and it seems that there were no American horror comic titles specifically intended for girls.

The difference between *Spellbound* and *Misty* lay in the degree to which they were prepared to transgress. As Graham Kibble-White puts it, "Where *Misty* would later succeed with its anything-goes mentality which allowed the cruelest of fates to be meted out to the most innocent of parties, *Spellbound* lacked that element of moral fecklessness" (217). *Misty* combined this carefree attitude with artistic elements such as irregular panel layouts (including borderless panels and panels with shapes reflective of the story's themes and motifs), splash pages (i.e. pages taken up entirely by a single picture) and nods to the work of Gianni de Luca, particularly his trick of populating a page with multiple drawings of the same character over an unchanging background, condensing the passage of time into a single moment to create psychological intensity and immediacy (Round 41–42). As well as these, there were illustrations that placed the reader inside the monster's point of view (or had the monster break the fourth wall to lock eyes with the reader), and storytelling with "hidden layers of diegesis," embedded stories and complex flashbacks (42).

Misty's titular host was a Gothic, vampire-esque woman who lived in "the Cavern of Dreams." The framing device for the comic was an enchanted pool, through which Misty could observe the trials and tribulations of girls dealing with supernatural problems, and narrate them for the reader. It quickly gathered a loyal following among children who found its fare more interesting than the girls' comics they were used to. One girl wrote in to say, "I used to be scared of ghosts and darkness. But when I started reading your comics I got less scared. Now every night I just look out for ghosts. And the darkness does not frighten me any more [*sic*]."[4] Another reader, after praising the comic, states, "My burning ambition is to see at least one of the following during my lifetime: A ghost, the Loch Ness monster, a Flying Saucer or a Yeti."[5] Another girl gets right to the heart of the matter: "I think your comic is the best out because it's exciting and not soppy."[6] Notable stories from the comic and its annuals included "The Cult of the Cat" and its sequel "The Nine Lives of Nicola"; the *Carrie*-inspired "Moonchild," and "The Four Faces of Eve," an entertaining variation on *Frankenstein*. *Misty*'s gleeful lack of moral restraint, combined with its stylistic flourishes, meant that many of its stories were genuinely unnerving.

The comic's depictions of vampires, however, were usually light-hearted, or at least sufficiently off-kilter to undermine the creatures' threatening nature to an extent. The story "Blood Orange" from the 1979 annual, for example, revolves around a joke implied in the title. Amy White, the daughter of a fruiterer, is helping her father run his stall in Covent Garden on Christmas Eve at the turn of the century; she accidentally sells a crate of specially-imported oranges intended for an eccentric customer named "R. A. Claud," replacing it just before he arrives to collect his order. When she accompanies him to his run-down mansion to help unload the crates, her curiosity gets the better of her and she discovers that the oranges Mr. Claud regularly buys from her father have been filled with blood.[7] Not only is her customer a vampire, but he is none other than Count Dracula himself. When he tries an unadulterated orange from the substituted crate, he accuses her of swindling him and prepares to make good the deficit by drinking from her. Luckily, it turns out to have been a dream: Amy fell asleep at her father's fruit stall while a nearby sandwich-board man was shouting advertisements for *Dracula* at the Lyceum Theatre, starring Sir Henry Irving.

The atmospheric "Hunt the Ripper" from issue 54 (17 February 1979), meanwhile, is set in the winter of 1888, with London in the grip of terror as Jack the Ripper continues to evade the police. A disheveled-looking stranger arrives at the Bristow lodging house looking for a room, and despite young Alison's protests and attempts to keep him out, her mother invites him in and offers him a room. Alison is very suspicious of the strange lodger, and with good reason: before he arrives, he has already arranged to have his luggage delivered to the Bristows' house; he only ever goes out at night, and he is extremely secretive. Alison suspects that he is the Ripper, but her attempts at snooping are thwarted by his keen senses. Eventually, she waits for him to leave and enters his room using her mother's pass-key. She picks the lock on one of his trunks, uncovering what she thinks is a dead body; at this very moment, the stranger returns and reveals that it is in fact his ventriloquist's dummy, Marianne. "Marianne" suggests that Alison inspect the other trunk, which is revealed to be full of earth. The stranger explains that this earth is from his homeland, and he has to sleep on top of it during the day: he is in fact Count Dracula, Alison now knows too much, and he intends to drink her blood. Fleeing the lodging house, Alison bumps into Jack the Ripper, and not knowing who he is, asks him for help. Dracula assumes that the Ripper is trying to steal his kill, while the Ripper takes Dracula for "another of those amateur detectives," and the two do battle for the remainder of the night, allowing Alison to escape. The outcome of the duel is not known, but we are told that there were no more Ripper murders after that night, and that Dracula did not make it back to his trunk of earth before sunrise: "In some dirty East End alley he must have withered to dust in the sun's rays" ("Hunt the Ripper" 15). Assuming this vampire was telling the truth about who he was, this must count as one of the strangest versions of the character ever published.

The prose story "To See a Vampire!," meanwhile, takes one of the vampire's traditional weaknesses to a bizarre extreme. Returning home from the cinema one night, sensible horror fan Karen and her sloppy, cheeky brother Eric pass by a cemetery, where they see a strange-looking man moving among the headstones. Eric goes in to investigate, planning to jump out and give Karen a fright when she follows; Karen, however, guesses what Eric is planning and keeps on walking, leaving him there on his own. Startled by a screeching owl, Eric flees the cemetery moments later and huffily refuses to talk about what he saw there. What he does not realize is that he was being stalked through the cemetery by a real vampire, and he only escaped because the stick from the choc-ice he had been eating in the cinema fell out of his pocket while he was running. Vampires, it seems, are vulnerable to injury from all kinds of wooden implements, not just stakes, and when the creature stood on the wooden lolly-stick it had much the same effect as a human standing on a nail.

In a great many *Misty* stories, the heroine is intuitive and curious: she almost instinctively knows that something is wrong, but her concerns are either ignored or dismissed by the adults around her. In "Hunt the Ripper," for example, Alison first tries to fob the stranger off by telling him that they have no vacant rooms, and it is her mother who invites him inside (without which, in some variations of the folklore, the vampire would not be able to enter at all); she even tells her mother outright, "Mum, I don't like him!," but to no avail (9). Realizing that she is going to have to deal with the threat on her own, the heroine usually then starts to investigate, or else just gives in to her own morbid curiosity, which lands her in more serious danger. The one thing that all these heroines possess is a willingness to believe in the supernatural, in spite of the disbelief of others, and *Misty* played up to this trait in its readers: it regularly published horoscopes, dream interpretation guides and articles on ghost stories and superstitions, as well as giving away "occult" or "supernatural" gifts such as charm bracelets and a "mystic circle" board game based on the signs of the zodiac. In "To See a Vampire!," Karen is cautious enough not to "tempt fate" by declaring outright that she does not believe in vampires, whereas her loudmouth brother repeatedly proclaims that there is no such thing; he ends the story humbled, but blissfully ignorant of the ironic situation he just stumbled through.

The Cassandra-like plights that arise out of this willingness to believe, of course, resonate strongly with children and adolescents who are not yet empowered to take action in a world run by adults, and in stories where the supernatural is involved, this sense of powerlessness is increased exponentially. This in itself may account for the popularity of these stories with young female readers: the girls in these stories can perceive problems that need to be addressed, but nobody will listen to them, in a grim foreshadowing of what the readers would experience in real life as they grew older. Furthermore, at the time these stories were published, the Yorkshire Ripper (later identified as Peter Sutcliffe) was still active, and the West Yorkshire Police were being criticized by feminist groups for indulging in victim blaming. Inspired by German and American feminist demonstrations, the Leeds Revolutionary Feminist Group organized "Reclaim the Night" marches in numerous cities across the UK on the night of 12 November 1977, denouncing the suggestion that women's movements should be restricted by men's violent behavior (encapsulated in the police force's advice that women should remain indoors after dark while the Ripper was at large). Without wanting to sound facetious, the echoes of this period can be read in these comics, which feature weird, predatory men, authority figures who fail to take the protagonists seriously, and an otherworldly hostess figure who asserts, on the inside front cover of nearly every issue and annual, that she owns the night: as she puts it in the 1980 annual, "[...] this is MY world and I am your guide" (*Misty Annual 1980* 2). *Spellbound* lasted for 69 issues before merging with *Debbie*, while *Misty* ran for 101 issues before being absorbed into *Tammy* (Chapman 123). The merged comic was published as *Tammy and Misty* until 1981, when *Tammy* acquired the sf/fantasy-oriented *Jinty* and dropped the *Misty* element altogether. Though the comic itself had come to an end, *Misty* annuals continued to be published until 1986.[8]

The British market for girls' comics was severely diminished during the 1980s, due partly to a general market contraction and partly to an industry-wide change of focus towards adult comics for predominantly male sf and fantasy fans. As a result, girls' comics were superseded by teen magazines (123). By 1997, the girls' comics that survived the contraction (such as *Bunty* and the merged *Mandy & Judy*) had substantially changed, including ethnically diverse casts, pop-culture references and explicit interest in romance in place of some of the more masochistic themes. The lead characters' narrative roles, however, remained mostly passive. Valerie Walkerdine (1984) argued that girls' comics prepared their readers for adolescent heterosexuality (which would then be addressed more directly by teen magazines), and John Hood-Williams later found that girls' comics of the mid-1990s contained strong elements of both, strengthening the semiotic link between them. Hood-Williams attributes this to marketing considerations, with the comics aiming to align themselves with social trends that saw girls "'growing up' earlier than they used to" and entering sexual relations at younger ages (90).

The Fangs of Draculass

Vampires were not limited to the pages of horror comics, however. There were plenty of British comics that deployed creatures of the night to humorous rather than terrifying effect, with the humor derived mostly from showing vampires, werewolves, ghosts and so on interacting with regular people in a variety of everyday settings and situations. *Shiver and Shake*, to take one example, ran from 10 March 1973 to 5 October 1974 (at which point it was absorbed into *Whoopee!*), and all of its characters were in some way derived from the tropes and stock characters of horror fiction, such as Frankie Stein, Creepy Car and Sweeney Toddler. From June 1975 to October 1976, *Monster Fun* filled the gap left by *Shiver and Shake*'s departure with its own cast of mischievous monsters, such as Kid Kong, Tom Thumbscrew, Teddy Scare and Gums (a shark with false teeth).

There were a handful of comedic vampire characters as well, with their powers, attributes and appetites serving as the basis for puns and visual gags. "Deadly Hedley, the Vampire Detective" (*Buster,* April 1981 to May 1983), created by Mark Rodgers and Martin Baxendale, was a somewhat camp private investigator who preferred tomato juice to blood and could change into a bat to pursue miscreants. Lew Stringer's "Vampire Brats" (June 1989 to September 1991) were a pair of toddlers with all the standard powers of their kind, who used their abilities to cause chaos for their human foster-family. "Dracula Dobbs" (May 1987 to September 1991) by Nigel Edwards, meanwhile, was a normal boy cursed to become an insatiable vampire each night, albeit one with a hunger for fast food rather than blood.

Much more in keeping with the spirit of vampires as inhuman predators was "Draculass: Daughter of Dracula," a small, green-skinned, sharp-toothed girl who moved from Transylvania to stay with her human relatives in Britain, the Joneses. As Draculass explains, the move was necessary due to her father being "er ... *gravely* indisposed."[9] The stories revolved around her cousin Maisie's futile attempts to control her as she went around attempting to bite the necks of all and sundry—however, her attacks were never fatal, her vampirism was not contagious, and she usually got her just deserts in the end. Created by Terry Brave and his wife Sheila (without whose input the character would have been a boy called "Draculad"), Draculass soon gathered a sizeable fan following, and Brave noted, in an interview for the Summer 1986 edition of the fanzine *Golden Fun,* that the character generated a large amount of fan-mail, "with many a reader (especially girls) exclaiming their sheer delight over the little vampire's fangs" (Irmantas 2014). Draculass's fangs are enormous and very strong, having the appearance of tusks, which certainly explains why people tried very hard to avoid being "pranged" by her. Her skin was green, but because her strips were not always printed in color, these enormous teeth were her defining visual characteristic. In one story, when she causes a ruckus at a circus, she makes amends with a performance in which she swings from the trapeze by her fangs, prompting one audience member to remark upon their strength.[10] One of her many visits to the zoo reveals that only crocodiles can match her for biting power.[11]

Her fangs are the source of her ability to cause chaos, and so it is hardly surprising that she is anxious about losing them. It is established, during a game of 'doctors and nurses' in which Draculass plays the patient (in order to bite the other kids), that she is terrified of dentists.[12] A few months later, faced with mountains of complaining letters from her cousin's victims, Maisie resolves to take her to the dentist and have her fangs pulled; a horrified Draculass tries to escape by running away and diving into a swimming pool, only to accidentally knock her fangs out anyway when she mistakenly dives into the shallow end (this is the only story where Draculass physically attacks Maisie, biting her on the hand in order to escape). We are told, however, that her fangs will have grown back by the following week.[13] Once this ability to re-grow her fangs is introduced, she starts to lose them more frequently, but they are emblematic of more than just her predatory nature. Draculass, while not exactly a tomboy, shows little interest in the trappings of traditional femininity valued by Maisie. As with most of Maisie's interests, Draculass finds such things boring and usually only goes along with her cousin under protest. When Maisie drags Draculass to a fashion show, for example, Draculass thinks the whole exercise is pointless until she sees the models' exposed necks and shoulders: a number of catwalk attacks later, and she has created a new fashion craze for thick hand-knitted scarves and balaclavas.[14]

It is also very strongly demonstrated that Draculass's vampire nature—the thing that sets her apart and makes her powerful, as signified by her enormous fangs—is what places her outside the realm of traditional British girlhood. The following month, when Maisie brings Draculass to a salon to get her hair done (in spite of Draculass's protests that her hair is fine the way it is), Draculass tries biting customers' exposed necks until Maisie knocks her teeth out with a mirror, at which point she grumpily settles down and allows the hairdressers to tend to her.[15] Though she might not conform to traditional expectations of femininity, however, that does not necessarily mean that Draculass is unfeminine. Rather, she expresses a different kind of femininity, somewhat similar to that which holds particular appeal for female vampire fans.

Brigid Cherry, building on previous sociological work on women within genre fandom, conducted a survey of female British horror fans and found that her respondents were especially attracted to vampires (42). From her survey, she derives a couple of reasons for this attraction. First, and probably fundamental to women's participation in any fan culture, the group dynamics of vampire fandom were more welcoming to women, being less male-dominated and exhibiting less sexist behavior (51). Vampire costuming was another attractive aspect of the fandom for Cherry's respondents (51–52), with some connecting it to dress-up games they had played as children (54). Many respondents were also participants in the Goth subculture, with the overlap expressly linked to horror fandom and the expression of an alternative mode of femininity: these fans, Cherry finds, model their looks on predatory female vampires and thus "adopt extremes of femininity in opposition to contemporary social norms" (52). Cherry argues that participating in vampire fandom allowed her respondents to "act out a fantasy," adopting an image that subverted traditional femininity with threat and menace, but was still feminine and somewhat glamorous. For some, it allowed for a "more extreme" articulation of femininity than is currently fashionable, hearkening back to bygone days of opulence and elegance. The respondents' answers demonstrated that traditional feminine interests can be subverted by an enthusiasm for horror, and yet, that subversive element remains feminine (54). In other words, adopting the mantle of the vampire allows for the expression of power without sacrificing the expression of one's gender identity, and the power in question is not limited to sexual manipulation: at the end of the day, the female vampire is not dangerous just because people are sexually attracted to her, but because she *is a vampire*. The use of costume props, such as vampire fangs and abnormally colored contact lenses, invokes this dangerous, powerful Otherness by rendering the wearer's appearance "monstrous" and emphasizing "non-conformity to current ideals of femininity" (52–53). It is hardly surprising, then, that many girls were appreciative of Draculass' fangs.

In many British comics of the time, it was commonplace for children to correspond directly with their favorite characters; in the case of *Monster Fun*, most of readers' letters were addressed to Frankie Stein, the "editor" of the comic as well as one of its stars, but occasionally other characters received direct communications too. Draculass was the subject and addressee of many children's letters.[16] On the letters page of issue 18, a girl wrote to tell Draculass that she might have found one of her teeth in a stream, and even sent it in to be identified. Draculass replied that the item was probably a stone, and bravely stated her intention to go see a dentist soon (to feed on his "scrumpy long neck," of course) (*Monster Fun* #18).[17] Another girl wrote in to ask if Draculass brushes her teeth; Draculass answered that not only does she brush them, she sharpens them as well (*Monster Fun* #35).[18] Another girl wrote in to say that she wished she had fangs like Draculass, so that she could frighten her brother as payback for his hogging the comics.[19] Some of the boys who wrote in seemed a bit wary of the character, one comparing Draculass to his French teacher ("because she is always after our blood!"), and another asking Frankie if Draculass had ever tried biting his Adam's apple; Draculass herself responded to the latter, thanking the reader for the suggestion and pointing out that "apples are good for your teeth!" (*Monster Fun* #38)[20] Some girls definitely picked up on this aspect of the character too: one girl wrote to ask Frankie to send Draculass to her school, to deal with an annoying (male) teacher (*Monster Fun* #52).[21]

Draculass shuns traditional femininity, but still performs a feminine identity. This can be seen in the story about her birthday: to prepare for her party, she puts on her best party dress ("All black!," of course), puts some flour on her face ("So I'm all pale and ghastly!"), sharpens her fingernails and fangs and gets the Jones residence looking "lovely and spooky" (*Monster Fun* #12).[22] The resonances with Cherry's findings are clear enough. Together with her fangs, her lack of interest in mainstream feminine pursuits and her instinct for causing chaos, Draculass exhibits oppositional, nonconformist femininity of the kind that drew Cherry's respondents to vampire fandom: most of Cherry's respondents reported that they were interested in vampires as young girls—to take two particular examples, one respondent stated that a childhood fascination with horror led her to listen to Goth music when she was fourteen (52), while another said that she used to make vampire costumes for her dolls when she was eleven years old (54).

Draculass might not be exactly "glamorous," but then, she is only a child. Even so, she poses some interesting questions about how children internalize and then grow into stereotypical gender roles. In one story, Maisie, having developed a crush on teen heart-throb Freddy Fabb, tries to get Draculass to share her interest; Draculass does not see the attraction until a trip to the cinema gives her a look at his "big juicy neck." She attacks the cinema screen in a frenzy, with the result that she and Maisie have to hide from a mob of irate fans.[23] In this instance, Draculass' desires run parallel to those of her sister and the other girls: though she ends up apparently just as obsessed with this celebrity as the rest of them, she is only interested in him because she wants to feed on him, an attraction that mocks romantic desire by ironically mimicking it.

In the following week's episode, the conflation of dietary and romantic desire is more pronounced, as Draculass outlines her preferences in victims (though her attacks were largely indiscriminate before). Using a somewhat out-of-place wine metaphor, she dismisses a "1926 vintage" city gentleman as "much too dry," while a 10-year-old schoolboy is "not mature enough" for her taste; at this point Frankie Stein jogs through the scene (reminding the reader that this is still a children's comic), but after this Draculass spies a 26-year-old "dreamy" teacher, and captures him with a lasso, intending to bring him home and lock him up in her cellar. Before she can do so, however, she is attacked by a gang of smitten schoolgirls, who rescue the handsome teacher and carry him away on their shoulders, trailing clouds of love-hearts (*Monster Fun* #51).[24] It is unclear whether Draculass is describing some nascent romantic feelings for the dreamy teacher, or if she really does intend to treat him like a bottle of fine wine, keeping him captive in the cellar and drinking his blood whenever the mood takes her. This ambiguity means that she is neither a typical girl nor a typical vampire, but it also places her outside of the "puppy-love" norm represented by the crowd of schoolgirls (who look almost identical to one another).

Overall, it is not difficult to see how Draculass might have appealed to girls who felt like they did not fit in (or did not want to); like other vampires, she demonstrated an alternative, powerful femininity. Alas, she did not last for very long. She was carried over into *Buster* following the 1976 merger, and lasted in her new home until December 1977, with occasional reprints in holiday specials until *Buster* finished publication in 2000.

Conclusion

It is not the aim of this study to argue that something was lost forever with the end of *Misty* and Draculass. Other comic books and strips have appeared in the interim which have similar appeal for girls and young women, for the most part without the dedicated use of horror tropes; if there is a relative paucity of female-centered horror titles, then as Danziger-Russell (2013) says, girls will most likely make do with boys' horror comics until an alternative tailored to their needs comes along. It is difficult to believe that there is an overall lack of horror heroines in comics, however, given the size of the globalized market for sequential art and the ready availability of comics on the Internet. Outside the sphere of comics altogether, stock horror characters are increasingly marketed to girls in the form of dolls (e.g. Mattel's "Monster High" franchise, in which all the characters are the children of classic movie monsters), and the TV show *Buffy the Vampire Slayer* still casts a long shadow over popular culture, spawning new imitators every year. It is a shame, however, that the likes of *Misty* ceased production in Britain during the 1980s: one wonders what stories could have been inspired by third-wave feminism, the riot grrrl music scene, Cool Britannia, "girl power" and other 1990s phenomena, not to mention the growing online activism of the twenty-first century. Draculass, had circumstances allowed her to continue, would also surely have found favor with a generation of girls who took pride in being outspoken and nonconformist. Every generation deserves a heroine with massive, sharp teeth.

Notes

1. For a fuller account of the political intricacies of the campaign against horror comics in the UK, see Martin Barker's *A Haunt of Fears* (1984).
2. Wertham is beyond the scope of this study, but his book *Seduction of the Innocent* (1954), in which he linked comic books to crime, juvenile delinquency and sexual "deviance," has made him something of a *bête noire* to the comics industry and fandom. The extent to which he directed the U.S. moral panic over comic books is debatable, but his status as a psychiatrist certainly lent credibility to the anti-comics campaign.
3. Furthermore, *Eagle* was intended to be the antithesis to imported American comic books: it would carry characters who could serve as role models for their young readers; it would be printed on high-quality paper, and its contents would "conform with modern educational theory, rather than run counter to it" (Henry 372–373).
4. *Misty* #31 (2 September 1978), 26.
5. *Misty* #54 (17 February 1979), 26.
6. *Misty* #64 (28 April 1979), 26.
7. This might have been a tribute to Errol Flynn on the part of the unnamed writer/artist. According to urban legend, whenever the Hollywood actor was banned from drinking alcohol on a film set, he would instead eat oranges that, unbeknownst to the producers or director, had previously been injected with vodka.
8. This was a common enough arrangement for defunct comics in Britain. For example, *Monster Fun* ceased to exist as a standalone comic in 1976, but *Monster Fun Annuals*

were published until 1985; *Shiver and Shake* annuals were published until 1986, despite the title's merger with *Whoopee!* in 1974.
    9. *Monster Fun* #1 (14 June 1975).
    10. *MF* #18 (11 October 1975).
    11. *MF* # 26 (6 December 1975).
    12. *MF* #24 (22 November 1975).
    13. *MF* #52 (5 June 1976).
    14. *MF* #67 (18 September 1976).
    15. *MF* #71 (16 October 1976).
    16. Two letters in particular touch upon Draculass' family and heritage. One girl, whose letter was published in issue 28 (20 December 1975), asked why the character's parents were never seen in the comic. Draculass replied only that they were in Transylvania, without elaborating on the events that obliged her to move to England. Another, much more pointed, letter in issue 60 (31 July 1976) asked, "Please can you tell me when you are going back to your real home in Transylvania? Because you have been on holiday with your cousin for a very long time." Draculass responded by saying that she liked England so much, she was planning to stay there.
    17. *MF* #18 (11 October 1975).
    18. *MF* #35 (7 February 1976).
    19. *MF* #46 (24 April 1976).
    20. *MF* #38 (28 February 1976). It should be pointed out, though, that Draculass did in fact target her male victims' Adam's apples from time to time, and had done so on a couple of occasions prior to this boy's letter. Clearly, the mental image of such an attack proved more disturbing than was intended.
    21. *MF* #52 (5 June 1976).
    22. *MF* #12 (30 August 1975).
    23. *MF* #50 (22 May 1976).
    24. *MF* #51 (29 May 1976).

WORKS CITED

Anonymous. "Blood Orange." *Misty Annual 1979*. London: IPC Magazines Ltd., 1978. 49–56.
Anonymous. "Hunt the Ripper." *Misty* 54. 17 February 1979. 8–15.
Anonymous. "Medical Notes in Parliament." *British Medical Journal* 2:4895. 30 October 1954, 1054–1055.
Anonymous. *Misty Annual 1980*. London: IPC Magazines Ltd., 1980.
Anonymous. "To See a Vampire!" *Misty* 64. 28 April 1979. 20–21.
Barker, Martin. *A Haunt of Fears: The Strange History of the British Horror Comics Campaign* [1984]. Jackson: University Press of Mississippi, 1992.
Brave, Terry. "Draculass: Daughter of Dracula." *Monster Fun* 1–73 (14 June 1975–10 October 1976); *Buster and Monster Fun* (6 November 1976–10 December 1977).
Chapman, James. *British Comics: A Cultural History*. London: Reaktion Books, 2011.
Cherry, Brigid. "Screaming for Release: Femininity and Horror Film Fandom in Britain." *British Horror Cinema*. Ed. Steve Chibnall and Julian Petley. London: Routledge, 2002. 42–57.
"Children's Publications (Prosecutions)." HC Deb 5 December 1974, vol. 882, 588–589.
Danziger-Russell, Jacqueline. *Girls and Their Comics: Finding a Female Voice in Comic Book Narrative*. Lanham, MD: Scarecrow Press, 2013.
Henry, Harry. "Measuring Editorial Interest in Children's Comics." *Journal of Marketing* 17.4 (April 1953): 372–380.
Hill, George E., and Estelle Trent. "Children's Interest in Comic Strips." *The Journal of Educational Research* 34.1 (September 1940): 30–36.
Hood-Williams, John. "Stories for Sexual Difference." *British Journal of Sociology of Education* 18.1 (1997): 81–99.
'Irmantas' (pseud.). "A Look at *Monster Fun* Strips: Draculass." *Kazoop!!* blog (kazoop.

blogspot.ie), 12 April 2014. http://kazoop.blogspot.com/2014/04/a-look-at-monster-fun-strips-draculass.html. Accessed 6 August 2016.
Kibble-White, Graham. *The Ultimate Book of British Comics*. London: Allison & Busby, 2005.
Misty Annual 1980. London: IPC Magazines Ltd., 1979.
Nolan, Michelle. *Love on the Racks: A History of American Romance Comics*. Jefferson, NC: McFarland, 2008.
Round, Julia. *Gothic in Comics and Graphic Novels: A Critical Approach*. Jefferson, NC: McFarland, 2014.
Walkerdine, Valerie. "Some Day My Prince Will Come: Young Girls and the Preparation for Adolescent Sexuality." *Gender and Generation*. Ed. Angela McRobbie and Mica Nava. London: Macmillan, 1984. 162–184.
Waugh, Coulton. *The Comics*. Jackson: The University Press of Mississippi, 1947.
Witty, Paul. "Children's Interest in Reading the Comics." *The Journal of Experimental Education* 10.2 (December 1941): 100–104.

Section Two: Negotiating Femininity and Identity

Jeepers Creepers
The American Vampirization of the Female Immigrant Teacher in Vampires Don't Wear Polka Dots

Sharon Pajka

Children's books treat vampires in a wide variety of ways. Rather than bloodsucking monsters, vampires in younger children's books are more likely to be reformed vegetarians, or lonely characters seeking companionship and acceptance. Children reading these books enjoy a slightly scary setting, while discovering sympathetic characters with whom they can relate and appreciate. Books such as *The Adventures of the Bailey School Kids* series introduce young readers to elements of Gothic literature, while helping them confront anxieties and fears of childhood, and allowing them to grapple with questions of identity.

The Adventures of the Bailey School Kids by Debbie Dadey and Marcia Thornton Jones with original illustrations by John Steven Gurney and reissued cover illustrations by Nathan Hale is a children's chapter book series for readers ages 7–10 published by Scholastic. With more than 80 books in the series, including "Super Special" editions, holiday editions, and a spin-off series, *The Adventures of the Bailey School Kids* is one of Scholastic's top bestselling series of all time with over 30 million copies sold. In each story, the Bailey School kids encounter a character who, based on their observations, might be a mythical or monstrous being. The reader is left guessing. The first novel in the series, *Vampires Don't Wear Polka Dots*, was published in 1990 and recently celebrated 25 years in publication. In 2015, the publishing company Quirk Books named Mrs. Jeepers, the Transylvanian teacher who may or may not be a vampire, as one of "the most terrifying teachers of Children's Literature." With or without vampires, children's literature reflects societal understandings of contemporary cultural norms and politics. Niemi, Smith, and Brown maintain, "in the case of how Western society regards teachers' work ... if we want to hide society's feelings about teachers, we should publish the message in children's storybooks" (74). Their research concludes that women are kept in powerless and objectified roles in the teaching profession (58); Mrs. Jeepers, as a character that is mostly observed, discussed, and criticized remains somewhat voiceless; while her appearance is arguably culturally normative for the late 1980s, her behavior and actions are rather compelling. Consequently, the role of the suspected vampire-teacher, Mrs. Jeepers, a foreigner teaching in an American public school system, becomes a model for analyzing the construction of gender, the representation of teachers in children's books, and the American response to immigrants.

Anticipating the Teacher

In the beginning of *Vampires Don't Wear Polka Dots* (*VDWPD*), the students anticipate the arrival of their new teacher. They worry she will be like a fictional character in a children's book that they had read (4). Considered "the meanest substitute teacher in the whole world," the character of Miss Viola Swamp appears in three children's picture books by Harry Allard and illustrated by James Marshall including: *Miss Nelson Is Missing!* (1977), *Miss Nelson Is Back* (1982), and *Miss Nelson Has a Field Day* (1985). The basic premise of these picture books is that their nice teacher is constantly being taken advantage of by her rude and misbehaved students who refuse to learn. One day this teacher does not come to school; instead, she is replaced by Miss Viola Swamp, a substitute and strict disciplinarian who overworks the poor students into submission. After several days, their teacher returns only for the students, who have learned to be more respectful, to rejoice in the homecoming. At the end of the book, it is revealed to the reader that Miss Viola Swamp is their teacher dressed in a disguise. Referencing the character Miss Viola Swamp appears as a passing allusion to another series of children's books; however, it reinforces that school teachers should be nice and not overwork their students, just as students should be polite and well behaved in class.

The problematic nice teacher dressed in a disguise also warns the reader to be cautious of being tricked by appearances. In addition to their conjectures of a fictional character joining their classroom, the Bailey School kids speculate that their new teacher might be a male wrestler, a profession filled with culturally dominant or hegemonic masculinity that includes "themes of aggression and violence..." (Soulliere n.p.). Miss Viola Swamp, described more as a drill sergeant who requires strict discipline, is harsh, authoritarian, and mean. There is not much contrast between the two. Eddie, one of the main characters, brags, "I can take care of any teacher—even a male wrestler!" (4–5). Readers understand that Eddie will become the bane of the classroom. He "holds simultaneous duel positions of powerless student and powerful male" as he asserts his masculinity by becoming the opponent of the teacher before even meeting her (Niemi, Smith, and Brown 72). The children fear the arrival of an overtly masculine male teacher, and they fear the arrival of a masculine female teacher. This conjecture by the children, as silly as it may be, admits their lack of understanding regarding teachers, and it points to the representations of teachers and their genders in children's books in the United States. Weber and Mitchell remind us, "There are few legitimate places of female power outside the home in our society to which young children are privy" (41). Additionally, "children's fiction tells us that we teachers are female workers who should take care of children, do what we're told, and keep the masks of teacher identity intact" (Niemi, Smith, and Brown 74). *VDWPD* both reproduces and challenges these portrayals of the female teacher.

Meeting Mrs. Jeepers

The elements of suspense that are quite noticeable in Gothic literature begin for the reader before the book is opened; the current reissued cover illustration has been updated to attract more contemporary readers. Yet, it also alters the reader's perception of the story. The original cover from 1990 includes a scene with Mrs. Jeepers standing between the desks of two of the main characters. The perspective is from the front of the classroom as if the reader were standing at the head of the room looking out at Mrs. Jeepers and rows of students in desks. Mrs. Jeepers offers a wry smile with one hand touching her necklace and another on her hip. Her body is facing the reader. All of the children pictured on the original cover are watching Mrs. Jeepers with their mouths slightly agape. The reissued cover illustration is more cartoon-like. It places the reader among the desks right behind two of the main characters, the only children now depicted on the cover. Mrs. Jeepers writes, "Rules" on the blackboard at the front of the classroom with a student whispering to another who is blowing his gum into a large bubble while staring at his teacher. Mrs. Jeepers' back is mostly to the classroom while she looks over her shoulder. She has the wry smile but she casts a large distorted shadow that includes claws.

The new cover is intentionally scary. It emphasizes the voyeuristic nature of the narrative; it demonstrates a visual *othering* of the teacher as Mrs. Jeepers no longer stands among the children but is placed in opposition to them; and it places the reader in the story by sitting this student directly behind the main characters. On both the original and the reissued cover, Mrs. Jeepers wears the polka dot dress that is noted in the title. Although the reissued cover includes an ominous shadow, it is more vibrant than the original and is dominated by the bright pink dress with polka dots, a whimsical outfit with bishop sleeves that the children believe would never be worn by a vampire. The back cover of the book includes a description of the plot:

> Teachers never last in the Bailey School third grade. And when Mrs. Jeepers takes over the class, the kids are sure she'll quit, just like all the rest. But the Transylvanian teacher has a strange way of getting what she wants. Now the kids are starting to wonder: Will *they* survive Mrs. Jeepers? [Dadey and Jones].

The message warns children, "There are some pretty weird grown-ups living in Bailey City"; the message is countered with a bright lime green background and a dark raspberry Showcard Gothic font. The details from the back cover juxtapose the weird adults who live in town with third graders that are in a constant state of transition. Overall, it is presented in a gender frame which lessens the reader's discomfort and uncertainty.

Odd Appearances

As with numerous vampire-characters found in literature, Mrs. Jeepers is an immigrant who hails from the land of Stoker's Count Dracula. Immediately, she is considered the *other* by her students who perceive her as being so different that she is "strange" (6); likewise, as a new teacher in a new school, Mrs. Jeepers witnesses many odd behaviors by the Bailey School kids who behave quite differently from school children in Transylvania (46). This early interaction reminds one of the passage in Bram Stoker's *Dracula* with the titular character telling Jonathan Harker, "Our ways are not your ways, and there shall be to you many strange things" (26–27). For Mrs. Jeepers entering an American classroom, presumably for the first time, there are many challenges. Yet, she views this as an opportunity for cross-cultural understanding; a way for both her and the children to appreciate their cultural differences in order to build trust, and a safe learning environment. The children view this as a classroom invasion.

The culture around us influences our consciousness. In *VDWPD*, the assumptions the children make are often based on appearances. In America, appearances matter and so it is important to discuss how vampires are traditionally depicted in literature and film since Mrs. Jeepers' attributes and wardrobe determine if she is or is not a vampire. Sherman explains, "When one thinks of vampiric figures, it's quite naturally a set of frighteningly sharp teeth that first comes to mind" (20) and further notes, "…the nails were long and fine, and cut to a sharp point" (23). Mrs. Jeepers' teeth are not mentioned nor are her fingernails, except to point out that she wears green nail polish (23). In dressing as a vampire, Sherman writes, "…the traditional Dracula ensemble of a black tux and/or tails, a long opera cloak, and the occasional hint of red," which is most often attributed to Hamilton Deane's 1924 stage adaptation of *Dracula* (34). Additionally, the cape was added for theatrical performances (Sherman 35), Mrs. Jeepers' fashion taste is quite different from the vampires in traditional portrayals.

Readers see her image on the cover and within the text seven times; and, her outfits including accessories are described in three different scenes. These images and descriptions present a wardrobe that is rather benign. Mrs. Jeepers is described as "kind of short" with "long red hair [that] was pulled back with a purple barrette. She [wears] a starched white blouse with a high collar" (Dadey and Jones 8), has a "strange accent" (6), and smiles with "an odd little half smile" (8). From the first illustration, Mrs. Jeepers wears a small bat brooch on her dress (7). Niemi, Smith, and Brown argue that teachers in children's literature have modest and conservative clothing that includes "the teachers' collars [being] high on their necks" (69). Mrs. Jeepers wears a high collar throughout the book. She always has long-sleeves most often under a shell top. In this regard, Mrs. Jeepers meets the expectations of appropriately covered clothing. With each outfit, Mrs. Jeepers' wears her "green brooch the size of a chicken egg" on a choker. This is the one article that the children most often mention. Some of them literally are mesmerized by the glowing brooch. Including the cover illustration, Mrs. Jeepers' entire outfit is only seen once at the very end of the book (76), somewhat of a letdown for readers anticipating the great monster-reveal. The only perceivably weird accessories that Mrs. Jeepers wears is the bat pendant on her dress (7), and a bat bracelet (45). Sika argues that we visually communicate our identities based on our fashion choices. Further, "What we choose to wear can determine rejection or acceptance into different social groups…" (47). Mrs. Jeepers' un-vampire-like attire, which negates the children's concerns of their teacher's identity, shows how assimilated she is in American culture, "She didn't look like a vampire today. She had on a bright pink-and-green polka-dotted dress with a bright green ribbon tied in her red hair. Her fingernails were even painted bright green. And at her neck the green brooch" (23).

The confusion caused by Mrs. Jeepers is further seen when she is late for class and the students begin to suspect that she was attacked by a ghost or a vampire. Their discussions focus on one of the movers carrying a long box which Melody points out was shaped like a coffin; Howie then adds that Mrs. Jeepers is from Transylvania, "and isn't that where Count Dracula lives?" (22). When Mrs. Jeepers arrives to class offering an apology and an explanation that she did not sleep well during the night, Melody pokes that vampires do not sleep during the night but during the day. In a response of frustration, Liza resorts back to fashion by responding, "yeah, but vampires don't wear polka dots" (23). Even with Mrs. Jeepers' origin, the speculations of a coffin-box, and her suspected sleep habits, her choice in clothing disproves her vampire-status. Aside from her whimsical polka dot dress, Mrs. Jeepers wears conservative and traditional attire for the late 1980s, when the book was originally published. The polka dot dress and her accessories show how assimilated Mrs. Jeepers becomes in American culture.[1] Her original outfits are plain and somewhat conservative, "a black dress with a high collar, and a bat bracelet" (44), which leads the children to confirm their suspicions that their teacher is indeed a vampire. Nevertheless, the novel concludes with the children looking back on their school year. Howie states that Mrs. Jeepers is "not *that* weird," while Melody laughs, "I can't believe we ever thought she was a vampire!" Liza once again adds, "Vampires don't wear polka dots!" (78) a reminder that clothing and appearances matter.

Aside from how the children in the story see Mrs. Jeepers as dressing, it is more important to analyze how readers see Mrs. Jeepers since all of the pictures in the book, except for the last show a partial illustration of the character. To clarify; Mrs. Jeepers is only shown once to have a clear, full body illustration. The children and the movers in the story are depicted having full bodies but Mrs. Jeepers is often shown behind a desk or from an angle that makes her difficult to be seen. One could read this as suspenseful and not seeing "the monster" makes readers anticipate the worst; however, such a depiction or lack thereof of the immigrant teacher cannot be read lightly. Equally, from the beginning of the text Mrs. Jeepers' voice plays a significant role. Eddie discounts his peers' accusations and states, "Mrs. Jeepers is just an ordinary teacher with a strange-sounding voice" (14). Eddie emphasizes the main aspect that differentiates Mrs. Jeepers from the former teacher Mrs. Deedee, a teacher who leaves the Bailey School while screaming; Mrs. Jeepers speaks very softly, barely above a whisper. Whispering can be perceived as uncanny, something that borders between that which is heard and that which sounds otherworldly but it is also a technique teachers have used to force students to pay attention. Right after the initial introduction, "Even Eddie, who always tried to act as if he weren't paying attention, leaned on his elbows and listened" (11). Her whisper does not function as disempowering but as influential. Perhaps Mrs. Jeepers uncanniness lies in her ability to command good behavior. Niemi, Smith, and Brown stress that the majority of children's books include teachers who are seen as pretty (76). The depictions of Mrs. Jeepers as both partially seen and partially heard present her as the *other*, which parallels with the expression, "Children should be seen and not heard." It is not necessary for her to speak as long as she looks tidy and attractive. Indeed, this is how Mrs. Jeepers appears to the children, an observation which dissolves the rooted American perception of foreigners being dirty.

Odd Behavior and the Home

A. Jackson writes, "Much has been made not only of the homelike qualities of the fictional schools of pop-Gothic texts ... but of the familiarity, the homelike-ness, of the school genre itself" (157). The school in the text is the only "home" offered for the children. The other home in the novel is the new teacher's, which is presented as a domestic double for the classroom. How they treat their space gives insight to how they respect the environment. Mrs. Jeepers is not privy to the children's suspicions of her. In class, she behaves like a regular teacher. However, after school one day, Eddie, Melody, Howie, and some of the other students walk down the street and become distracted when they learn that someone has moved into the Clancy estate, pictured as a dilapidated house of American Queen Anne style architecture. This shocks them since they consider the house "creepy" and "haunted with ghosts and vampires" (Dadey and Jones 16). While the students are deliberating over who would be "crazy" enough to live in such a house, "they all turned to see Mrs. Jeepers smiling at them" (16). She invites the children in a similar way to Count Dracula's "Welcome to my house! Enter freely. Go safely, and leave something of the happiness you bring!" (Stoker 22). But instead of entering the home excitedly, all scatter except for Eddie and Melody. Offering excuses of going home to do their homework, Mrs. Jeepers reminds them that she did not assign any. They are hesitant about entering. While they obey social etiquette of being polite to their teacher, they also understand the dangers. Ken Gelder cautions in his book *Reading the Vampire*, "the vampire's function is to cross back and forth over boundaries that should otherwise be secure" (70). Here Mrs. Jeepers is asking the children to cross a boundary. Albeit their new teacher, she is still considered a stranger.

Children's books and fairy tales such as *Hansel and Gretel* remind children of the dangers of visiting a strange woman's home. Readers feel anxious and elated by the idea of breaking the boundaries and visiting a teacher's home. By entering Mrs. Jeepers' residence, they are visiting a foreign land where they do not know the rules; they are gaining insight about their new teacher, something that should make them feel more comfortable; yet, Melody feels that Mrs. Jeepers is even more different than she originally expected. Eddie, having seen the inside of the Clancy estate, continues to reject Melody's insistence that living in that particular house does confirm anything about Mrs. Jeepers. He responds, "All right, maybe she is a little strange for wanting to live in the old Clancy place, but that doesn't mean she's weird" (Dadey and Jones 20).

Originally unenthusiastic about entering Mrs. Jeepers' house, the children later return to break in as a way to prove bravery and to find out what is inside the coffin-shaped box. Because none of the children trust that Eddie will follow through, Melody goes with him. They sneak into the basement, locate the box, and try to lift the lid. The box is locked and since the two of them are unable to see any type of latch, Melody wonders if the box is "locked from the inside." Arguing about the location of a lock, they suddenly hear a "thump" (39). The children look around and determine that the sound must have come from inside of the box. They flee. The next day, Melody and Eddie share their story with their classmates. The students argue that Mrs. Jeepers must be a vampire or that she is married to Count Dracula. Mrs. Jeepers enters the classroom dressed in black and wearing a bat bracelet, which again reinforces their belief of vampirism. Mrs. Jeepers' clothing and accessory choices continue to dictate whether or not she is perceived by the children as a vampire (44). When Eddie misbehaves, "determined to show Mrs. Jeepers who [is] boss, he knocks papers off the desks and begins to pop his bubble gum in class" (50). He burps and by the time he mocks a classmate who is participating in the math relay game, Mrs. Jeepers has had "quite enough" of his behavior (57). Eddie becomes enthralled by the green brooch and hardly moves the rest of the class, while Mrs. Jeepers continues the lesson. At the end of class, he does not appear to remember what has happened; his peers are convinced that Mrs. Jeepers hypnotized him.

Howie decides that they need to "do something about Ms. Jeepers" since "Mrs. Jeepers is a witch or a vampire or something" (60). He consults a book, *Vampires and Witches: The True Story* that he checks out from the public library, which leads him to decide that they must use garlic as a form of protection. He is only able to bring garlic salt to school. Hoping this will do the trick, he convinces Melody to help him sprinkle it around the classroom. Once the class begins, Mrs. Jeepers has a severe allergy attack. Liza suggests "major house cleaning" since that is what her mother does when she has an allergy. She continues, "Maybe I should go get the custodian" (67). The class resumes after a custodian sweeps the room clear of the garlic salt. By the time that Mrs. Jeepers has recovered, Eddie's behavior has severely escalated. Mrs. Jeepers "very quietly" insists that the two of them go into the hall to discuss his behavior. When they return, "…Eddie looked as white as a ghost" (75). After school, the children meet to discuss what happened in the hall. Melody and Howie make wild assumptions about what Mrs. Jeepers did to Eddie but he refuses to reveal any details stating, "I'll never make her mad again" (78). Much of the class time is wasted by the children's misbehavior, forcing Mrs. Jeepers to focus on classroom management over lessons. When she does, she is perceived as a monster. Marshall argues that children's literature offers readers "the devaluing of teaching as 'women's work' or 'child care'" (460).

Domestic Responsibilities

From Mrs. Jeepers' initial introduction, readers' view of the classroom includes children "slouched in their chairs" (Dadey and Jones 8). The classroom is disheveled and the children are combing their hair, picking their noses, and chewing gum. The class resembles more of a student lounge than a place of learning. The former teacher could not manage the domestic responsibility and Mrs. Jeepers' domestic qualities are tested. Mrs. Jeepers' response may have more to do with her own domestic skills that appear to be much different from other adult females the children have experienced. When Eddie and Melody are escorted into the main hall of her house they discover, "a huge cobwebbed-covered chandelier ... massive wooden staircase ... [and] the dusty blood-red carpet" (19), they notice how different their new teacher is from others. Mrs. Jeepers' home is in need of as much attention as the unruly Bailey School classroom. Her view of the home is one that needs work but is full of potential, a reading that one can transfer to her view of her classroom space. Mrs. Jeepers inviting the children to her home is a quality one might find in a nurturing female mother; yet, her lack of domestic skills reveals a dualism that evokes uncanny feelings and suspicion. *Otherness* is continually constructed throughout the novel based on the intersectionality of Mrs. Jeepers being a Transylvanian female teacher. The morning after the students have broken into her home, Mrs. Jeepers arrives to a noticeably messy classroom. She recounts a story of her childhood in Romania about the importance of respecting others by keeping an environment and oneself neat in appearance (46). While the children have seen Mrs. Jeepers' untidy home, they still are expected to keep the classroom clean, a conjecture that because Mrs. Jeepers lives alone she is not disrespecting anyone with the untidiness of her home.

The children in *VDWPD* have their own expectations about teachers, especially since they have been through quite a few. Returning to the book description from the reissued back cover, a reader initially may be sympathetic since these kids are constantly abandoned by their teachers. From an educator's perspective, the plot description is a bit disconcerting since a higher teacher-turnover can result in lower student performance; yet, some studies show that teachers tend to be more productive when they start in a new school and that turnover is beneficial when less effective teachers leave (Ronfeldt, Loeb, and Wyckoff 6). Faculty retention is not an obvious concern to the reader but it does set the tone of change; and, to many young children, change can be terrifying. Yet, readers quickly learn that it is the students, not the teachers, who are to be blamed for the lack of teacher-retention. Perhaps the back cover should read, "Will Mrs. Jeepers survive the Bailey School kids?" From the beginning, readers are guided by an omniscient student narrator. In a flashback, we observe former teacher, Mrs. Deedee, who after placing her hand in a desk full of shaving cream begins screaming at the children. Her response out of frustration along with her exit from the profession, as we are told that no one has seen this teacher since, includes an ominous threat to the children, "I want you to know that you will pay for it. Someday, you'll get yours! Somebody, somewhere, will make you pay" (Dadey and Jones 2).

The U.S. Department of Education, National Center for Education Statistics show that of the public school teachers who were teaching during the 2011–12 school year, 84 percent remained at the same school. Only 8 percent left the profession during the following year (2016). Mrs. Deedee's exit seemingly follows the percent of public school teachers who cited the manageability of their workload and the general work conditions as reasons for leaving the profession. Approximately 7 percent of teachers left the profession between 1987–88 and 1988–89 (1997). Mrs. Deedee's exit certainly is not the norm since she cackles as she leaves the classroom. Her response borders more on madness than being "weird."

Teachers in American Public Schools

Historically, the United States American public school system varies by location due to local public government control. Elementary school typically includes kindergarten through sixth grade. Public elementary school teachers instruct between twenty and thirty students of diverse learning needs in basic arithmetic; English grammar, spelling, and vocabulary; and, the fundamentals of other subjects. The students often remain in one classroom throughout the school day, except for specialized programs, such as physical education, library, music, and art classes. From the description in the text, the Bailey School children experience the average American elementary school. The profile of Mrs. Jeepers parallels much of the data from the U.S. Department of Education. Traditionally a female-dominated profession, the U.S. Department of Education, National Center for Education Statistics reveal that between 2011–12, 76 percent of public school teachers were female; and 44 percent of the teachers were under age 40 (2016). The statistics from the early 1990s do not vastly differ. In the early 1990s, 73 percent of public school teachers and 75 percent of private school teachers were female with the vast majority of these female teachers being in positions of elementary education (1997). Further, average age for public school teachers in the early 1990s was 43 years. The research also shows that the majority of teachers continue to be white (87 percent in the early 1990s).

Representations of Teachers in Children's Literature

In her research on the representation of teachers in contemporary adolescent literature, Amy Cummins explains that there are three types of teachers: the entertainer, which would include the lecturer or performer that transfers information from the teacher to the student; the hegemonic overlord who is unconcerned with student empowerment and follows lessons strictly and didactically; and, the liminal servant, who empowers students to question the dominant power and be involved in their own learning (39). Cummins emphasizes that the latter category is the most effective and argues, "The more effective teachers [in children's literature] are characterized by use of critical pedagogy" (37). In addition, Cummins suggests, "The more favorably depicted teachers help students develop their identities and resist dominant and oppressive educational paradigms…" (37). Critical pedagogy is a teaching approach inspired by Marxist critical theory that endeavors to assist students in questioning and challenging the posited domination. In more practical terms, the goal is to challenge the conservative traditionalists' status quo. Niemi, Smith, and Brown share that the new "alien teachers" use non-traditional methods of teaching that are "portrayed as significantly better than the [other] teacher's methods" (Niemi, Smith, and Brown 64). The xenophobic children comment on liking how Mrs. Jeepers' teaches; yet, they still remain uncomfortable with her being their teacher. Through Mrs. Jeepers' actions in *VDWPD* and in the series, she includes learning activities found in a constructivist classroom, including learning as a socially constructed active process. Many of the characteristic views of critical pedagogy are consistent with a constructivist approach to education. Mrs. Jeepers does not lecture her students but engages with them so she is not "the entertainer," nor does she behave like an overlord. Arguably, Mrs. Jeepers behaves more in line with the label of the liminal servant who encourages her students to think independently and question authority.

While this would have been perceived as a somewhat radical approach to teaching in 1990 which political conservatives could consider dangerous, Mrs. Jeepers has limited authority even within the classroom. Niemi, Smith, and Brown reveal that female teachers in children's literature rarely interact with the subject matter and that the focus is on their outward appearance being "young and beautiful" with dispositions "described as patient, kind, helpful, and liking children" (Dadey and Jones 69). Initially, Mrs. Jeepers does not receive such labels but once classwork begins the narrator adds, "Mrs. Jeepers seemed to be a pretty fun teacher" (10). And, Mrs. Jeepers does interact with the subject matter. For example, during the social studies lesson, she shares information about her home country of Romania and her "family's estate at the foot of the Transylvanian Alps" (11). Later in the story, she has her students play math relay games, something in which her students are enthusiastic to participate.

Monsterizing a female teacher is not uncommon in children's literature. Marshall argues, "The female monster educator in popular cultural texts offers a corporeal curriculum that seeks to discipline the body of the teacher and to obfuscate the radical potential of teachers as professional women" (460). Further, she argues that the focus of these stories is on the female educator who shows some type of significant horror. The plot uses the school as the main setting for the child to connect with the "monstrous-feminine" (Creed cited in Marshall 462). Monsters just as new teachers disrupt the order of a place. Stories with monster-teachers are cautionary tales that offer moral and/or didactic content; they include women that act as surrogate mothers; and they show female teachers as nurturers (463). Our constructions of mothering and monstrosity are closely associated with "the monstrosity of the female pedagogue [being] predominately defined by [a female teacher's] refusal or an inability to properly mother her students" (464). Mrs. Jeepers does not have children of her own although she has been married. This lack of motherhood marks her as unfeminine. Returning to the illustrations of Mrs. Jeepers, readers see that she is not presented as a whole woman.

The male gender dominance is still present in the classroom from the start. The other adult present in *VDWPD* is Mr. Davis, the Bailey Elementary principal that is described as "something like an egg with two legs [who] wore dark-rimmed glasses and was completely bald" (Dadey and Jones 6). Male principals nearly always oversee female teachers in children's literature (Niemi, Smith, and Brown 63). Mr. Davis enters the classroom for introductions warning the children that if they do not behave for the new female teacher they will have to deal with him. He undermines her authority by asserting his own. The visual rhetoric is clear from the illustration. Mr. Davis wears suspenders and is supposed to be perceived by the reader as a friendly character. While standing at the front of the classroom, one hand is firmly touching the teacher's desk commanding authority and showing ownership of the domain. This arm separates him from Mrs. Jeepers who is standing by his side. His other hand points to Mrs. Jeepers, a gesture that is both impolite and historically connected to administering a hex, which is likely how the characters perceive their new teacher: a hex.

Smith asserts, "Fear thrives on distorting the familiar: nothing is more terrifying for a child than to find that ghosts, aliens and bad fairies can haunt a real bedroom, a school, a neighborhood" (131). The arrival of a pretty, female teacher who dresses the part is the familiar; yet, the children are suspicious of Mrs. Jeepers' true identity and attempt to figuratively unmask her. The students begin to discern what they know from what is hidden. During her social studies lesson, Eddie interrupts Mrs. Jeepers commenting that her last name does not seem to originate from Romania. The research of Niemi, Smith, and Brown parallels with the novel: "interactions between students and teachers were also gendered in that the expected power differentials that rightly occur between student and teacher were, in many cases, negated by the students' positioning of their opposite-sex teacher as an object of heterosexual gaze" (67). Eddie challenges Mrs. Jeepers by asking for the consequences of disobeying the new classroom rules. Mrs. Jeepers smiles, flashes her green eyes, and responds, "I hope you never have to find out" (Dadey and Jones 9–10). Eddie continues to voice authority in the classroom but the more that he challenges Mrs. Jeepers the more mysterious she becomes to all of the children. Marshall posits:

> The construction of the female teacher educator through the perspective of the schoolboy matters because the discourse of feminine monstrosity moves beyond the confines of [...] books and into familiar debates about gender and education. These female monster teacher narratives envision elementary classrooms as spaces overrun with the wrong kind of women who punish "natural" boyish urges to move (or to throw airplanes) [471].

Mrs. Jeepers is seen as the wrong kind of teacher: foreign and vampiric. Eddie has a history of misbehaving and scaring off teachers. He controls the classroom in a similar way as Principal Davis: undermining the female authority in the room. Weber and Mitchell believe that children's books include tropes of the monster-teacher because boys are uncomfortable with having a woman who is not their mother in charge of them. Further, they argue, "Women with power may be perceived as threatening…" (41). There are numerous images and accounts of horrifying female characters within media and why they should be put in their place.

Aside from Liza, who continues to be supportive of their new teacher, Eddie is the only other student who continually denies that Mrs. Jeepers is anything but a regular teacher. Part of Eddie's insistence may be because he is still operating under the familiarity of past experiences. She looks similar to his former teachers; therefore, he should be able to scare her into leaving the Bailey School. He is baffled by his peer's assertions that Mrs. Jeepers is unique or different as that would mean that his plan would not come to fruition. Throughout the text, Eddie misbehaves and expects Mrs. Jeepers to respond in a way that other teachers have responded. Yet, she completely ignores him; and, "Eddie wasn't used to being ignored, especially by a teacher" (25). A. Jackson asserts, "A sense of identity, or the possession of a sense of self, is shown to depend quite a lot on being noticed…" (160). Eddie makes noises with his mouth and even drops his math book; he wiggles his hips while at the pencil sharpener to make his peers laugh. Even the illustrations of Eddie shows his eyes looking up toward the front of the classroom as he misbehaves hoping to catch a glimpse of his teacher's reaction. Mrs. Jeepers' response to each infraction is to say in nearly a whisper, "That is quite enough" (Dadey and Jones 30).

Through the characters interactions, readers see that the male characters especially Mr. Davis demonstrating his dominance in the classroom, and the student Eddie who continually misbehaves, are the female teacher's greatest obstacles. The interference in Mrs. Jeepers' teaching is an invasion of her space similar to the way the students break into her home. While they consider her the intruder, the children are the ones who continually overrun her space. Cummins (2008) argues, "Gender has long been a primary concern of critics who examine Gothic literature, and it has been consistently present in the discourse even as other issues become primary to critical attention, such as race, class, [and] national identity..." (178). Marshall contends, "Monstrosity also relies on racial and ethnic stereotypes that intersect with these constrained images of femininity" (466). Mrs. Jeepers endures the oppression for her gender and of being a Romanian. The students fear Mrs. Jeepers because they immediately view her as an "*other*," even though they cannot articulate why. Mrs. Jeepers does not follow the expectations of traditional American women: married with children, nor does she follow certain American ideals. While Americans fear immigration, an irony considering the country predominately is made up of immigrants, the child-characters more explicitly fear that which they do not understand: Mrs. Jeepers is a new teacher but because she does not behave like their past teachers, she must be a vampire; Mrs. Jeepers is female but because she does not behave like a traditional socially-constructed female, she must be a vampire. And, of course, the stereotypes are contradicted and even invalidated by Mrs. Jeepers' wardrobe.

Vampiric Immigrant

Readers never discover whether or not Mrs. Jeepers is a vampire; however, her character is constructed by the perceptions of the child-characters in the text in a similar way that Count Dracula is constructed in Stoker's novel. Both texts include characters to represent the fears and anxieties of their audiences. For example, the British fear foreigners invading their land in *Dracula*, while the American school children fear an immigrant as their new teacher in *VDWPD*. While readers might recognize these contemporary negative depictions and dismiss them as harmless stereotypes, these portrayals can become a part of the unconscious of members of our society. If books continually reinforce stereotypical depictions of those from a particular culture or minority group, individuals belonging to the group could be typecast and discouraged into a limited way of being. This is true for the depiction of Transylvanians in literature. Generally speaking, Americans have a limited understanding of Transylvania and its people. Researchers agree that reading books about characters that are different is a benefit to young readers who may only experience diversity within literature. When these texts offer accurately, well-rounded portrayals of diverse characters, they help readers understand diverse cultures and experiences; and readers develop empathy and acceptance of those previously viewed as *others*.

Unfortunately, mainstream children's books have a tendency to stereotype and include clichéd portrayals. Even the invasion literature that was popular pre–World War I continues to creep into contemporary American children's books. The Bailey School kids try to convince each other that Mrs. Jeepers is strange. She, indeed, is a stranger to them. When she initially introduces herself, Mrs. Jeepers explains that when she immigrated to the United States she changed her name. Although somewhat typical for immigrants coming to the United States, not knowing Mrs. Jeepers name or identity escalates their motivation to unmask her true self. Readers also learn that Mrs. Jeepers' family "was forced to leave" her country but does not share any more details, which leads to the four characters speculating why they had to move (Dadey and Jones 11) She is now shrouded in exotic mystery. The Bailey School kids' speculations intensify from the broad accusation of her family being criminals to the charge that her family is made up of jewel thieves. This seems to be a rather extreme leap for the students to make regarding their new teacher; however, it is a deeply rooted American stereotype of Eastern Europeans who believe that "Gypsies," a pejorative term in itself, come from Romania; and that these people are thieves (Morse et al. 321). The characters do not distrust Mrs. Jeepers because she is from a vampiric race but because she is an immigrant. Only Liza shows any kind of sympathy to Mrs. Jeepers. She comments that she believes Mrs. Jeepers "smiles because she's nice. And her accent is really neat!" (Dadey and Jones 12).

Viewing the illustrations, all of the characters are white except Melody who is portrayed as African-American. Acknowledging the current institutional racism inherent in American society, Melody would more likely feel the effects of being treated as an outsider more than any of her peers. Yet, after the two male characters in the story, Melody makes the most judgments against Mrs. Jeepers based on her Transylvanian heritage. Melody is unable to transfer any shared feelings of difference. To Melody, Mrs. Jeepers is not just different but is foreign and does not belong in the classroom.

From media, it appears that the United States' "nativist extremist" groups dominate the country. The Southern Poverty Law Center describes these groups as "anti-immigration organizations that go beyond mere advocacy to confront suspected undocumented immigrants and those who hire or help them" (2014). The number of "nativist extremist" groups was quite high in 2010 with 319 groups. By 2015, there were only 17 groups; unfortunately, the decline is not necessarily a reflection of diminishing hatred directed at immigrants coming to the United States. The activism groups are simply unnecessary as mainstream political groups and state legislatures have fundamentally incorporated the issue into their platforms (2016). The United States is a nation of immigrants with people coming from all nations. Inscribed at the base of the Statue of Liberty, Emma Lazarus's poem, "The New Colossus" offers an encouraging message to immigrants seeking refuge. Lazarus's poem reads, "Give me your tired, your poor, your huddled masses yearning to breathe free, the wretched refuse of your teeming shore. Send these, the homeless, tempest-tost to me, I lift my lamp beside the golden door!" The ideals from the poem do not necessarily translate to the immigration policy in the United States, nor do they translate to the American's views of immigration or immigrants. Yet, a shortage of qualified teachers throughout the States has resulted in school districts employing qualified international teachers. These immigrant-teachers face the same adjustment challenges of all immigrants: new language, new rules and laws, and new customs.

The Western stereotypes of Transylvanians are vast. As Andras argues, "Most westerners have no concept of the contributions made to Transylvanian culture by its Romanian population..." (1). Further, she cites Kaplan, "the very word Transylvania conjures up images of howling wolves, midnight thunderstorms, evil-looking peasants, and the thick, courtly accent of Count Dracula, as portrayed by Bela Lugosi" (149). This view of Transylvania "as the land of vampiric monsters" is not based on the collective conscious of Eastern Europeans but constructed in the West (8). The young characters reflect American societal views when they connect Mrs. Jeepers' nationality to stereotypes that have been reproduced continuously in literature and film. Light concludes, "Stoker's novel both expressed and constituted a place myth of Transylvania as a sinister and marginal location where the supernatural runs wild.... Transylvania has become synonymous with the supernatural in the Western popular imagination" (760). *VDWPD* follows this place myth with the children quickly labeling Mrs. Jeepers as a vampiric immigrant.

Final Thoughts

With children's books being full of stereotypes and clichéd portrayals, and while their readers are indoctrinated in a culture that cautions children to beware of strangers, it is easy for them to make assumptions based on appearances in *VDWPD*. Overall, Mrs. Jeepers is benign. She enforces good behavior. Beyond that, she is just different. And, in a country full of difference, it is not an aspect Americans value. Mrs. Jeepers does not have fangs nor does she drink blood. She dresses slightly eccentrically for the students' taste but she also dons a polka dot dress which completely baffles them. She does not have the typical characteristics of a vampire; yet, Mrs. Jeepers does seem a little strange. She lives in a rundown Victorian mansion and keeps a box that resembles a coffin in her basement. The children believe a strange sound came from the box but did it? Mrs. Jeepers also wears a green brooch that appears to mesmerize her students. Does she have hypnotic powers of mind control or is she simply a teacher trained in behavior management? Readers never discover what is in the box in her basement, why the green brooch transfixes some of her students, or how she was able to get Eddie to behave. The novel does not end with all the answers tied up in a neat little bow. Mrs. Jeepers is never truly unmasked by the children. Unlike other monster-teachers in children's literature, she will remain at the Bailey School; she is not asked to leave nor is she replaced. Mrs. Jeepers is not revealed to be any kinder at the end of the text than she was at the beginning. Following the research of Niemi, Smith, and Brown, Mrs. Jeepers is the perfect outlier.

While researchers argue that women are kept in powerless and objectified roles in the teaching profession, Mrs. Jeepers pushes against these constructions. She is an independent woman who lives alone. She sees the beauty in old architecture and while living on a teacher's salary understands that any sprucing up will come with time. While depicted as a stereotypical immigrant in children's books, she tolerates unruly American children never raising her voice above a whisper. Unlike other monster-teachers in children's literature, Mrs. Jeepers creates a safe learning environment. She interacts with the subject matter. She has the students participate in hands-on learning activities such as the math relay games, and shares information about her home country of Romania during the social studies lesson on the first day. Mrs. Jeepers was always open and welcoming even inviting the children into her home. In the end, the children survive Mrs. Jeepers and she is seen as a fun teacher whom the Bailey School kids end up enjoying, even when they cannot quite overcome their perceptions of her as a vampire. Perhaps that is the lesson in the entire series: immigrants are not necessarily dangerous even if they are not like us; perhaps we can learn from them. Mrs. Jeepers is a different kind of female and arguably a role model for young girls who do not necessarily want to grow up to become the women they are expected to become. With the limited illustrations, we do not see Mrs. Jeepers as a whole woman but as a vampire who wears polka dots.

Note

1. The 1980s actress and teen superstar Molly Ringwald could have been Mrs. Jeepers' American style icon considering they both don red hair, oversized hair bows, brooches worn at the very top of a buttoned collar shirt, not to mention both being *pretty in pink* in their dresses.

Works Cited

Allard, Harry, and James Marshall. *Miss Nelson Has a Field Day*. Boston: Houghton Mifflin, 1985.
_____. *Miss Nelson Is Back*. Boston: Houghton Mifflin, 1982.
_____. *Miss Nelson Is Missing!* Boston: Houghton Mifflin, 1977.
Andras, Carmen Maria. "The Image of Transylvania in English Literature." *Journal of Dracula Studies* 1 (1999). https://kutztownenglish.com/journal-of-dracula-studies-archives/. Accessed 21 July 2016.
Anonymous. "Active 'Nativist Extremist' Groups in the United States." *Southern Poverty Law Center*. 2016. https://www.splcenter.org/fighting-hate/intelligence-report/2016/active-nativist-extremist-groups-united-states. Accessed 17 February 2016.
Anonymous. "'Nativist Extremist' Groups Decline Again." *Southern Poverty Law Center*. 25 February 2014. https://www.splcenter.org/fighting-hate/intelligence-report/2014/%E2%80%98nativist-extremist%E2%80%99-groups-decline-again-0. Accessed 21 July 2016.
Anonymous. "7 Misconceptions about Romania." *Transylvania Hostel*. n.d. http://hostelcluj.com/misconceptions-about-romania/. Accessed 21 July 2016.
Arata, Stephen D. "The Occidental Tourist: *Dracula* and the Anxiety of Reverse Colonization." *Dracula: Norton Critical Edition*. Ed. Nina Auerbach and David J. Skal. New York: W.W. Norton, 1997. 462–470.
Boundless. "Gender Roles in the U.S." *Boundless Sociology*. Boundless, 8 Aug. 2016. https://www.boundless.com/sociology/textbooks/boundless-sociology-textbook/gender-stratification-and-inequality-11/gender-and-socialization-86/gender-roles-in-the-u-s-498-7851/. Accessed 31 October 2016.
Bousalis, Rina Roula. *The Portrayal of Immigrants in Children's and Young Adults' American Trade Books During Two Peak United States Immigration Eras (1880–1930 and 1980–2010s)*. Graduate Theses and Dissertations. September 2014. http://scholarcommons.usf.edu/cgi/viewcontent.cgi?article=6386&context=etd. Accessed 21 July 2016.
Cummins, Amy. "Beyond a Good/Bad Binary: The Representation of Teachers in Contemporary YAL." *The ALAN Review* 39.1 (2011): 37–45.
Dadey, Debbie, Marcia Thornton Jones, and John Steven Gurney. *Vampires Don't Wear Polka Dots*. New York: Scholastic, 1990.
Gelder, Ken. *Reading the Vampire*. London: Routledge, 1994.
Henke, Robin, Susan P. Choy, Xianglei Chen, Sonya Geis, Martha Naomi Alt, and Stephen P. Broughman, "America's Teachers: Profile of a Profession,1993–94, NCES 97–460," U.S. Department of Education, National Center for Education Statistics. Washington, D.C.: 1997. http://nces.ed.gov/pubs97/97460.pdf. Accessed 21 July 2016.
Hinkle, Linda. "Bloodsucking Structures: American Female Vampires as Class Structure Critique." *MP: An Online Feminist Journal* 2.2 (2008): 19–26.
Jackson, Anna. "Uncanny Hauntings, Canny Children." *The Gothic in Children's Literature: Haunting the Borders*. Ed. Anna Jackson, Karen Coats, and Roderick McGillis. London: Routledge, 2008. 157–176.
Jackson, K. *Match Quality, Worker Productivity, and Worker Mobility: Direct Evidence from Teachers* (Working Paper No. 15990). Cambridge, MA: National Bureau of Economic Research. 2010.
Kaplan, Robert D. *Balkan Ghosts: A Journey Through History*. New York: Vintage Books, 1996.
Koester, A.W., and N.O. Bryant. *Fashion Terms and Styles for Women's Garments*. Corvallis, Or: Extension Service, Oregon State University, 1991.

Light, Duncan. "Dracula Tourism in Romania: Cultural Identity and the State." *Annals of Tourism Research* 34.3 (2007): 746–765.
Marshall, Elizabeth. "Monstrous Schoolteachers: Women Educators in Popular Cultural Texts." *Feminist Media Studies* 16 (2016): 460–477.
Morse, Jedidiah, Aaron Arrowsmith, Amos Doolittle, Enoch G. Gridley, William Hooker, and Joseph T. Buckingham. *The American Universal Geography, Or, A View of the Present State of All the Kingdoms, States, and Colonies in the Known World: In Two Volumes.* 6th ed. Vol. 2. Chicago: Thomas & Andrews, 1812.
Niemi, Nancy S., Nancy Brown, and Julia B. Smith. "The Portrayals of Teachers in Children's Popular Fiction." *Journal of Research in Education* 20.2 (2014): 58–80.
Ronfeldt, Mathew, Susanna Loeb, and James Wyckoff. "How Teacher Turnover Harms Student Achievement." *American Educational Research Journal* (February 2013): 4–36.
Sherman, Aubrey. *Vampires: The Myths, Legends, and Lore*. Avon: Adams Media, 2014.
Sika, V. "Fashion for Feminists—How Fashion and Dress Shape Women's Identities." *Buwa: A Journal on African Women's Experiences* 2.2 (2013): 47–52.
Smith, Anna. "The Scary Tale Looks for a Family: Gary Crew's Gothic Hospital and Sonya Hartnett's the Devil Latch." *The Gothic in Children's Literature: Haunting the Borders.* Ed. Anna Jackson, Karen Coats, and Roderick McGillis. London: Routledge, 2008. 131–144.
Soulliere, Danielle. "Electronic Journal of Sociology." *Masculinity on Display in the Squared Circle: Constructing Masculinity in Professional Wrestling*. 2005. http://www.sociology.org/content/2005/tier1/soulliere.html. Accessed 21 July 2016.
Stoker, Bram. *Dracula*. New York: W.W. Norton, 1997.
United States. National Park Service. "The New Colossus—Full Text." *National Parks Service*. U.S. Department of the Interior, n.d. https://www.nps.gov/stli/learn/historyculture/colossus.htm. Accessed 24 Aug. 2016.
U.S. Department of Education, National Center for Education Statistics. "Introduction and Chapter 2." *Digest of Education Statistics, 2014* (NCES 2016-006). http://nces.ed.gov/fastfacts/display.asp?id=28. Accessed 21 July 2016.
U.S. Department of Education, National Center for Education Statistics. (2014). *Teacher Attrition and Mobility: Results From the 2012-13 Teacher Follow-up Survey* (NCES 2014-077). http://nces.ed.gov/pubs2014/2014077.pdf. Accessed 21 July 2016.
Weber, S., and C. Mitchell. *That's Funny, You Don't Look Like a Teacher! Interrogating Images and Identity in Popular Culture*. London: Falmer Press, 1995.
Wing Bo Tso, Anna. "Representations of the Monstrous-Feminine in Selected Works of C.S. Lewis, Roald Dahl and Philip Pullman." *Libri & Liberi*, 1.2 (2012): 215–232.

Under Her Batwings
Jung's Shadow Aspect as Depicted in Monster High *and* My Little Pony *Vampires*

Jacquelyn E. Bent

Recently, there has been an uprising among the undead. Vampires, universally feared and reviled predators, have seemingly transformed. Once believed to terrorize at nightfall, draining blood from their hapless victims, they have seemingly moved on to other pursuits. The vampire has become a "friendly" revenant. A reminder to others, perhaps, not to judge a fanged creature by its incisors. More importantly, the vampire serves as a metaphor that we all cast a shadow; one that should not be repressed or denied. The purpose of the vampire in contemporary children's media will be explored with a particular emphasis on representations that appeared in the reboot of *My Little Pony: Friendship Is Magic* (MLP) and *Monster High* as well as how these representations correspond to Jungian theory of the shadow aspect of the psyche, and his theory of individuation.

Venture into the local toyshop and take note of the proliferation of fangs, batwings, and coffins. Certainly this would be reasonable for Halloween, or a tourist trap in Romania, but it becomes harder not to notice that even the local Toys 'R' Us has taken on quasi–Gothic flair. The vampire has been culturally appropriated. No longer a source of terror, children are actively encouraged to embrace the vampire. The vampire has become ubiquitous. On oddly pastel pink or yellow batwings, they bring with them a message that is largely intended to be positive or B+, depending on your tolerance for bad puns. There has been a very substantial change in how the vampire is perceived. Rather than inducing fear, longing for immortality, or being a source of sexual seduction, the vampire is viewed as a variant on the species.

A variant that has some unique dietary restrictions and need for intensive sun protection. Depictions of the vampire in children's media are hardly new and include *Sesame Street*'s the Count, who is largely helpful and curiously amused by the act of counting, Count Chockula, whose only evil deed seems to be a yearning to convince children that a marshmallowy chocolate cereal is a healthy breakfast option, and the affable Count Duckula, a vampire duck who subsists on vegetables. In young adult books such as Harris' "Southern Vampire Mysteries" series (aka True Blood), the vampire is a metaphor for accepting something that is different. The vampires largely want to co-exist with humans, and many of the humans who feel out of place among their species, such as Suki Stackhouse, find a sense of acceptance among the vampires of Bon Temps. In the past four decades, the modern vampire has undertaken a change into a kinder, approachable undead ambassador. Over the past six years, in fact, the vampire motif has seemingly been adopted as a symbol encouraging tolerance of "others" in children's media, in particular.

There has been a long-standing fascination with the vampire legend. The vampire traditionally represented something dark, forbidden, and otherworldly; it was both seductive and despicable. It may well be that man's fascination with the vampire has something to do with the difficulty humanity has reconciling their own shadowy tendencies with cultural and societal norms we're expected to adhere to. Carl Jung, a protégé of Freud spoke at length about the shadow aspect. The shadow is the side of man we deny; insecurities, fears, hostilities, deviancies that we would never share, and often reject is part of our psyche. Jung also proposed the idea of individuation. The notion that for an individual to be whole, they would need to integrate all aspects of their psyche. This included descent into the depths of one's shadow to integrate those qualities with their persona; their more "outward" facing self. According to Jung (1935), "The aim of individuation is nothing less than to divest the self of the false wrappings of the persona on the one hand and the suggestive power of primordial images on the other" (Schmidt 2). The shadow referred to here as the primordial images consists of many of the negative aspects of one's personality including fears, insecurities, atavistic tendencies, guilt and other things most people would like to suppress. However, Jung also believed the shadow to be the seat of creative endeavors and honest evaluations of the self and others. It was not meant to be ignored, but to be integrated via individuation. While there is debate as to whether this would happen instantaneously or as part of life-long development remains open to debate (Morgan). Jung was said to be inspired by the ancient Greek philosopher Heraclitus whom he adopted the concept of enantiodromia from which roughly translates to running counter to, or opposite of. According to Trinh and Kolb, Jung was influenced by this belief in a need for a unification of opposites within the self. Failure to do so would result in an imbalance; caused by suppression of those aspects of ourselves we have either denied or repressed coming out and wreaking havoc.

The shadow aspect was typically perceived as negative, and therefore was also believed to be evil. However, according to Jung, this is an oversimplification of the shadow aspect. He believed that a failure to assimilate this aspect of ourselves results in conflict on both an individual and potentially a far grander scale, creating hostility and having the potential to lead to war. According to Jung, embracing the shadow aspect of the self would lead to greater mental health, relief of depressive symptoms and ultimately, improved self-esteem, self-acceptance and self-awareness (Morgan). Interestingly, according to Schmidt, a lack of integration led to neuroticism, a trait that is curiously present in some of the post-modern vampires found in *Monster High* and *MLP*. Look no further than the *Monster High* cabal—intended for 6 to 12 year olds—who were conjured by Mattel in 2010 for a variety of new age monsters, in particular, vampires. The message associated with these "monsters" is that one should embrace their uniqueness; celebrate their ghoulishness.

According to the *Monster High* literature prepared for parents there is a particularly strong emphasis on tolerance. More precisely explained on the *Monster High* site, "Monster High is a school where teenage monsters from all walks of unlife are accepted, just as they are … what makes this school special is the community where imperfections are scary-cool and embracing everyone's differences is encouraged" (*Monster High*). It would appear that the monster has become a metaphor for the embracing of flaws, differences, uniqueness, and imperfections. The *Monster High* characters include werewolves, mummies, ghosts/poltergeists, mer- and moth-people, gorgons and more. A veritable hodgepodge of myth, legend, and cultural phenomena. These toys are geared toward females aged 8 and up, however, their aesthetic tends to also appeal to tweens and older. On an episode of RuPaul's *Drag Race All-Stars 2*, a reality television program where drag queens compete for drag superstardom, contestant Adore Delano was quoted as saying she wants to look like a *Monster High* doll (Delano 2016).[1] Their appeal is seemingly near universal.

The intention behind the marketing of *Monster High*, while admirable, is also rather misleading. A quick view of the profile of Draculaura, one of the most popular *Monster High* characters, demonstrates this inconsistency. She is raised by a single father (Dracula), is a vegan, and is "totes optimistic." She is also quoted as saying she loves smiling and making others happy (*Monster High*). Draculaura's vamp friend, Elissabat, is also described unsurprisingly as someone who loves girly/frilly clothes. She is an actress who has severe stage fright and also appears to be a vegetarian who cites blood oranges as her favorite food (*Monster High*). Heavy-handed would be an understatement. These creatures of the night appear to be so far removed from those of legend, they are totally banal. The message that emerges is that to be accepted you will be stripped of your supernatural tendencies and instincts. Packaged for mass-consumption by people who do not want the slightest whiff of evil or otherworldly for their children's toys. Tamed and broken; these creatures lose their lust for the sanguine and upon closer inspection are de-fanged for "our" protection. What makes these dolls "unique" appear to be lifestyle choices, such as their diet, and in some cases family dynamics. On the surface, a message that seemed truly commendable does not really appear to be. It is unclear how a dietary choice is meant to translate into embracing the uniqueness of the individual, including their flaws and imperfections. Rather than aggression or bloodlust, it would seem Mattel have simply glossed over the vampire's nature in favor of promoting a diet.

With so many adolescents suffering eating disorders, it would seem that this is a less than ideal focal point; a concept that has been explored by Schild who suggests that the body composition of the *Monster High* dolls reinforces unhealthy body image to females. She proposes that the design and characterization of *Monster High* dolls significantly reinforce gender stereotyping, as well as romanticizing death to adolescents, including proposing that death is an acceptable alternative to treatment for eating disorders. She has pointed out that media, including the *Twilight* books and films, equally send messages to pre-adolescent and adolescent teens that seemingly glorify unhealthy relationships and death. While it is harder to agree with the sentiment that the dolls reinforce the idea that death is more preferable than treatment, eating disorders are far too complex to suggest this being a possible cause for why those affected avoid treatment. Schild makes a number of valid points, in particular, concerns about emphasizing unrealistic body shape/image, as well as reinforcing gender stereotypes like gossiping, and fashion. There is a particularly strong emphasis on female's appearance (14) including the ever present discussion of make-up and even issues with body hair, at least for the werewolf characters, such as Clawdeen Wolf (*Monster High*).

Certainly this shift in using the monstrous for marketing is not entirely new. Prior to the *Monster High* specter, the *Living Dead Dolls* crawled forth from the abyss in 1998 (Mezco). These dolls, however, were not intended to be cute, positive, and cuddly. They were marketed toward adult consumers of collectibles and consisted of cinema-inspired characters, spoofs of horror film characters, as well as those of urban legend and post-modern Gothic culture. There was a niche market that Mezco capitalized upon and to great effect. The dolls' profiles suggest that they are openly murderous and evil in their intent and remain wildly popular. Funko, also founded in 1998 as a bobble head[2] manufacturer, around 2005 expanded their line of collectible toys which now include a vast range of pop culture characters such as those from horror films, cartoons including MLP, and popular films (Funko). It certainly made sense for a company like Mattel that has in recent years struggled to maintain profitability to jump on the proverbial monster bandwagon. As of 2016, however, the profit margins for Mattel and *Monster High* have begun to dwindle (Armintal), suggesting that this particular toy trend may have abated. Mattel was hardly alone in attempts to capture the monstrous zeitgeist, however. Sanrio, the multi-billion-dollar Japanese company that brought us such harmless and universally adored characters as the Little Twin Stars, Hello Kitty, and My Melody, who first appeared in the 1970's eventually added an apparently sinister critter known as Kuromi in 2005. Kuromi is depicted as the proverbial Jekyll to My Melody's Ms. Hyde.

My Melody, for the uninitiated, appears as an adorable little bunny that wears a red cap on her little bunny ears and has delightful sheep and mouse associates. Kuromi, also painfully cute, is however, different. Unlike My Melody, she wears a black cap on her bunny ears. Her cap has a skull on it, and she has been depicted as a bunny with fangs, though it is not entirely clear where the Sanrio marketing ends and fan art begins. According to Sanrio's biography on Kuromi's official Facebook she is a tomboy, troublemaker and likes to cause mischief. It is also stated on the official Sanrio site that one should not be intimated by Kuromi's tough exterior; she remains girlie (Sanrio). This seems to suggest there is something unfeminine about being tough. Further, her birthday is Halloween and she is described as My Melody's rival. Curiously, she also has a tail not dissimilar to that of a red devil, qualities you do not typically see in a Sanrio character.

Admittedly, Sanrio has been known to take creative license with bunny and kittens before. For example, Hello Kitty is allegedly a little girl, not a cat, something that came as a tremendous surprise and confusion to most people when it was announced. Kuromi, however, is a particularly atypical departure in character development for Sanrio. The critters, some of whom have been around for over forty years, have always been depicted as sweet, friendly, and helpful. Menacing is something new. According to the official Facebook for Kuromi, she is in fact secretly very girly, likes romance novels, shallots, and good looking men. Appearances, once again, are deceiving. While we are lulled into believing she is naughty, even malevolent, the truth is she is not, though the mention of her sexual orientation more than suggests homophobia on the part of Sanrio. The authors of Kuromi's biography are quick to point out that her being a tomboy should not be misconstrued. Not to worry! She strictly adheres to gender stereotypes. She loves cooking, and her aforementioned love of shallots, while related to garlic, may suggest that any depictions of her with fangs are purely coincidental; likely a fan-created variant. Ultimately, she is not vampire or vampire-adjacent. In fact, she is not even a "bad girl." She is tame, and girlie; only appearing naughty. Also curious, as with

Monster High, Sanrio's characters have a near universal appeal. While originally intended for children, typically little girls, Sanrio has maintained its worldwide success by appealing to all ages.

A variation of this kinder, gentler vampire trope was recently depicted on the cartoon *My Little Pony: Friendship Is Magic* (*MLP*). *MLP* first emerged in the 1980's as collectible toy ponies (Valiente and Rasmusson). They came in a variety of pastel colors and promoted harmless activities such as grooming one's mane and shopping, ostensibly for more *MLP* merchandise. In 2010 *MLP* was re-imagined under the watchful eye of Lauren Faust (Valiente and Rasmusson 90).[3] Faust wanted *MLP* to be more than a brand. She wanted to incorporate messages that included embracing one's unique abilities and imperfections as well as encouraging friendship (90), not dissimilar to the *Monster High* message. She wanted a character driven show that appealed to female audiences as she felt this demographic was largely neglected (Faust in Tekaramity n.p.). The "Mane Six" characters were developed by Faust in collaboration with the toy manufacturer Hasbro who had been motivated by recent successes of the Transformers cinematic reboot of the 1980s cartoon of the same name. (Hart n.p.).

These ponies are meant to be fully realized; kind yet flawed creatures that extol the magic of friendship. More specifically, the Mane Six includes three "sub-species" of ponies: Pegasus —winged ponies who have the ability to fly; unicorns—whose talents typically include the ability to use magic; and earth ponies—that have talents like all the other ponies, but cannot fly or use magic (Hasbro). Though it should be pointed out that each pony, regardless of sub-species, has what is known as a "cutie mark" (Hasbro) that denotes what his or her unique ability is. Interestingly, cutie marks emerge around the time of what would be the humanoid equivalent of being a pre-teen, when puberty typically begins. Additionally, each member of the Mane Six has a particular quality known as an "element of harmony" that corresponds to a specific facet of friendship they are "responsible" for curating (Hasbro). These elements including loyalty, honesty, and laughter.

The Mane Six consist of the following characters: Pinkie Pie, an earth pony who loves to laugh and have celebrations with friends. She is never without her party cannon and frequently, and much to the chagrin of her friends, breaks out into song. She is known to break the "fourth wall" and talk directly to the audience during the program. She is responsible for the element of harmony known as laughter (Hasbro). Fluttershy, a painfully shy, neurotic Pegasus who is afraid to fly, has tremendous love for animals as well as a great talent with caring for them, including an ability known as "the stare" which enables her to "mesmerize" animals. She is responsible for the element of harmony—kindness (Hasbro). Rarity, is a fashionista unicorn with a flair for the dramatic, as well as a keen design sense, who is responsible for the element of harmony—generosity. Apple Jack, an earth pony who is honest and hardworking, and helps her family run an orchard known as Sweet Apple Acres. Apple Jack is responsible for the element of harmony—honesty. Rainbow Dash, an ambitious, quick flying Pegasus who dreams of joining the Wonder bolts; the Pegasus equivalent of the Blue Angels for like of a better analogy,[4] who makes everything 20 percent cooler, and is responsible for the element of harmony—loyalty (Hasbro). And finally, Twilight Sparkle, a unicorn who starts as a loner, who focuses only on her academic studies of magic and does not see the point of friendship. She is responsible for the element of harmony—magic (Hasbro). Eventually, during her time living in Ponyville, a suburb of Equestria, the country where *MLP* takes place, she meets the other members of the Mane Six and learns the importance of friendship. This is accomplished through a series of misadventures and allegories about how one cannot be an island unto themselves (Hasbro). These messages include embracing your friends' differences, flaws, and uniqueness as well as loyalty and honesty. Eventually, Twilight becomes an alicorn princess, a unicorn/Pegasus hybrid, after completing a number of trials requiring she save Equestria, Canterlot, Manehattan and, most importantly, friendship (Hasbro).

The ponies are strong characters. They are empowered females, who never require the intervention of male ponies to save their hides (Valiente and Rasmusson 91–92). This is not by accident and, in fact, a point of occasional criticism of the *MLP* brand. The only "regular" male characters include the likes of Spike, a baby dragon-assistant of Twilight Sparkle (Hasbro). He is often depicted as loveable and well meaning, but also prone to fits of jealous rage and gluttony. Overall, male characters appear minimally (Valiente and Rasmusson 93), and at times are a significant nuisance. Discord, a chimeric being of pure chaos that has historically brought, for lack of a better term, discord to Equestria is a good example of this. He also brought along chocolate rain, so he is not all bad. Over time, in fact, he is brought, albeit reluctantly, into the Mane Six' inner circle by way of Fluttershy, at the request of Princess Celestia, who believes everyone deserves another chance to redeem themselves. Fluttershy even lets him live with her for a time. Curiously, Discord is also depicted as very jealous, possessive, and resentful, especially over Fluttershy having other friends or outside interests. Male depictions are frequently less than flattering, it would seem; portrayed as befuddled, cranky, jealous, and voracious.

Oddly, these seemingly sexist characterizations have not inhibited the show from capturing the hearts and minds of a largely male, 18–25-year-old demographic affectionately known as bronies (Hale n.p.). Though the original purpose of the show was to provide story-driven, compelling characters for girls and a bit of nostalgia for their mothers, it has far exceeded those expectations, particularly with a male audience. The popularity of the program has also spawned a number of televised films, an upcoming feature length cinematic release, a considerable range of toys, and collectibles, including a humanoid version of the ponies known as Equestria Girls (Hasbro), and, most strikingly, "brony" conventions (Hale n.p.). It seems ironic that a show intended to empower female audiences has been so universally embraced by adult males instead. While not an immediate goal of Faust, she strove to prove that programming designed by females for females could have a larger appeal, something she managed to great effect. Alongside this, the show has incorporated a host of themes including the historical (Native American Buffalos) and the mythical (minotaurs and hydras), but also the supernatural.

The *MLP* episode, "Bats," features Fluttershy and her unique talent for communicating and caring for animals. Vampire fruit bats had invaded Apple Jack's apple orchard, Sweet Apple Acres, and were wreaking havoc on her apple crops. She enlists the Mane Six for help. There is a disagreement over how to dispatch the bats. Fluttershy suggests that a portion of the orchard be devoted to the bats, as a sanctuary of sorts, so that they can peacefully coexist. Something that does not appeal to Apple Jack. It is decided, instead, that a spell will be used to alter the bats' appetite for apples. Fluttershy is asked to use her special ability known as "the stare" to essentially hypnotize the animals, while Twilight Sparkle uses a spell to alter their appetite. The spell appears to have worked, in the short term, and the bats are no longer a threat to Sweet Apple Acres. Or so it is thought. Overnight, the orchards appear to have been attacked again. It is assumed something has gone wrong with the spell, which frustrates Twilight greatly. She prides herself on her ability to use magic to solve problems. The ponies decide to "stake out" the orchard to see the bats in action. This time, however, there is one lone bat hanging from a tree. Upon closer inspection it is not a bat, rather it is Fluttershy, who hisses at them and flies off. She appears to have vampire fangs, and displays aggression that is not at all consistent with Fluttershy's typical demeanor. The ponies are at a loss of how this could have happened or what to do.

Fluttershy, as you may recall, is sweet, to the point of being slightly annoying. She is shy, she does not like flying, much less hanging upside down from a tree. She certainly is not known for hissing or growling at her friends, nor does she typically have fangs or glowing red eyes. Also very notable of the vampire motif, her feathered Pegasus wings are transformed in to more bat-like membranous wings. Eventually, the ponies are able to resolve the problem of Fluttershy, but there are some unintended consequences. The new and perhaps slightly improved Fluttershy, AKA Flutterbat as she was called by Rarity at various points in the episode, seems to have greater balance in her psyche. The short-lived "darker" Fluttershy has left its mark and Fluttershy may be all the better for it. Fluttershy claims not to recall what it was like to be her darker self; however, at the end of the episode, when she smiles, her fangs re-emerge suggesting otherwise. She has known, however briefly, what it was like to embrace an atavistic side of her nature, to be unbridled, if you will. She was not only aggressive and single-minded in her pursuit of apples, but she put herself first. She did not concern herself with how her actions might affect others, something very unlike Fluttershy. Equally, the other ponies were frightened of her and her change in demeanor, something Fluttershy had never experienced before, though, in a previous episode where she tries to learn to be more assertive, she does say rather nasty things to Pinkie Pie and Rarity. It only serves to upset them, not make them fearful. In that episode, ultimately, she recognized that she had become a "monster" and did not like herself being overly assertive. This time, however, the change seems to be welcomed by Fluttershy.

The message was quite a curious one for a show that encourages friendship and kindness. In fact, it was quite exciting. Embrace your dark side. It does not make you bad, ostensibly, rather it makes you more "you." By denying your whole self, you live a life of needless fear, and miss out on many things that life has to offer. While the darker element should be tethered, it is necessary to not only explore but to engage actively with one's shadow to be a fully-integrated being—a provocative message, especially for something that was originally intended as a children's cartoon.

In a subsequent *MLP* episode entitled "Scare Master," Fluttershy's dark side re-emerges during Nightmare Night festivities, Equestria's equivalent of Halloween. In a series of incidents, it appears that the rest of the ponies are looking forward to the frights that accompany Nightmare Night; however, most of the evening has been a bust. Fluttershy implements some fantastic ideas for scaring her friends in all manner of ways. This includes allusions to the film *Psycho* down to the psychotic mother in the basement. It is revealed that since she has embraced her dark side, she has a better understanding of fear and what motivates it. This knowledge is used much to her friend's delight. By the episode's end Fluttershy informs her friends that while she appreciates her friends, and wants them to be happy, inducing fear in others is not really her idea of fun. Even when her friends are having a good time she'd rather not participate in Nightmare Night in the future. It would seem that individuation has taken place; while Fluttershy is more complete and has a better understanding of the pony condition, including a positive role of fear and excitement, she would rather not play along. And that rather than succumb to the pressures to please her friends she is able to assert herself, something she had previously struggled to do.

The depiction of Fluttershy and her transformation from neurotic to more fully integrated is quite striking in its similarity to that of Jung's concept of individuation brought about by integration of the shadow self as part of the psyche. She had previously been depicted as incredibly nervous, fretful, and unable to assert herself; she struggled to embrace her talents, as well as downplaying her immense abilities with animals. As a Pegasus she is quite literally afraid to fly and because of her severe shyness she frequently avoids activities that she would otherwise enjoy. In fact, there have been story arcs where she has jeopardized not only her own safety and well being, but that of her fellow ponies due to the severity of her fears and insecurities. They are often all consuming. The transformation of Fluttershy, after being turned into a vampony, creates a balanced, richer, more fully realized Fluttershy. This new dimension to Fluttershy gives her greater insights into herself, as well as enables her to function better as a whole. In essence it had been a therapeutic tool to become a "vampony," even if the spell cast by Twilight Sparkle ostensibly removes that which made Fluttershy "vampy." She is transformed. She has tasted the "forbidden fruits" her shadow side had to offer and by the episode's conclusion it was clear that Twilight's spell was not 100 percent effective. Curiously, this is information Fluttershy decides not to share with her pony pals, but clearly embraces.

In contrast, Draculaura seems to be at odds with her vampire self. She is a strict vegan, who is disgusted by blood. It is unclear how she feels about garlic, though the author did try to find information about this. In many ways she is actually depicted as a very stereotypical girl. She loves fashion, hanging out with her friends, dressing her pet bat, Count Fabulous, up in cutesy clothing, and pleasing other people. Her bio, listed on the *Monster High* official site, is rather saccharine. Things that are important to her are ensuring her friends' happiness and seeing the good in the world. This myopic worldview is not unique to this vampire. Draculaura's bestie, Elissabat, also has a rather insipid and stereotypical worldview. She loves fruit and acting despite her terrible stage fright, and loves dressing up in girlie clothes. Though immortal, they seem incredibly devoid of the world-weariness one has come to expect from the vampires of yore. In fact, for creatures who are listed as over 1,000 years old (Mattel), neither demonstrates much in the way of depth, education, or understanding beyond eye shadow and fashion.

Unlike Fluttershy, Draculaura does not seem to have integrated her shadow aspect with the rest of her personae. While she has fangs, and cannot see her reflection in the mirror, one should not be concerned. She has adapted and does not find that this interferes with her ability to apply lip gloss. Incidentally, the blurb about the lip gloss is quite literally something Mattel included in her biography. In terms of her style and make-up one would describe it as faux-Gothic, but as described by Draculaura, "sweet with just a little bite" (Mattel), thus ensuring that she is as non-threatening as possible. The emphasis on the character, as well as the other creatures is that while they may appear "different" they are very much stereotypical, even vain, mostly female characters. While there are male characters, referred to as

Mansters, as with *MLP*, they play little role. Throughout, especially with Draculaura, it appears that people pleasing is incredibly important to her. It is probably a first in vampire cannon that a vampire could be described as a doormat. Draculaura has not achieved individuation. If anything, she is vulnerable to break down, as she is unable to reconcile her darker elements with those that are more socially acceptable. Even when she is surrounded by other monsters, she feels a need to conform to a human societies standards of behavior. It is unclear how this depiction of a vampire translates into a message of accepting one's ghoulishness that is promoted quite conspicuously on the *Monster High* site.

The theme that is emerging from these characterizations is to embrace who you are, fangs and all. However, closer examination reveals that this is often only the case if what makes you "unique" falls within acceptable cultural guidelines. There is no blood-sucking vampire to be had. Rather she is transformed into an apple obsessed pony, an extremely fashionable, optimistic vegan, who strives to please others, who adheres to gender stereotypes or in the case of Kuromi, who is actually not a vampire at all, but rather a mischievous tomboy who adheres strictly to gender stereotypes. What is particularly sad is that this also reinforces for young girls that to be accepted you must forgo your dark side. Any urge that runs counter to what is acceptable for a young "lady" must be quashed and sublimated into something more socially acceptable. The use of dietary restrictions as a metaphor for self-control and reinforcement of ideal behavior is disquieting.

Admittedly, some of the storylines of *MLP* have been altered to satisfy child development specialists who work as part of a team of consultants for the show. Faust was quoted as lamenting a number of the restrictions on how the *MLP* stories could be developed to ensure that the subject matter of *MLP* never ventured into edgy territory due to standards and practices associated with children's programming (Tekaramity 93). As *Monster High* was also developed for children, aged 8 and up, it can be assumed the dolls design and personae's have been heavily influenced by child development experts who no doubt had a hand in how the monstrous characters progressed. Despite all of the bluster about uniqueness and acceptance there is often a lamentably unpleasant reinforcement of cultural norms and gender expectations that belies the use of the eerie and supernatural in children's cartoons and toys.

Arguably, there is some support for the notion of being yourself, even if it does not conform to the desires of others. Notably in the *MLP* episode "Scare Master," Fluttershy embraces who she is more fully. She has a dark side and seemingly she has become well acquainted with the power evoked by this dark side. She exhibits a creative flair for inducing fear in others, for example. Still, these are facets of her persona that she does not wish to employ. For example, her ability to use her creativity to evoke fear in others; even though that is what is desired by her friends while celebrating Nightmare Night, is not what she would like to do, and she makes this very clear. She respects their right to enjoy being scared and to revel in that fear. They too must respect that she does not enjoy being scared or scaring others and does not want to participate. It is a breakthrough for her, certainly. Fluttershy asserts herself, something she has struggled to do. However, it feels as though there remains a compromise and an unwillingness on the part of the storytellers to truly embrace the more integrated Fluttershy. Especially, since the side of her that she chooses to disavow ultimately, is dark and fear-inducing.

Ultimately, the message the vampire represents in these toys and cartoons is a disappointing one. It appears that girls can be different, unique and flawed providing they do not stray too far from cultural norms and expectations. Hasbro has made slightly greater strides. In particular, with the reboot of *MLP* there have been substantial gains toward encouraging self-acceptance, as well as developing a fan base of male constituents for a show that was developed with female children's sensibilities in mind. However, there is still much that needs to be done. Perhaps, as mentioned earlier, standards and practices intervened, determining that certain themes and message are not suitable for the intended audience of female children. That may, ultimately, be part of the problem. Often, the notion of being different and embracing those differences is conditional. You can be unique and different; providing you adhere to culturally accepted ideals and remain a "good girl."

Notes

1. "RuPaul's Drag Race AllStars 2." Logo, 2016. http://www.logotv.com/shows/rupauls-all-stars-drag-race.
2. A bobblehead, which can also be known as a nodder, wobbler or bobble head, is a type of collectible toy. Its head is often oversized compared to its body.
3. The target audience for the show is ages 4–12.
4. The *Blue Angels* are the United States Navy's flight demonstration squadron, with aviators from the Navy and Marines.

Works Cited

Delano, Adore. Facebook Page, 23 March 2016. https://www.facebook.com/AdoreDelanoOfficial/videos/1144450158901336/. Accessed 1 August 2016.
Funko. "No Title." *Abous Us*. N.p., 2005. https://funko.com/pages/about-us. Accessed 1 September 2016.
Hale, Mike. "Galloping Once Again into a Rainbow Sunset: 'My Little Pony: Classic Movie Collection' Rears Its Head." N.p., 2014. http://www.nytimes.com/2014/01/19/movies/homevideo/my-little-pony-classic-movie-collection-rears-its-head.html?_r=0. Accessed 1 September 2016.
Hasbro. "The Mane Six." N.p., 2010. http://mylittlepony.hasbro.com/en-ca/ponies. Accessed 30 July 2016.
Mezco. "About." 2016. N.p. http://www.mezcotoyz.com/. Accessed 1 September 2016.
Monster High. "Characters." N.d. http://play.monsterhigh.com/en-us/character/index.html. Accessed 1 August 2016.
Morgan, Speer. "The Shadow." *The Missouri Review* 33.3 (2010): 5–7.

Sanrio. "Kuromi." N.p., 2016. https://www.sanrio.com/pages/character-goodies-kuromi. Accessed 1 September 2016.
Schild, Heather D. "Anorexia/Bulimia, Transcendence, and the Potential Impact of Romanticized/Sexualized Death Imagery." *Center for the Study of Ethics in Society*. Kalamazoo: Western Michegin University, 2014. n.p.
Schmidt, Martin. "Individuation." *Society of Analytical Psychology*. 1935, 1–5. https://www.thesap.org.uk/resources/articles-on-jungian-psychology-2/about-analysis-and-therapy/individuation/. Accessed 1 September 2016.
Tekarmity. "Exclusive Season Retrospective Interview with Lauren Faust" N.p. 2010. http://www.equestriadaily.com/2011/09/exclusive-season-1-retrospective.html. Accessed 1 September 2016.
Valiente, Christian, and Xeno Rasmusson. "Bucking the Stereotypes: My Little Pony and Challenges to Traditional Gender Roles." *Journal of Psychological Issues in Organizational Culture* 5.4 (2015): 88–97.

Metamorphosis of the Blood
Vampiric Femininity in Contemporary Children's Fiction

CHLOÉ GERMAINE BUCKLEY

Introduction

Throughout literary history, vampires have connected social and/or sexual deviance to disease. They "encompass a broad range of all things that defy normative constructions of nation and health" and connote "a variety of fears attached to sexuality and disease" (Fink 417). In nineteenth-century Gothic the vampire "disease" incorporated a pathologized femininity; the emaciated bodies and degenerate appetites of female vampires metaphorically and thematically connected femininity to sickness. As Aspasia Stephanou argues, "vampire females are imagined as bodies open, uncontrolled, sick and dangerous" (97). This essay explores how children's fiction has inherited these connections between vampires, femininity and sickness, developing and reworking the tropes of nineteenth-century vampire narratives in response to feminist critiques and rewritings. Examining three novels published between 1980 and 2010, this study will argue that the "nomadic" ethical outlook of children's Gothic offers innovative responses to the problematic and ambiguous construction of femininity in vampire narratives.

Late nineteenth-century vampire narratives suggest a connection between femininity and sickness through their depiction of vampiric females. Typically, a young woman, who has become the chosen prey of the vampire, succumbs to a mysterious wasting illness transmitted via the blood. In these stories, when the young female finally succumbs to the vampiric contagion, she turns into a femme fatale, a Gothic "vamp" whose sexuality threatens patriarchal ideals of femininity, the bonds of marriage and proper (or, healthy) lines of descent. Conventional vampire stories suggest the moral weakness of femininity, depicting women who are easily seduced, "voluptuous temptresses who desire to infect all the men who enter their lives" (Wisker, "Vampires and School Girls" n.p.). Vampiric femininity is thus characterized by figurative ambiguity; fetishized ideals of beauty and passivity degenerate swiftly into a patriarchal nightmare of a corrupt and corrupting female body that is the "embodiment of disease and threatening sexuality" (Stephanou 13). The vampire tales of Joseph Sheridan Le Fanu and Bram Stoker, in particular, establish enduring tropes (of female victims and female vampires) found in many subsequent vampire fictions.

Room 13 (1987) by the British writer, Robert Swindells, *Blood Sinister* (1996) by British writer, Celia Rees, and *The Reformed Vampire Support Group* (2009) by Australian writer, Catherine Jinks, draw on many of the tropes associated with the vampiric feminine from Le Fanu's *Carmilla* (1872) and Stoker's *Dracula* (1897), while reworking and contesting others. Both *Room 13* and *Blood Sinister* insist upon the necessity of vanquishing the vampire, who is the source of disease and contamination. Both twentieth-century novels conclude by returning the assailed female victims to full health. Despite echoing a nineteenth-century connection between the vampire and the "at-risk" female body, though, these books also resist the confines of pathologizing discourse. In *Blood Sinister*, the vampire is not merely pitted against the doctor, but is also a doctor himself. This change blurs the moral lines established in Bram Stoker's *Dracula*, which set up a contest between the "crew of light" (led by the doctor, Van Helsing) and the degenerate, superstitious Count (Craft 111). In *Blood Sinister*, the young female protagonist must not only escape the clutches of the vampire, but also the medical institution over which he presides.

The Reformed Vampire Support Group goes further in overturning the pathologizing discourse of vampiric femininity, refusing an ending in which the diseased female body must be cured. In this novel, the protagonist accepts the vampire as an essential part of herself, rehabilitating her body by acknowledging its new functionality afforded by the vampiric "condition." Indeed, Jinks's novel exploits most fully what inheres in nineteenth-century vampire narratives, but which those narratives work to repress or expel. That is, the potential for vampiric contagion to cross or dissolve binary divisions between animal/human, feminine monstrosity/masculine humanity, and between superstition/science. *The Reformed Vampire Support Group* explores the potential for what Stephanou identifies as "change, decay and transformation" in vampire contagion narratives (75). However, rather than employ this potential in the deconstructive sense suggested by Stephanou, in which the vampire can "dissolve identity," Jinks's rehabilitated vampire suggests the potential for a positively embodied femininity.

The Nineteenth Century: Carmilla *and* Dracula

Before I explore the children's novels in more detail, I want to unpack a little further how nineteenth-century vampire narratives forge a connection between femininity and illness with a view to better tracing how these connections develop in contemporary fiction. Laura, the protagonist of Le Fanu's female vampire novella, *Carmilla*, and Lucy Westenra, who dies from the attentions of the eponymous "Count" in Stoker's *Dracula*, exhibit symptoms that accord with the extreme limits of an idealized bourgeois femininity: passivity, weakness, and a consumptive beauty. *Carmilla* is a key text in establishing the tropes of the vampiric feminine because it focuses on two women, the vampire and her victim. Its unusually frank depiction of feminine vampiric desire also offers a complex insight into and response to late nineteenth-century discourses of femininity. Laura, a young woman living with her aging father in isolated Styria, Eastern Europe, narrates the novella. After a carriage accident near the grounds of their *schloss*, the family takes in a beautiful young aristocrat named Carmilla. Carmilla preys upon Laura, who becomes increasingly unwell. Before the vampire Carmilla kills Laura, however, the family discovers the true nature of their visitor. The male characters (including Laura's father and the family doctor) track her to a tomb in the ruins of her ancient family home and destroy her body, freeing Laura from the vampiric contagion that threatened to kill her.

The relationship between Carmilla and Laura, and the contagion that passes between them, produces links between femininity and vampiric "illness." Carmilla represents idealized feminine beauty, but the language used to describe her links this beauty to a pathologized weakness: "her ways were girlish; and there was always a langour about her, quite incompatible with a masculine system in a state of health" (Le Fanu 226). Femininity as illness spreads from Carmilla to Laura, whose confined existence makes her easy prey. Just as feminine beauty and domestic confinement are pathologized through the vampire narrative, so too is the idea of intimate female friendship, explicitly suggestive in the text of non-normative sexuality.

Laura is both attracted to and repulsed by Carmilla's behavior, which is portrayed as that of a suitor. Thus, vampiric illness is not only physical, but also psychological, implying sexual "inversion" (to use the term employed by nineteenth-century "sexologists") as well as "hysteria," as described by nineteenth-century medical texts. Writing in 1877, American physician Weir Mitchell asserts that a "hysterical girl is a vampire who sucks the blood of the healthy people about her … surely where there is one hysterical girl there will soon or late two sick women" (35). If vampire contagion is a "feminine" contagion of mind and body, this is in part because of the feminization of contagion in popular and medical discourse of the late-Victorian period, especially in writings about sexual disease and hysteria. This was a period of the pseudoscientific discourse of "degeneration," of the rise of the "New Woman," and an associated moral panic over sexually transmitted diseases, fired by the "Contagious Diseases Act" of 1864. The depiction of Carmilla and Laura's relationship responds to these anxieties. Helen Stoddart notes how the "tremulous" Laura "repeats the 'infectious' gestures" of Carmilla, speeding up her own victimization and contagion (19). Carmilla gains control of Laura's "infected" mind to access her body and precipitate her "hysterical degeneration" (19). Thus, in Le Fanu's tale, a language of infection pervades the depiction of vampiric femininity, with Carmilla as its degenerate center.

In *Carmilla* the vampiric feminine is deeply ambiguous, leaving space for contemporary interpretations and innovations. Certainly, many critics have read the text as Queer, offering resistance to patriarchal and heteronormative systems. For example, Wisker argues that the story leaves room for a positive interpretation of Laura and Carmilla's relationship and suggests that Carmilla's undecidable feminine/masculine coding problematizes received notions of women's passivity ("Female Vampirism" 154, 150). Ardel Haefele-Thomas notes that the text has become an iconic "Lesbian Vampire" story, but argues that Le Fanu "struggle[s] with a profound sense of ambivalence" (96). Despite provoking readers' sympathy with Carmilla, the text ultimately suggests the necessity of her destruction to expel the monstrous threat of miscegenation, incest and queer sexuality (Haefele-Thomas 107). Wisker likewise recognizes this late nineteenth century imperative to punish transgressive women and (re)assert normative notions of femininity: "Threats of impurity ... appear in imagery that demonizes women, portraying them as half-snake, half-human, product of a fear of contagious disease and a continued failure to suppress unlicensed lust" ("Female Vampirism" 153). Associated with the asp, her blood is a poison to the pure Laura, and Carmilla must be punished. The text's disgust for Carmilla (as sexual "invert" and sexually promiscuous "New Woman") operates through the language of disease and infection. Although Carmilla resists this pathologizing figuration (she wryly notes that "Doctors never did me any good"), ultimately, patriarchal and medical authorities triumph (Le Fanu 230). Indeed, in the second version of the text, the whole narrative is framed as a medical "case study" from the papers of a Doctor Hesselius. Thus, the vampiric feminine becomes a passive object for medical analysis within a patriarchal moral system.

Bram Stoker's *Dracula* attempts to write over the ambiguity in Le Fanu's depiction of the vampiric feminine. In this later novel, the "threat" of female intimacy is expelled by the substitution of a female vampire for the male Count and by the interruption of the intense friendship between female characters, Mina and Lucy, when the latter succumbs to the Count's disease. Stoker also heightens the importance of the doctor, with key roles in the destruction of the vampire given to Van Helsing and Dr. John Seward. Indeed, Van Helsing's medical authority dictates how the signs of vampirism exhibited by Lucy's body should be interpreted and treated. As in *Carmilla*, the pathologizing of the feminine body, and of the vampiric contagion as a "feminine" contagion, is emphasized through Lucy's illness, the symptoms of which resemble that of consumption. As Stephanou notes, in nineteenth-century medical and literary texts, consumptive bodies were associated with the feminine and the feminine was likewise fetishized as the consumptive body, with its pale skin, rosy cheeks and emaciated frame (86). A similar fetishization of Lucy's body emerges in *Dracula*. She is so weak that she is hardly able to turn her head, and passively accepts the ministrations of Van Helsing and Seward. Her skin is chalky; her gums are pale and drawn, and her "stertorous" breathing and soft whispers figure silence and passivity (Stoker 194). Seward comments that Lucy looks at her most beautiful in death, positioning her as a passive fetish object, still, silent, and looked upon.

Of course, becoming a vampire does not allow Lucy to escape a patriarchal representational system that confines, pathologizes and punishes women. Even when she returns as a voracious vamp, with seeming sexual agency, her sexuality functions in the service of a male vampire; she hunts so she can spread the Count's contagion. Marking her out as a diseased body—newspaper reports of a "Bloofer Lady" responsible for sick and missing children hasten the "crew of light" to destroy Lucy in an act of public health as well as moral necessity. Stoker's depiction of Lucy is thus patriarchal and punitive, particularly in the violent scene where she is staked and beheaded by her former lovers. Lucy dies in service of a moral imperative; she dies so Mina can be saved from the Count and recuperated into patriarchal and heteronormative structures.

The depiction of Lucy Westenra is informed by social and medical contexts of the late nineteenth century. Men's attitude to women in the novel "epitomizes shifting cultural anxieties at the moment when a long-standing ideological conception of proper femininity comes under ... attack" (Prescott and Giorgio 487). "Proper femininity" in this context denotes a construction of gender placed under increased social and medical scrutiny at the end of the century. Pseudo-scientific ideas about inherited characteristics and criminality, popularized by Lombroso's *Criminal Man* (1876), and the bleak diagnosis of fin-de-siècle culture offered by Max Nordau in *Degeneration* (1892), fed reactions against attempts by women to gain increased social, political and sexual freedom. The "symptoms" of Lucy's vampiric femininity echo those attributed to the degenerate "New Woman" as depicted in the popular press. Her increased sexual appetite, for example, suggests the disease of "erotomania." When Lucy asks her fiancé for a kiss in the moments before her death, Van Helsing hastily steps between them "like a lion at bay," to prevent her contaminating Arthur (Stoker 195). After death, Lucy figures as a dangerous excess beyond normative femininity and Kathleen Spencer notes that her impure appetites make her the scapegoat of the novel (209). Her death cleanses the male community from the pollution of the vampiric disease and it (re)asserts the bounds of normative femininity. Yet, at the same time, Lucy also reveals how idealized femininity—fetishized as passivity and weakness—is itself already pathologized by patriarchal systems of representation.

The vampiric feminine of nineteenth-century Gothic is composed of ambiguities and anxieties about "normative" femininity, which form the basis for the depiction of vampire females in subsequent literature. There is not time here to trace a history of vampire fiction, but I do want briefly to mention the period from the 1970s to the 1990s, when vampire narratives gained popularity largely through the innovation of women writers. As Gina Wisker asserts, this period of popularity saw a number of "feminist revisions of the [vampire] myth" from writers such as Angela Carter, Anne Rice and Poppy Z. Brite ("Vampires and School Girls" n.p.). Following this, children's writers such as Caroline B. Cooney and R. L. Stine began to adapt the vampire narrative for children's horror fiction. Cooney and Stine wrote for Scholastic's horror labels, *Point Horror* and *Goosebumps*, which dominated the popular fiction market in the UK and the U.S. in the 1980s and 90s. Swindells' *Room 13* (1989) emerges as part of the success of this mass-market horror fiction. Swindells also anticipates the innovations of twenty-first century children's Gothic, drawing on Gothic's literary heritage by borrowing aspects of *Dracula*. As I have noted elsewhere, twenty-first century children's Gothic is explicitly intertextual, using the strategies of metafiction, pastiche and parody (Germaine Buckley 2). Set in Whitby, with nods to the town's "Dracula" tourist trade, *Room 13* evokes Gothic literature and the figures of nineteenth-century vampire tales. Likewise, Celia Rees' *Blood Sinister* (1996) rewrites the London portions of *Dracula*, as well as borrowing from later film adaptations. Jinks' *Reformed Vampire Support Group* (2009) strays furthest from nineteenth century Gothic literature, completely recontextualizing, and so transforming, vampire tropes in its exploration of a new form of vampiric femininity.

1980s–1990s: Room 13 *and* Blood Sinister

Room 13 is both school story and vampire story and thus its patterning differs to the nineteenth-century vampire Gothic discussed above. Swindells merges the tropes established by Sheridan Le Fanu and Stoker with the early twentieth-century genres of "school story" and "mystery." The book follows a group of schoolchildren (aged around 12) on a residential trip to Whitby. Fliss, the main character, senses that something is not quite right about the boarding house where they are staying. When another girl in the group, Ellie-May, falls ill, Fliss investigates. She discovers a room at the top of the house that only appears after midnight—the eponymous "room 13"—home to an ancient vampire who has Ellie-May under his thrall. With the help of three classmates, Fliss destroys the vampire before Ellie-May succumbs to her wasting illness. Alongside the school story and mystery elements, which position Fliss as an active heroine, the book borrows aspects of nineteenth century pathologized vampiric femininity in its depiction of Ellie-May, whose plight echoes that of Lucy in the Whitby portions of *Dracula*. Thus, Swindells establishes two orders of femininity, active and passive; healthy and vampiric.

Ellie-May succumbs to the vampire's bite and influence, which manifests itself as a listless sickness, a mysterious contagion that the teachers cannot diagnose. However, the sexual elements implicit in *Dracula* are effaced. Ellie-May does not exhibit signs of sexual desire as Lucy does when she nears death. Instead, she becomes weaker, doing nothing except looking "pasty" and "awful" with "dark smudges, like bruises, under her eyes" (50, 58). Like Lucy, Ellie-May has no appetite and so very little agency in the text. As Tamara Heller and Patricia Moran argue, in women's writing and feminist thought, appetite is agency, or voice, and eating represents power (2). Stephanou also suggests that "control over the feminine is achieved by disciplining female hunger" in traditional vampire narratives (76). While Ellie-May displays none of Lucy's thirst for blood or other "unnatural" appetites, her emaciated body suffers the same patriarchal punishment. She is utterly passive and voiceless, walking in her sleep unwittingly to the "Room of Doom" and its "Bed of Dread." When Fliss interrogates Ellie-May the girls speaks in a barely audible whisper: "Tablets make me sleepy. Give me dreams … horrible dreams" (89). Where Lucy's passivity briefly metamorphoses into a vampy sexuality, Ellie-May fades. No longer acting as the scapegoat in a sexual morality tale, Ellie-May simply does nothing.

There are elements of the cautionary tale here, though, as the novel echoes late twentieth social anxieties surrounding the figure of the pedophile. In her study of the "bogeyman," Marina Warner notes that the cannibalistic figure of the "child abuser and the paedophile" emerges in late twentieth-century bogeyman tales (38, 385–386). Certainly, Swindells's vampire draws on this archetype; young girls are his food of choice. A local tells Fliss the story of "Little Meg," a former inhabitant of the house and victim of the vampire, before lamenting that "now he's got bairns—a fresh lot practically every week" (130). Thus, although the child characters' sexuality is largely absent, there is a backgrounded sexual threat that emphasizes Ellie-May's weakness and silence, since it positions her as the passive victim of child sexual abuse.

While Ellie-May remains paralyzed by pathologized weakness and voiceless listlessness, Fliss takes up the role of plucky heroine.

As in *Dracula*, *Room 13* opposes two women: a "bad" girl and a "good" girl, though their figurative resonances differ greatly. Stoker's good girl and bad girl represent different ideals of femininity: Lucy's dangerous sexuality is destroyed while Mina's wifely devotion is recuperated into the domestic sphere. In Swindells, Ellie-May is a "bad" girl in that she is selfish and something of a bully, while Fliss is thoughtful and caring. Their opposition is not necessarily moral, though. Rather it is a more a matter of agency and passivity demanded by the generic conventions Swindells mixes. Agency is afforded to Fliss because she operates in the role of heroine typical of a "mystery" or girls' adventure story, rather than as a figure of the vampiric feminine. The character of Fliss sits within a long tradition, which originates in late nineteenth-century girls' fiction and includes annuals and comics, of plucky heroines exerting power (within the limits of the story). Though often conservatively moralistic, these girls' tales construct heroines to equal their male counterparts in solving mysteries, bringing criminals to justice and returning order. Wisker calls them "subversive schoolgirls" because their "energetic activities ... question and trouble the conventional representations of women's lives in the movies and magazines of the period" ("Vampires and School Girls" n.p.).

Fliss also gains agency because she remains uncontaminated by the vampiric contagion. She is healthy and so is able to take charge, outwitting even the adults who have failed to protect Ellie-May: "'Grown-ups are so stupid,' she muttered. 'They never believe anything you tell them. If Ellie-May goes in that cupboard again tonight it may be too late to call her parents'" (95). Fliss takes the lead, directing a group of three other children (including two boys) to overcome their fears and destroy the vampire lurking in the attic of the boarding house. She appears to have been "chosen" for this purpose, and so anticipates the figure of the vampire slayer popularized by *Buffy the Vampire Slayer* in the late 1990s. Fliss represents a different femininity from the vampiric listlessness embodied by Ellie-May. She is plucky, active, and mobile. In this sense the vampiric feminine remains threateningly "Other" in this text, and is expelled at the end of the novel by the defeat of its source. When the children leave the boarding house having staked the vampire, Fliss notes that the morning is "just perfect.... An enormous weight had been lifted from them and they walked on air" (154). This cleansing of the boarding house and subsequent return of Ellie-May to health echoes the trajectory of *Dracula*, albeit having replaced the male "crew of light" with a plucky schoolgirl heroine.

Celia Rees's *Blood Sinister* (1996) offers a more complex response to the vampiric feminine, merging the agency of the plucky heroine and the weakness of the victim into one character. This heroine is Ellen Forrest. She is confined to her grandmother's house next door to Highgate Cemetery in London, suffering from a mystery disease of the blood. Ellen finds the teenage diaries of her namesake and great-great-grandmother, a famous doctor. Reading the diaries takes Ellen into a late nineteenth-century vampire Gothic story, in which the corrupt Count Szekelys preys upon the young Ellen Laidlaw. In the present-day narrative, Ellen's condition worsens and she comes under the care of a sinister medical specialist, Dr. Stacey, who is keen to confine Ellen to his private medical institution. As Ellen learns more about her grandmother's fight with the vampire, she realizes Dr. Stacey is Count Szekelys. Working with a male friend and a young nurse, Ellen outwits the doctor and manages to lay the vampire to rest once and for all, curing her disease in the process.

Blood Sinister echoes nineteenth-century vampire Gothic in its description of Ellen's "mystery sickness" (Rees 7). Like Lucy and Laura, she has neither physical strength, nor appetite, sleeping for hours, too weak to walk far, the "condition" having sapped all her energy (43). However, since it is focalized through Ellen, the narrative voice offers her agency denied to Lucy Westenra. Ellen rails against being an "invalid" and hides her symptoms so her grandmother will allow her out of the house. There is no "crew of light" attending to Ellen; she must save herself. She is pitted directly against the vampire in a contest of wills and ingenuity. Though Ellen struggles to overcome the lethargy and passivity imposed upon her body by the blood contagion, she draws strength from her ancestor. Thus, the patterning of *Blood Sinister* connects rather than opposes two women, positioning them both as victim-cum-heroine in their joint struggle against the vampire.

As Stephanou points out, blood is "a metaphor for descent" in *Dracula* and classic vampire tales (2). Likewise, *Blood Sinister* is concerned with inherited blood, both that which is contaminated with vampiric disease and that which is pure. Ellen is linked by blood, which forges a supernatural connection, to her proto-feminist ancestor, a "pioneering woman doctor" (Rees 11). As well as providing Ellen with knowledge and courage, this female line of descent is also the source of her blood disease. This complex and ambivalent figuration of bloodlines adapts the notion of maternal blood lineage found in *Carmilla*, where Laura's (maternal) kinship with Carmilla makes her particularly vulnerable. The female vampire's corrupted blood is associated with her degenerate foremothers, but also establishes kinship and sympathy between the girls. Ellen is linked to her great-great-grandmother through blood, by an uncanny resemblance, and through a supernatural connection that allows her to "become" the other Ellen (82). Ellen Laidlaw's diary offers messages for her descendant. In one passage, she asserts that "I must learn to trust my own emotions, not their judgment" (16). This textual connection between the girls thus validates feminine emotion, rather than working to suppress it as is the case in *Carmilla* and *Dracula*, where pathologized women (hysterical and sick from vampiric contagion) must capitulate to the knowledge and strength of male characters.

Blood Sinister also muddies the representation of medical authority found in *Carmilla* and *Dracula* and so begins to undermine the pathologization of vampiric femininity. Even in these earlier texts, medical science gives way to superstition in the face of the vampire, but the "cleansing" role of the doctor is paramount in expunging the contagion and so "curing" the imperiled feminine body. As Stephanou argues, in vampire narratives "empirical language is confounded by the presence of the vampire, the strange stirrings of the blood, and the occulted mysteries of the bite" (2). In *Blood Sinister*, doctors are baffled by Ellen's disease and it is only her own—supernatural—investigation that reveals the truth. More than this, though, doctors and medical institutions become sources and sites of danger. In the nineteenth-century timeline, Ellen's father's obsession with curing Count Szekelys' blood disorder recalls the mania of Mary Shelley's Victor Frankenstein. As the "rational" male scientist comes under the thrall of the vampire, his weakness and obsession put his daughter in harm's way. The medical institution over which he presides echoes Dr. Seward's asylum near Carfax Abbey in *Dracula*, resembling more a "crypt than a place to nurse the sick," "more like a prison than a hospital" (Rees 14, 31). Typifying Gothic claustrophobia, the medical institution and Ellen's father's experiments within its tomb-like walls, do little to aid the girl in her struggle against the Count. Indeed, it is only years later, when Ellen publishes her father's papers as part of her own research, that his contribution to medical science (the discovery of blood types) is recognized.

In the present-day narrative, Dr. Stacey's private institution, Cedar Lodge, is likewise compared to a tomb and prison. He refers to its previous function as an asylum, suggesting further contiguity with Carfax Asylum in *Dracula*. However, the overseer in this case is not a vampire hunter, but the vampire himself. Ellen knows that being trapped within the walls of the building and the medical bureaucracy of the institution will rob her of her voice and agency once and for all. She learns that many patients referred there never recover. In this modulation of a Female Gothic narrative of entrapment, Cedar Lodge offers the same Gothic claustrophobia of the nineteenth-century asylum, while the modern-seeming imagery of blood packs and intravenous drips take on the same sinister association as the glass bottles and rubber tubing of Ellen's great-great-great-grandfather's illegal transfusion experiments in his basement laboratory. Throughout the novel, medical apparatus represents the pathologization discourse by which passivity is imposed upon the female body and so must be refused. Thus, medical institutions and doctors become ambivalent in *Blood Sinister*, a strategy that works to question the authority given to characters such as Seward and Van Helsing in *Dracula* and their control over the pathologized feminine body.

At the same time, the book presents advances in medical science as necessary to enlightenment and progress, suggesting a feminist message about women and girls' contribution to this traditionally male-dominated realm. Ellen's great-great-grandmother is famous for the discovery of the "Rhesus Factor" in blood and credited with saving the lives of many pregnant women and babies. Ellen's grandmother recalls that she was "always frightfully busy.... What with the practice, hospital work and her research—she worked almost up to the day she died. Exceptional woman" (37). This recollection emphasizes the busy activity, agency and strength of the elder Ellen, providing a stark contrast to the listlessness, weakness and passivity imposed upon the younger Ellen because of her disease. In this sense, the medical discourse of *Blood Sinister* echoes aspects of the pathologizing discourse of nineteenth-century vampire Gothic; it insists upon a healthy, uncontaminated female body. Like *Room 13*, the ending of Blood Sinister requires the destruction of the vampire and cleansing of its contagion. Again, this is complex since Ellen's contaminated blood also seems to be what connects her to the past, and allows her access to the knowledge that saves her life. Nonetheless, just as Mina Harker's blood connection to the Count must be severed in *Dracula*, so must Ellen's blood be cleansed so she can become empowered.

As in *Room 13*, the predatory vampire and his contagious blood sickness is also linked to the threat of pedophilia. In the nineteenth-century narrative, Ellen notes the disappearance of children, while she herself is courted by the "predatory" Count as he grooms her for vampiric transformation and kidnaps her. In the present-day timeline, Stacey's treatment of Ellen constitutes the exploitation of a vulnerable child in his care. In one scene, the narrator describes the "creature" on Ellen's bed, its wings spread over "tumbled bedclothes," feeding while Ellen sleeps (81). Here, the vampire represents a predatory contagion that must be expunged so Ellen can inhabit an active, healthy feminine body. The closing pages of the book suggest the same notion of cleansing and healing as *Room 13*: "Dr. Frank Stacey, formerly the Count Szekelys, was dead. Whatever power he had over the living died with him. The wound on Jenny's neck disappeared. ... The greatest proof was Ellen herself. Her health was completely restored" (196). Unlike in *Dracula*, where transgressive females are destroyed and imperiled women returned to domesticity, this cleansing of vampiric contagion allows for a feminist-inflected figuration of femininity. Ellen is determined to follow her great-great-grandmother's example: "It would not be easy, there was a very long way to go, but in the end she would be a doctor. It was in her blood" (199). There is no room for the vampiric feminine here, only normative, healthy and active female bodies. Though some aspects of the pathologized figuration of femininity found in nineteenth-century vampire Gothic are challenged, *Blood Sinister*'s recourse to a foreign "other" and predatory sexual threat as the source of blood contagion does nothing to rewrite the xenophobia of the original text. Indeed, *Blood Sinister* follows the same trajectory of *Dracula* in its need to expel a "foreign" contagion to maintain the "health" of the native population (Stephanou 15). *Blood Sinister* offers a rich, if not always satisfactory, response to the figuration of vampiric femininity found in nineteenth century vampire Gothic.

A key text linking Swindells and Rees with twenty-first-century children's Gothic is the popular television series, *Buffy the Vampire Slayer* (1997– 2003). Although not strictly a children's television show, it was watched by pre-adolescents as well as adults and innovated the tropes of the vampiric feminine through its figure of the eponymous teenage heroine. Buffy is not a vampire, but, as Wisker argues, she is on the "edge" and her supernatural character of "slayer" offers "a new take on women in vampire fictions. The representation of the feisty virginal schoolgirl interweaves with the image of the female recalled from vampire and other horror tales" ("Vampires and School Girls" n.p.). *Buffy* draws on contemporary feminist vampire figures who break taboos and refuse to capitulate to traditional conceptions of femininity. As such, *Buffy* operates as a waypoint between Swindells and Rees' fiction and Jinks's 2009 novel. In *Buffy*, vampirism is still a horrific "disease," but the series incorporates feminist revisions of the vampire myth in the way it shows that women's power is both possible and positive.

Drawing on Kristeva's *Strangers to Ourselves* (1988), Wisker suggests that feminist vampires of the 80s and 90s offer the potential for celebrating otherness. She asserts that the feminist vampire offers "a popular, deviant alternative sense of youthful energy and of teenage rebellion" ("Vampires and School Girls" n.p.). This critical and cultural turn towards the vampire as embodying attractive Otherness rather than functioning as a bogeyman has its effect on children's fiction. In vampire narratives written about and marketed to young women, the ideas of contagion and corruption begin to metamorphose. Wisker's use of the word "energetic" in her analysis of *Buffy* suggests the nature of this metamorphosis. In the twenty-first century vampiric femininity casts off its nineteenth-century languidity and becomes physically active and kinetic.

Twenty-First Century Vampire Femininity: The Reformed Vampire Support Group

The Reformed Vampire Support Group offers a markedly different figuration of vampiric femininity to the 1980s and 90s. The postmillennial period in children's and young adult fiction is characterized by innovation and proliferation of Gothic forms, including heightened intertextuality and self-reflexivity (Germaine Buckley 2). Partaking in the strategies of parody and pastiche characteristic of twenty-first-century children's Gothic, *The Reformed Vampire Support Group* transposes the vampire narrative into the world of the everyday. The heroine is a 51-year-old vampire trapped in a teenager's body, struggling to cope with the daily "medical emergencies" associated with her "condition" (Jinks 52). Jinks uses parody and humor to strip elements of fetish from vampiric femininity. At the same time, she draws on the idea of medical management to foreground the pathologization of the feminine, and its continuing association with weakness and passivity. Through Nina's commentary, Jinks metamorphoses the pathologizing language of nineteenth-century vampire Gothic into the modern language of disability. Vampiric illness is a manageable "condition" rather than a metaphysical contagion.

At first, the prognosis seems bleak. Nina makes ends meet as a vampire by writing salacious supernatural fiction. Unlike the heroine of her novels, Zadia Bloodstone, Nina feels powerless. She attends weekly "reformed vampire" support group meetings at a local church, sustains her life by drinking the blood of guinea pigs, and struggles with lethargy, nausea and a host of other health problems. However, when one of the support group, Casamir, is murdered by a self-styled vampire hunter, Nina is instrumental in persuading the other vampires to act. Their investigations lead them to uncover a secret werewolf smuggling ring and brings them into contact with some dangerous gangsters. *The Reformed Vampire Support Group* refuses an ending in which the vampiric contagion must be cured for the female character to find agency and power. Instead, the novel stages Nina's "rehabilitation" and her vampiric condition comes to be framed as a potentially affirmatory embodiment of femininity.

At first, the representation of Nina's vampirism as a disability seems to echo the connection between femininity and weakness found in *Carmilla* and *Dracula*. However, alongside the expected language of languidity and illness, Jinks offers alternative figurations of femininity, allowing Nina to experiment and so escape from the confines of pathologizing discourse. The novel opens with excerpts from Nina's latest *Bloodstone* book, which parodies supernatural fiction such as Laurell K. Hamilton's *Anita Blake* series (1993—present) and *Buffy the Vampire Slayer*. Though explicitly parodic, the character of Zadia merges nineteenth-century vampiric femininity (pale skin, draped in a black cloak) with the kinetic energy and ingenuity of Buffy Summers. Since her vital organs regenerate "at lightning speed," Zadia thinks nothing of sustaining bullet wounds while fighting kidnappers (Jinks 1). In contrast, Nina is "an entirely different species of girl" (Jinks 3). The fetishized aspects of vampiric femininity quickly dissipate in Nina's wry account of her unglamorous life, which includes "uncontrollable bouts of vomiting" and hair "matted with blood and saliva" during the messy process of feeding from a guinea pig (3, 73). Whereas in nineteenth-century vampire narratives, "consuming appetites for food and sex define the identity of the female vampire" (Stephanou 14), Jinks infuses the consumption of blood with pathos and parody, demystifying the consumption process and so forging a route to recuperating Nina's condition as acceptable bodily practice. Like Ellen in *Blood Sinister*, Nina expresses frustration with her condition, with not being able to "do the simplest thing without risking a full-blown haemorrhage. *God* I'm sick of it" (14). This frustration, along with the demand to act precipitated by the mystery plot, propels Nina into the search for an alternative figuration of vampiric and feminine identity.

Like Ellen, Nina comes into conflict with a male doctor, who is also a vampire. Dr. Sanford is self-appointed "lord and master" of the support group (Jinks 5). A physician in his human life, Sanford invents the enzyme supplements that Nina ingests daily. He also dictates acceptable behavior to the group as part of the medical management of their condition. This includes not taking public transport, never going out in public without a "sponsor" (to avoid being tempted to drink human blood) and staying as close to home as possible. Nina notes that none of them have "travelled more than a handful of kilometres in the past thirty years" (69) and bemoans the confinement imposed by Sanford's medical management. She complains that "being a vampire is ... like being stuck indoors with the flu watching daytime television, for ever and ever" (5). Initially, Sanford has authority and Nina capitulates to his medical readings of her body, since he has a "keen eye for physical changes" to her condition (29). She also accepts the comparison Sanford's regime suggests between vampirism and being a recovering alcoholic or "junkie," agreeing that not all vampires "(let's face it) can be trusted" (52). As the novel progresses, though, Nina increasingly challenges Sanford and the limitations he imposes upon her. She wants the space to self-manage and explore the limits (and capabilities) of her condition. Her rebellion enacts a process of "deterritorialisation" akin to that described in the "nomadic" philosophy of Gilles Deleuze and Félix Guattari. Nina seeks escape from a confined position within in a striated structure via a vector of motion and transformation (Deleuze and Guattari 451). Jinks's blending of vampire Gothic with mystery and action allows the space for this deterritorialization.

During the novel, Nina investigates Casamir's murder, plans a dangerous road trip to the outback and confronts a violent gang of kidnappers. These events interrupt Nina's regulated existence and energize her. After rearranging her mother's basement as a "safe house" for the support group, for example, Nina notes that "though I could hardly stand up.... I felt that I'd exhibited a degree of energy and enthusiasm that you don't often see in a vampire" (60).

The hermeneutic mystery plot acts as a force of propulsion, forcing Nina to become active and mobile. In this way, she echoes the characters of Fliss and Ellen, though the agency afforded the Gothic heroine within the mystery plot can also can be traced to Ann Radcliffe's eighteenth-century novels. These early Gothic heroines experienced mobility despite their social and physical incarceration. They "scurr[ied] up to the top of pasteboard Alps, sp[ied] out exotic vistas, penetrate[d] bandit-infested forests … [they] scuttle[d] miles along corridors, descend[ed] into dungeons, and explore[d] secret chambers" (Moers 126). The road trip, in particular, offers the most overt opportunity for deterritorialization, forging Nina into an example of what Deleuze and Guattari designate the "war machine of metamorphosis" (420). Although the demands of her vampiric condition have not changed (she cannot endure daylight; she needs to feed from animal blood; she is prone to fits of weakness and nausea), Nina uses her body to carve a "creative line of flight" from her restrictive everyday existence (Deleuze and Guattari 492). The road trip, during which Nina rescues a young male werewolf, is representative of deterritorialization happening at the level of embodied identity and Sanford's disapproval only serves to emphasize its importance. Nina is keen to avoid the psychological degeneration she has come to recognize in the vampires around her. The symptoms of this "degeneration" differ greatly to those imagined in nineteenth-century vampire tales. Nina is not afraid of contracting hysteria or erotomania, but of "retreating" from an engagement with the world: "Your interests become hopelessly circumscribed; your energy trickles away" (71). The road trip demonstrates the affordances of nomadic identity, deterritorializes Nina from her physical and psychological confinement and demonstrates a way to live with her bodily condition beyond the pathologizing confines of medical management.

The action-packed denouement of *The Reformed Vampire Support Group* shows Nina embracing the affordances of the vampiric condition and stages her metamorphosis into a positive embodiment of vampiric femininity. In a physical encounter with the kidnappers, Nina uses her vampiric abilities (including her night vision) to gain the advantage over her enemies. However, instead of besting them in combat as Zadia Bloodstone might, Nina uses empathy to solve conflict, talking a recently infected vampire into accepting his new state. Nina's success in resolving the conflict between the vampires, the werewolf and the kidnappers is a result of her stated choice to become "active and empathetic and dependable and involved" (Jinks 76). She offers a far more affirmative account of her vampiric identity than earlier in the novel:

> "Being a vampire doesn't mean that you're *finished*. I used to think so myself, but I don't anymore." Though I was talking simply to keep him occupied…. I was also speaking straight from the heart. "You can still live like a human being, even if you're

a vampire," I continued. "Even if it is a lot harder to be energetic and excited, and involved, it can still be done. I've *seen* it done" [337].

Nina's metamorphosis into a nomadic subject like that described by Deleuze and Guattari, Rosi Braidotti and others, involves a "mutation" and a merging of the vampiric with the human, and of the "feminine" with the "masculine." In Deleuze and Guattari's account, a "mutation" in code, in language, or in biological life, prompts variations and transfers within and between cells, species and languages, offering the chance to challenge hegemonic structures (261). Similarly, Nina's mutation of vampiric femininity challenges normative conceptions of the feminine and imagines a form of embodied subjectivity that echoes Braidotti's feminist-inflected account of nomadism (15).

Braidotti's nomadic subject embraces the conditions of its material body, and recognizes identity as "becoming" rather than "being." Nina's vampiric femininity is a "'becoming' body, a dynamic and changing entity" (Braidotti 5). Nina represents subjectivity undergoing metamorphosis; she is "becoming" without a fixed destination. The "becoming" state of nomadism is exemplified by Nina's teenage body, which will remain in the transitional state of adolescence. Sanford scoffs at Nina for being "stuck in a teenage time warp," but her body-in-process represents the opportunities of nomadism (Jinks 7). This not-yet mature body is a positive figuration of twenty-first-century vampiric femininity, embracing openness, transformation, and empathy. In this way, Jinks's vampiric feminine continues the process identified by Stephanou in other, recent feminist vampire narratives, which offer "representations of embodied subjects who resist patriarchal discourses and reconfigure the positivity of difference" (77).

Conclusion

This essay has traced the ways vampiric femininity has figured in children's literature. Late twentieth-century children's Gothic inherits the tropes of nineteenth century vampire Gothic, with its punitive and pathologizing construction of femininity. However, these children's novels explicitly rewrite elements of their source texts, paving the way for a more determined overturning of a pathologized femininity (as weakness, voicelessness, confinement) in twenty-first-century children's Gothic. This development is both a metamorphosis of blood and of genre. In her study of parody, Linda Hutcheon asserts that parody produces a "transformational synthesis" between old and new texts (38). The merging of vampire Gothic with other genres popular in children's literature as well as a parodic reworking of traditional vampire tropes, produces a transformational synthesis apparent in the work of Swindells and Rees, and more fully realized in *The Reformed Vampire Support*

Group. In this latter novel, Nina's ironic self-awareness and reflective narration along with the parodic recontextualization of traditional vampire tropes, creates a new figuration of vampiric femininity. Jinks places her female protagonist on a trajectory towards deterritorialization, like that proposed in the nomadic philosophy of Deleuze and Guattari, imagining a vampiric "condition" that affords agency, power and mobility for feminine bodies.

WORKS CITED

Braidotti, Rosi. *Nomadic Subjects: Embodiment and Sexual Difference in Contemporary Feminist Theory*. Second edition. New York: Columbia University Press, 2011.
Craft, Christopher. "'Kiss Me with Those Red Lips': Gender and Inversion in Bram Stoker's *Dracula*." *Representations* 8.1 (1984): 107–133.
Deleuze, Gilles, and Félix Guattari. *A Thousand Plateaus*. London: Bloomsbury, 2013 [1987].
Fink, Marty. "AIDS Vampires: Reimagining Illness in Octavia Butler's *Fledgling*." *Science Fiction Studies* 37.3 (2010): 416–432.
Germaine Buckley, Chloe. *Twenty-First-Century Children's Gothic: From the Wanderer to Nomadic Subject*. Edinburgh: Edinburgh University Press, 2017.
Haefele-Thomas, Ardel. *Queer Others in Victorian Gothic: Transgressing Monstrosity*. Cardiff: University of Wales Press, 2012.
Heller, Tamara, and Patricia Moran. "Introduction." Ed. Tamar Heller and Patricia Moran. *Scenes of the Apple: Food and the Female Body in Nineteenth- and Twentieth-Century Women's Writing*. Albany: State University of New York Press, 2003.
Hutcheon, Linda. *A Theory of Parody: The Teachings of Twentieth-Century Art Forms*. London: Methuen Publishing, 1985.
Jinks, Catherine. *The Reformed Vampire Support Group*. London: Quercus, 2009.
Le Fanu, Joseph Sheridan. *In a Glass Darkly*. Ware, England: Wordsworth Editions, 1995.
Mitchell, Weir. *Fat and Blood: And How to Make Them*. Philadelphia: J.B. Lippincott, 1877.
Moers, Ellen. *Literary Women: The Great Writers* (1978). Oxford: Oxford University Press, 1985.
Prescott, Charles E., and Grace A. Giorgio. "Vampiric Affinities: Mina Harker and the Paradox of Femininity in Bram Stoker's *Dracula*." *Victorian Literature and Culture* 33.2 (2005): 487–515.
Rees, Celia. *Blood Sinister*. New York: Scholastic, 1996.
Spencer, Kathleen. "Purity and Danger: *Dracula*, the Urban Gothic and the Late Victorian Degeneracy Crisis." *ELH* 59 (1992): 197–225.
Stephanou, Aspasia. *Reading Vampire Gothic Through Blood: Bloodlines*. London: Palgrave Macmillan, 2014.
Stoddart, Helen. "'The Precautions of Nervous People Are Infectious': Sheridan Le Fanu's Symptomatic Gothic." *Modern Language Review* 86.1 (1991): 19–34.
Stoker, Bram. *Dracula*. London: Penguin, 1994.
Swindells, Robert. *Room 13 and Inside the Worm*. New York: Random House, 2000.
Warner, Marina. *No Go the Bogeyman*. New York: Vintage, 2000.
Wisker, Gina. "Female Vampirism." *Women and the Gothic: An Edinburgh Companion*. Ed. Avril Horner and Sue Zlosnik. Edinburgh: Edinburgh University Press, 2016. 150–165.
_____. "Vampires and School Girls: High School Jinks on the Hellmouth." *Slayage* 1.2 (2001): n.p.

Problematic Parenting
Tweens and Vampire Fiction
Leslie J. Ormandy

Introduction

Judging by the tremendous popularity of books such as Darren Shan's *Cirque du Freak* series (2000–2009), Siena Mercer's series, *My Sister the Vampire* (2007–2016), Anne Hodgson's popular series, *My Baby-Sitter's a Vampire/or a Monster/or Has Fangs...* (1994–2012), Justin Stomper's series, *The Vampirates* (2007–2013), among myriad others on the bookstore shelf, preadolescents (tweens) are attracted to vampires. This attraction to horror stories featuring vampires, and an entire pantheon of other supernatural monsters, can cause parents discomfort. After all, the horror genre, by its very nature, features children much like their own, fighting creatures that have much more personal power than their own children possess. Professor of philosophy Stephen Asma suggests that "The monster is a beneficial foe, helping [children] to virtually represent the obstacles that real life will surely send [their] way" ("Monsters and the Moral Imagination" n.p.). Given the world in which children now live, a world of terrorists and school shootings and the constant threat of war, children are far too familiar with human monsters.

Parents concerned about their children's horrible reading choices might take some comfort in knowing that their children are reading material that helps them learn to deal with the human monsters in a non-threatening environment. Asma further states that monsters stories perform a specific psychological function for the readers; "After Freud, monster stories were considered cathartic journeys into our unconscious, everybody contains a Mr. Hyde, and these stories give us a chance to 'walk on the wild side.' But in the denouement of most stories, the monster is killed and the psyche restored to civilized order" ("Monsters and the Moral Imagination" n.p.). Joni

Richards Bodart furthers the discussion regarding the horror genre by adding that "Horror stories allow [readers] to [experience] emotions that usually [they] are required to control.... [The reader] can by proxy indulge in violent acts, give in to [their] fears, and exercise power over others that [they] can't do in the reality" (xxvi). Thus, horror books are, through offering a wide range of material to tweens in which they face a wide variety of possible experiences, allowing them to try out a broad range of emotions and behaviors, both acceptable and unacceptable, from the comfort of their own couches—a low cost life-training: price determined by the cost of the book.

This essay focuses upon the vampire, a creature which renowned scholar, Montague Summers, stated was, "a pariah even among demons" (xxi), exploring the roles assigned to parents (and other authoritative adults) in tween literature and speculating how supportive, or non-supportive, adult figures influence tween readers at the pivotal moments in which they distance themselves from previous dependent relationships to the parents and confront the ultimate "Others"—the vampires. This study suggests that observing and interacting with a wide variety of parents and parental stand-ins, such as teachers or authoritative adults who are both like, and unlike their own, allows the tween a distanced and less emotionally traumatic experience concerning growing up and eventually leaving home. Since tweens comprise the broad age group from 6 to 12, and their book choice is dependent upon their reading level, I have chosen to include a wide age-sampling of tween vampire books in this study: chapter books (ages 5–9ish), early readers (ages 6–9ish), and middle readers (ages 9–12ish).

By their very nature, tweens share a kinship with the vampire, for the tween, like the vampire, is transitioning into an age group in which different—more self-directed—patterns of behavior are expected of them; a need reflected in the vampire stories they read featuring children like themselves. The same agency shift is seen in tween books that focus on the problems of vampire children within vampire families. For all tweens in these books, both human tween and vampire tween, parents and the home-life play an increasingly smaller role as friends and school play an increasingly important role in their lives. While this decrease in parental power is a necessity since the children are being prepared for eventual entry into the adult world, the tween often feel confused by constantly fluctuating messages. Francis Bauer observed that "There [is a] tendency [by parents and society] to propel the child toward maturity and independence ... before he [or she] is ready for it.... Then adult ambivalence becomes apparent when [adults] reverse the process [as the child approaches] adolescence" (148). One need only utter the words, "Helicopter parent," to make it clear that adults have issues with the increasing independence of their children as they both encourage and discourage it at the same time. Is it any wonder that the tween years, ranging from six to twelve years old, are confusing since the parents appear unable to allow the growing children agency? This ambivalence toward the child's independence can be observed by tweens in the patterns of relationships shown between the adult characters and the tween characters in the books they read.

One of the functions of texts is to assist the reader to construct new ideas. This function is especially true in tween narratives where books are utilized to inform tweens what their roles will be in the social world they are maturing into. Mark Johnson and George Lakoff state that, "The concepts that govern our thoughts are not just matters of the intellect. They also govern our everyday functioning, down to the most mundane details. Our concepts structure what we perceive, how we get around in the world, and how we relate to other people" (qtd. in Asma *On Monsters* 13–14). There is safety in making this interpretation, and in attaining information, via books. At the least, stories in which tweens confront vampires are recognizably fictional so real-life tweens need not fear the supernatural "Other"—although according to recent data, many of the younger tweens might have a problem understanding that fictional creatures such as fairies or monsters, are unreal (Marterelli, Gurtner, and Mast 2014). Through their books, tween's are able to have a distance from the characters and actions read in the story. Because the characters and plots are happening at a distance, they can safely observe the relationships between characters, and mull over both the positive and negative results of actions, which might be expected if they are caught slipping from their room to meet friends and wander the local haunted house after curfew. A book provides an ideal venue for a more complex form of rote memorization as well since the material is engaged with several times: through discussion of the story, thought about the story, or rereading the story, all of which allow embedding in the long-term memory center of the brain. Unlike traditional rote memorization regarding the probable results of misbehavior, the narrative offers a readily recognizable context which offers it more staying power; especially in the chapter books which almost always feature settings which will be familiar to the tween, such as school or home, and experiences such as dances or parties. Timothy Lintner speaks to the value of utilizing literature as a teaching tool, believing it has the "potential to transit certain core values such as tolerance, diversity, and inclusiveness" (200). Books are powerful tools through which adults can offer tweens behavioral information as they are renegotiating "power relationships with parents, teachers, or other authority figures—[as well as with peer groups]" (Overstreet 15). Through the book choices made by the reading tweens, vampires are catalysts to actions which teach our children how to belong to our society.

Plots and Patterns

There are two distinct plot structures used throughout horror literature featuring supernatural characters, according to Noel Carroll in his groundbreaking classic, *The Philosophy of Horror: or Paradoxes of the Heart*. The two patterns consist of the "Complex Discovery" and the "Discovery" patterns. The main elements of the "Complex Discovery" pattern are "Onset," "Discovery," "Confirmation," and "Confrontation." The books that fit in this category begin with the "Onset" period in which the monster is introduced to the reader, although not perhaps to the narrative character. When the plot enters the "Discovery" period, people, usually children, realize supernatural monsters might exist. Moving into the "Confirmation" period, the protagonists realize there really is a monster present and they must address the situation. And the plot climaxes at the "Confrontation" process, in which the protagonists attempt to, and usually do, destroy the monster. The "Discovery" pattern leaves out the "Confirmation" step—to the protagonists: the monster exists, is discovered, and is fought/destroyed. Unless the text presents pretty much only vampires, adults are normally not privy to the "Onset" or "Discovery" steps—adults become active in the plot after the "Confirmation" or "Confrontation" step only if they are aware of the monsters at all.

The representation of parents in "tweens'" books morph as the tween ages from six years old to twelve years old, and it makes no difference if the narrative is a human versus vampire narrative, a human learns of vampires narrative, or a narrative focusing on the vampire tweens; the basic plot devices regarding the parents' role[s] remain the same. The basic parental roles discussed in this study are limited to four of the many possible variations; the two most common—the busy parents and the abandoned parent; and the two which I consider most interesting—the heroic parent/relative or transitional adult, and the dead parent. The busy parent plot device is by far the most common, occurring across all age groups of children's fiction from chapter books to young adult. It features parents who are too busy with their own lives to properly engage with their children. One would suspect that the sudden shift from attentive parents to parents who are increasingly less hands-on would assist in allowing the novel's children space for their adventures.

This plot device will be discussed as it is featured in the early-reader, *Vampire Island* (Griffen 2007), but it is also charmingly presented in *The Vanishing Vampire: A Monsteriffic Tale* (Lupar 1997), *HELP! I'm Trapped in a Vampire's Body* (Strasser 2000) *The Little Vampire* series (Sommer-Bodenburg 2012), and countless others. Books for all age groups inform the tween that if they, by choice or accident, become a vampire, they must leave the parents, family, and peers in order to forge a new vampiric identity. And likewise these same plots inform the readers that they must abandon their siblings, extended family, and peers to become a vampire, in every one of these narratives meant that one was somehow deficient as a human. The study utilizes Darren Shan's *Cirque du Freak* series for examination, since the power of this series is backed by the 2009 film *Cirque du Freak: The Vampires Assistant*. The voluntary self-ejection from the parent and family is amusingly presented in *The Vanishing Vampire* (which also utilizes the busy-parent plot device); *Ghosts of Fear Street: How to Be a Vampire* (Stein 1996); and *Never Bite a Boy on the First Date* (Summers 2009).

Transitional adults (heroic non-parental adults), who assist tweens as needed in the fight against the vampires, are utilized in early readers and middle readers to showcase the idea that adults can be caring and attentive, standing alongside the tween to battle the vampire. Usually, the transitional person dies heroically attempting to save the children. With this plot device, three things hold true: the vampires are monsters, the heroism of adults is stressed, and the ultimate triumph is due to the children. This study focuses on the popular Scholastic series by Sebastian Rook, *Vampire Plague* (2003–2004), to see how this plot device works. The least used, but perhaps most powerful, plot device allowing emotional visualization in urging tweens to distance themselves from their childish relationships to their parents, and encouraging them to develop self-reliance is the dead-parent plot device. This device is used very successfully in the exceedingly popular series by Justine Stomper, *The Vampirates* (2007–2014). With this device, usually one of the parents died long before the story began, and then the remaining single parent dies leaving the children to find new homes and relationships with non-relations. Again, this device is rare in this sort of fiction—although increasingly common in young adult fiction.

Busy Parent

The young reader of the book is expecting to meet monsters in his or her book—and usually they have the presumption that these monsters are not positively inclined. They do not necessarily attain the level of badness which would place them in the apocalyptic "Evil monster" category, yet they do present to children what for many readers is the sad reality of modern lives; parents who while providing for physical needs, have little time left over from their own lives to connect with their child as the child has come to expect from their pre-preadolescent years. Thus there is an overabundance of children's literature—of all ages past picture book stage—which feature parents blithely unaware of what is occurring in their children's daily lives after the parent[s] sends them to bed or to school. These parents are failing to properly connect with, and monitor, their children. According to Patterson and Forgatch, "Research has shown that parents who cannot provide adequate answers to questions [regarding whom their children are with, or where they are] tend to have adolescents who are at risk for drifting into deviant peer groups, substance abuse, or engaging in delinquency" (61); or perhaps becoming vampire slayers. The inattentive parent motif is so common a plot feature that one wonders if the adult writers realize on some level that their writing replicates tweens actual experiences. At the least these books offer the tween assurance that other tweens are living the same randomly supervised experience and surviving it.

The parent's jobs, of course, play a role in the lack of supervision that parents' exhibit. Matthew F. Bumpus, Ann C. Crouter, and Susan McHale posit that "Parental social withdrawal following a day's work at a demanding job may make it more difficult for parents to keep track of their children's experiences and/or less comfortable for children to self-disclose to their parents with the result that parents know less about their children's daily lives" (38). This lack of parental awareness and direct supervision can be seen to inform children's unwillingness to share the details of their lives and is clearly depicted in *Vampire Island*. It is an early reader featuring a family of vampires who were inadvertently turned into vampire bats via witchcraft during an "Old World" plague. The parents attempt to be attentive when they are present, demanding that their children, Maddy, Lexie, and Hudson all have breakfast together and show up for dinner—a fruit-diet meal which is shared by all—and that the children do their homework and assigned chores. But the parents also are involved in their quite successful dog-walking business, their own relationship, and in the rock band they have formed, "The Dead Ringers." They allow the children unsupervised time, expecting them to conduct themselves with behaviors based upon 300-plus years of experience as a family group. It is at this point that the parents fail in their parenting since rules that were successful for immortal, ageless children are not necessarily those which will work for newly aging tween children. (The previously immortal fruit-bat family is now mortal due to giving up blood consumption when they moved to the "New World" of Manhattan, and thus the children are now experiencing preadolescence with all its turmoils).

The adult vampires as well as the tween vampires appearing in this text, are all experiencing the same transition the human reader is having since they are all passing through the same aging process, yet in many ways the adults are fitting in more readily than their children. Adults, by and large, get to limit their associations to those they wish, children do not; children are forced to socialize with human children, mainstreaming in school with human children at who are the apparent human age of each vampire tween. In this, while the parents are indeed more focused on their own new experiences and opportunities, they are rather set up to fail. If, as Patterson and

Fogatch suggest, the role of every parent is to "get their children ready to be socialized by the major forces outside the family" (9), Mr. and Mrs. Livingstone are, due to their immigrant, non-human status, unable to comply.

The story line is told diary style, with each child taking turns narrating their own section, and thus presenting only their own perspective on her or his own action. Each child feels as though she or he is totally different from everyone else, even within their own family; and each child does possess differing vampiric powers now that they are off the blood-diet that had kept them aging only one human year per century. Maddy is now eleven years old, and has inherited the "'urge [which] had been passed onto her to slay the pure-blood vampires, the fruit-bat vampires natural enemy. This urge "made her different from all her family" (Griffen 2). Maddy also is the only member of her family that craves the energy of blood. This need to consume small portions of blood is something she has kept from her parents, although her siblings are aware of it. She feels that her parents would force her to stop satisfying her blood-urge, even though she satisfies it Renfield-like, only through small beetles and other insects. For the most part, Maddie's character demonstrates how easy it is to keep secrets from busy parents or to deflect their questions on the somewhat rare occasions they notice something afoot.

Lexie, at thirteen years old, is feeling a new urge; she has a crush on a classmate. Lexie laments the emotional and physical distancing she feels is now growing between family members. Even more she laments not fitting in with her own, human age group. Like many of the human tweens, she feels that she "'Doesn't fit in anywhere!'" (69). Lexie recognizes the distance from her classmates caused by her actual large age difference, she "Doesn't even speak the language of her classmates" (61). She is an outcast at her school due to her odd superhuman abilities—sticky hands and throwing power—and is teased unremittingly by the popular girl who threatens constantly to expose her as "odd." Given the various jobs and activities which prevent the unnamed adult parents—they are never granted names—from supervising her siblings, Lexie is forced to step into the gap, and try and keep them from obviously standing out as supernatural creatures, and try to keep them safe from their own urges; Maddie to slay vampires, and Hudson to be an environmental warrior.

The nine-year-old Hudson, in spite of being so handsome that everyone automatically grants him the popularity which is due to the very attractive, feels that "'sometimes the differences take up more space than sameness'" (84), even within his own family. His familial difference is more marked than Maddie and Lexie's. Hudson is still able to transform into a bat at night while the rest of the family lost that ability when they arrived in the New World. He is tasked by an older, supposedly wiser, fruit-bat friend, Orville, to be the "Young Protector" (22) to all the small animals that live in the parks on Manhattan; in fact, he is tasked with being the eco-warrior destined to save the earth from humanities waste. Like Maddie and Lexie, he keeps his destiny secret from his parents; he feels as though they would not understand, or would attempt to stand in the way of his destiny.

While the parents are also dealing with the dual problems of being vampire and being immigrants, the children note repeatedly their lack of attention, and each responds slightly differently. Maddie eats illicit bugs, and is even able to locate and slay the true-blood vampire family who has moved in across the street, all without her parents noticing. Lexie is bullied at school, falls for a werewolf boy, and is forced to parent her siblings since her own parents are inadequate to the task at hand. And Hudson, the youngest, sneaks relationships with others of their own fruit-bat vampire race since his parents have decreed he should not. The parental abdicating of attention is often replicated in the reader's lives, and they have the opportunity to see how other tweens respond to it—and the consequences of those responses.

Abandoned Parents

This category of tweens who are turning into vampires and running away from home, abandoning their families and peers, is used in all post-picture book vampire literature and is often combined with the "busy parent" modality. This literature features tweens who abandon home because, by force or choice, they are becoming vampires. The normal reasons for running away include the psychological, which "assume[s] that the child ... has poor impulse control, and is deviant. The social environmental viewpoint, in contrast, assumes that the family is the cause of the child's leaving. Most recently, the socio-psychological viewpoint adopts a combination of the psychological and the social environmental reasons" (Spillane-Grieco 159). Becoming a vampire is not on the normal list of reasons why tweens run away, but depending on the author, the psychological and social reasons might influence a tweens' choice to become a vampire—if they are not forcibly inducted into the undead. Arguably, the very fact that the tween runs away due to fear of harming their family post-turning speaks to the psychology authors attribute to vampires: Poor impulse control and deviant behaviors.

While the abandoned parent plot device appears in all tween literature in which the tween is turned into a vampire, book one of Darren Shan's *Cirque du Freak* series: *Cirque du Freak: A Living Nightmare*, offers a clear look at the reasoning that leads the tween to abandon home. This series presents "Nice" parents, parents who are involved in their children's lives, and establishes Darren Dalton, the main character, as somehow deviant—in not fitting into his "nice" family quite so well. This is done through establishing that while Darren, as are his best friends, are willing to steal ("borrow") money from family members to have the money to attend a "Freak" show. Mrs. Dalton, Darren's mother, upon learning about the "Freak Show" which Darren brings up, explains that Freak Shows are demeaning to people who are just handicapped in some way. Mrs. Dalton asks him, "'How would you like it if you were stuck in a cage for people to look at?'" To which Darren replies, "'Huffily.... I'm not a freak!'" An adult will recognize the disconnect in this conversation; the parent and child are speaking of two different angles to the issue: Mrs. Dalton is speaking of the "wrong" sort of people who attend the show—nice people do not treat anyone as "Freaks," while to Darren, the issue is not the character of the viewer; to him, if a person is a "Freak," it is perfectly all right to cage and pay to view them.

Darren is beginning to distance himself from his "nice" family, which is essential if he is to become the savior vampire called for in the series. This distancing from his family continues when, after an evening spent doing things with both of his parents which establishes their loving relationship with him, Darren sneaks out to attend the "Cirque" performance. The movement toward "bad" continues after the show when he steals the Tarantula, Madam Octa, from one of the performers, Mr. Crepsley. Darren wants it to be his pet, so he takes it. He furthers his bad actions by hiding the spider in his bedroom because he knows his parents will not approve of either the theft, or the spider, or the lying. Darren was correct in his assessment of his parents, since not only is the spider poisonous, it is stolen. His parents are attempting to raise a son who follows normal morals—and not stealing other's belongings is an edict of the nice society they are attempting to make him a part of. Darren's parents—although they are clearly making an attempt to interact and support his emotional and character development—are unaware of his turn to the wrong side.

Tweens are aware that there are consequences for bad behaviors, and for Darren those consequences begin once he has moved from the cultural construct of the approved "nice" category into the problematic and ill defined "not-nice" category. To further the plot, the spider bites his friend, Steve, who wants to become a vampire, and Steve will die without medicine only Mr. Crepsley can provide. Darren must now confess to his theft to Mr. Crepsley in order to request his medicine. Consequences for not being a good tween began as Mr. Crepsley turned Darren into a half-vampire as a punishment for theft, and in exchange for the medicine that would save Madam Octa's victim, his best friend Steve. The consequences of Darren's actions continue as the transition to vampire progresses. At first after becoming a vampire, he did not feel that much different; in fact, he acquired additional speed and strength. But as the transition continued, he discovered the vampiric desire overwhelming his human qualms—as a vampire, he wants to drink blood.

His first experience with this need was a public one. His friend Alan was injured playing soccer, and before Darren knew what he was doing, "[he] had covered the cut on his leg with [his] mouth and was sucking out his blood and gulping it down. This went on for seconds. [His] eyes were closed and the blood filled [his] mouth. It tasted amazing" (Ch. 28 n.p.). He had become a deviant: a freak. People watched his behavior with horror—the same horror used toward the "Freaks." Only when he found himself wanting to attack his sister, tracing, "the outline of her neck with [his] fingers.... His tongue slow[ly] licking the around [his] lips and his belly rumbl[ing]" (Ch. 23 n.p.) did he face the truth; he is now a threat to his family and his loved ones. He must abandon his family and his friends—a sort of heroic choice in some ways as he puts their safety ahead of his own need for security and blood.

Darren's relationship moved away from his parents long before he became a vampire although that is what forced him to fake his own death so that he could leave them with closure and himself with no parents searching for him. His parents, in this case, did no wrong with which the reading tween can identify. They have been loving to both their children; concerned for them, yet willing to allow them space for their friends and hobbies. The only item which could be pointed at was Mrs. Dalton's lack of understanding that she and her son were speaking of two different things in their original discussion regarding the Cirque du Freak. The parents have been the very model of the "Normal" parent. They have been what every tween thinks he or she wants: Parents who provide, listen, and love. In some ways, it is the parent's insistence on their own norm that lead Darren into trouble. If Mrs. Dalton, or the various teachers who responded regarding the show, had responded differently, perhaps Darren would not have felt the need to be sneaky about his attending the "Cirque du Freak." If she had responded to his interest with a more moderate, let's talk, or "what do you think?," the monologue might have become a dialogue in which Darren felt his opinions heard, even if not necessarily validated. But, of course, textually, Darren had to leave home to save his family. He had his own destiny to fulfill.

Heroic Adults

Just as society has trained tweens to the belief that adults will assist them if their own parent is unable to do so, it has trained adults to assist children who evidence serious need and ask for aid. Sharie McNamee and Faith Wesolick, in their "Brief Report on the Heroic Behavior of Carnegie Medal Heroes...," note that there is a pattern of decisions which are key to deciding to risk one's own wellbeing in the aid of others. They state that this process,

"Requires four sequential factors, [which] Staub (2003) defined as follows: a) a perception of someone's needs, b) empathy with that person, c) a realization of what needs to be done and, and d) critically, a decision that he or she is responsible to take that action, a decision heightened when there is a risk in helping" (171). Several adults in Rook's *Vampire Plague* series are able to suspend their disbelief in vampires, and demonstrate their belief in the tweens' narrative, heroically stepping forward to aid and protect the protagonist children (and to prevent the upcoming vampiric Armageddon). In the first novel of the series, *Vampire Plagues: London 1850*, Harrison Cole and Edwin Sherwood die to allow Benedict Cole (Ben), to escape the original vampire attack; and Professor Aldensnap will risk death to aid the protagonist tweens, the wealthy brother and sister, Benedict Cole and Emily Cole, and the street urchin, Jack Harkett, who has befriended Ben and Emily.

This narrative begins in the Yucatán with the accidental release of the vampire God, Cammeratoz, from his burial temple when the archeological expedition led by Ben's father, Harrison Cole, and his de-facto uncle, Edwin Sherwood, and the wealthy Sir Donald cause a cave-in in the cave/temple in which Cammeratoz had been held. Cammeratoz has the power to possess the bodies of victims so that their personalities reflect his own evil which is lodged within them. Sir Donald, usually kind and jovial with Ben, changes after the cave-in allowing the possession of Sir Donald. He is now cold, distant, and a hard taskmaster to all. He forces the others to gather his bats (vampire minions in bat form) into crates to ship to London where he plans to establish a foothold on world domination. On the trip through the forest, many of the Mayan porters abandon the expedition—they believe in vampires and recognize the signs of the upcoming vampiric Armageddon, suggesting to the reader that the less-civilized Mayan's are somehow closer to the supernatural than the very civilized British. Ben's father is killed in an attempt to save his son from being turned into a vampire, and Ben makes his way ... hidden in the same ship that carries the vampires back to London, hoping to warn people about the vampiric threat. His first action on arriving in London is to notify the police of the threat. He is not taken seriously by the police due to their inability to believe in the supernatural entity: the vampire. His innocent sister, Emily, and the adept street urchin, Jack, believe in Ben's warning, and together they set out to destroy the vampire God and prevent Armageddon.

The first adult willing to suspend disbelief regarding vampires is Professor Aldensnap whom they visit for assistance in translating the "how-to-destroy vampires" manual left behind by the Mayan priests a thousand years earlier. Professor Aldensnap listens with intelligence and interest as Jack tells him, "We know that people are dying out there and we think those vamp—

er, those bats—is to blame. Ben here saw them in action in Mexico, and now they're here in London" (112). Professor Aldensnap not only listens, he accepts their first-hand experience, and assists them to, temporarily, defeat the vampires in London. Thus far, the assistive adult Professor Aldensnap has survived, and the series has a fairly happy ending in that all three children, and the assistive, heroic adult survive. Book two, *Vampire Plagues: Paris*, moves into darker territory.

Friends now, the children accompany Professor Aldensnap to Paris, where he is to attend a "symposium on Mayan civilization" (39) which allows the introduction of the next protector, Vicomte de Montargis, and the Vicomte's young daughter, Veronica. Thus far, not counting all the nameless victims who are not really on the reader's "care-list," only Ben's father and Ben's acting uncle, Edwin Sherwood have died protecting him. In Paris the helpful adult toll rises. The vampires were not defeated in London, just forced to have a new base of operations. Soon after introducing the children to the Vicomte, Professor Aldensnap is found dead in the Louvre Museum, drained of blood with his throat torn out; both the Vicomte's and his own papers about Cammeratoz stolen. The concerned Vicomte, who now suspects that vampires might be real, then takes the British children under his care since they are now orphans in a strange country. Cammeratoz's attention is now firmly on the children, and soon after the Vicomte fosters them, Jack is kidnapped. The wealthy and influential Vicomte is to exchange the one item they have found, a piece of a statue, which might assist in Cammeratoz's defeat, for Jack's return. In case the reader does not grasp the depth of caring demonstrated by the Vicomte it is spelled out. The Vicomte says, "with a brave smile.... It seems I am to be a hero after all"(137). This allows the tween readers to experiment vicariously with the idea that parents love them enough to sacrifice their own lives to protect the tweens. And that some other adults might not be so bad either. They might listen to the tween, as did Professor Aldensnap, relate to the tween's experience, assist the tween in performing necessary arming to battle evil entities, even when the adult knows that doing so risks his or her own life. But overall, parents do love one.

Dead Parents

The death of a parent—or any loved one—is a hard experience, and for the characters in the books, it is no different. Katrina M. Powell discusses the fear often felt both of, and by, displaced persons who are forced to move to new locales. "As bodies move, the identities they inhabit also move" (300); they have to construct new selves to deal not just with the move, but to construct new selves to deal with the new people. This leads to "complexities as identities interact and move across space and time as they are displaced [to new] 'home[s]'" (300). Dead parents, at least as patterned in these stories, offered unconditional love and support to the now-orphaned tween, and even if not—all issues are forgiven at death. Ayers, Sandler, Wolchick and Haine, through their 2013 analysis of trauma and childhood, declared that "Parental death is 1 of the most traumatic events that can occur in childhood, and several reviews of the literature have found that the death of a parent places children at risk for ... negative outcomes" (112). Arguably, the adult writers of these books offer totally dreadful new respectable "families" to the characters in these books. They offer placement in public care facilities such as orphanages, or prospective adoption by really, really self-serving individuals as large among the possible negative outcomes. The death of the parent[s] force[s] the character[s] to face the necessity of moving into a new environment, one with many different rules and patterns to follow.

The expectations of the adults offering to "take them in" are suspect. This is most obvious in the non-vampire Lemony Snicket series, *A Series of Unfortunate Events*, but the same unfortunate trope can be read quite clearly also in Justine Stomper's series for middle-readers/young adults, *Vampirates*. This study will only examine the dynamics set in motion through the death of the parents in the first volume: *Vampirates Book 1: Demons of the Ocean*. Through the clearly stated desires of both prospective caretakers, Polly Pagett and Mr. and Mrs. Busby, the narrative reinforces the idea that adults have their own reasons for taking care of children, and these needs do not always include the child's own desires. In this case, the children's understandings of the reasons of the prospective caregivers are the major factors driving the male and female twin protagonists', Connor and Grace Tempest, to run away to sea. With the death of their father, lighthouse keeper Dexter Tempest, the children—twins—are shown to be destitute and homeless and are forced into "care." The readers are experiencing this loss second hand, reading about it, and yet they are practicing how they would deal with this if it occurred to them. The existing research suggests that, "although there is little evidence that cathartic expression of emotion is necessary for all children, when children feel they must inhibit the expression of negative emotions they would like to express, they are more likely to experience greater mental health problems" (Ayers et al. 115). The twins are never allowed to deal with their emotions at their father's death. They are instead forced immediately to move into new "care."

It is their shipwreck loss of each other that drives the first book of the series, much more than the father's death. The novel expresses the love of the single-parent father toward the children, and their fulfilling and beloved life with him in one sparse, not quite nine-page prologue, before jumping ahead seven years to his funeral. Those seven years of child growth and parental relationship are left unexpressed, which of course allows the tween reader to fill in the blanks as he or she wishes. An argument can be made that this lack of addressing the missing years is due to the needs of the author to move the plot along, and the death of the parent allows the reader to enter the real plot of the book: bad substitute parenting with villagers who the children know or good substitute parenting with pirates.

The negative options are those which lead the twins to run away, and they are immediately presented to the reader at the actual funeral. There are two "care" options shown, both in a negative light. The first is the county orphanage where the matron, Polly Pagett, looks forward to their arrival because they offer free labor opportunity: "The boy looked exceedingly strong. He could be put to work at the harbor. And the girl … she was sharp as a tack. No doubt she could stretch the orphanages ever-dwindling budget" (17). The second option is equally grim: adoption by Lachlan Busby, the bank manager, and his wife, Loretta Busby, who have been unable to have their own children, and want children to form into their desired skill and personality shapes to leave as legacy. At the funeral, Lachlan Busby and his wife place themselves carefully in a location to observe the twins. He "has plans for the twins" (17) the reader is told. Lachlan Busby is attaining the twins for his wife; his own attention will remain fixed on his ledgers since he does not approve of the lack of forethought regarding their economic wellbeing shown by their father, and will not do the same. It will be his wife's business to shape the tweens into personalities suitable for the rise in rank—from lighthouse keeper's children to banker's children.

Connor, at school at least, wears the appearance of a popular boy, but in reality both twins are set apart—social isolates, outsiders, because their dad's wife was from outside the village and the parents had kept themselves to themselves. The twins raised jealousy in the community: "they were talented in ways [the townsfolk's own] kids were not" (18). The narrative plot, of course, requires that the twins refuse to accept their prospective fate, so Grace informs the eager potential father, "My brother and I do not need new parents. It's very generous to offer us new parents, it really is, but we'll do just fine on our own" (25). As many children experiencing the abrupt shift to a new family—especially ones with very negative options offered to them— think about doing, Conner and Grace choose the third option—one not readily practicable to most of the readers: they run away. In this case, they do not run away to join the circus or to live among the homeless, they escape to sea; where of course a storm comes up and sinks them. They are both rescued by pirates—just two totally different sorts.

It is with these new substitute families—families built on peer relationships—that the children find new homes. Connor is rescued by human pirates, while Grace is rescued by "Vampirates." Both children now must learn to exist in their new environments—totally new environments that they have no control over and which are totally separate from their former existences. It is unclear if this is a positive or negative positioning for the tween reader. What is clear; however, is that each child has been placed in the ideal setting for their skill set to earn each one membership in their new family structures. Connor, athletic, strong, brawny is now among pirates where he is fully capable of learning their trade and earning a place in their pirate family. The ship is a patriarchal structure, as his newly assigned best mate, Bart, informs him. "Everyone pitches in. The captain's kind of old school, a bit irregular, but he treats us like his own family" (85). But as in the Orphanage which he has avoided only by fleeing, Connor has to earn his way into this family. His belonging, his continued existence, depends upon his actions: acceptance is not unconditional. In fact, it is only after the first piratical engagement in which he participates, that the pirate Captain, Captain Wraith, states, "We could never make up for your loss, Mister Tempest, but if you cared to think of us as such, we could be your new family. Not to replace your real one—we could never do that—but all the same to look out for you and give you a place in the world. To reassure you, you are not alone" (135). The Captain repeats this statement two pages later, "Mr. Tempest; we are all family here" (137). Connor has found a home with set rules and known consequences, but never has to deal with the two-facedness of the townsfolk. Here the conditional acceptance is out-front.

Grace Tempest has landed with the fictional Vampirates, whose shanty she has grown up singing; repeating over and over the phrase:

> You'd better be good, child—good as gold,
> As good as good can be.
> Else I'll turn you in to the Vampirates
> And wave you out to sea [Frontispiece].

Having chosen the third option, the twins run away to sea, but why is it she who lands with the Vampirates instead of Connor? In spite of the reader's fears for her—and her brother's fear for her safety—Grace is protected by the Captain through the auspices of Lorcan Furey, who is to keep her safe in her cabin with her presence unknown by the many Vampirates who inhabit the ship. Grace, unlike her brother, is not called upon to use her "cleverness" in a positive way. In fact, her efforts to discover more about her captor/saviors lead her constantly into more danger—and causes her to create more problems for the Vampirates' Captain who seeks her safety. To earn her keep here, she is to do nothing, to live in a drugged, but safe, cocoon. Her constant refrain, the need to find her lost brother, lead her to ignore the proffered family and their acceptance of her. Does the tween reader catch that Grace's life is predicated upon an acceptance of un-agency? Every time she acquires agency, it causes her trouble. Only in the third book do her skills come into play. Like Connor, she laments the loss of her sibling much more than the loss of her father. But then, she buried her father; her brother is lost, lamented, but not dead to her since she did not witness his death.

The series continues the theme of the Tempest Twins earning acceptance among their various seafaring found families, and their learning to accept these found families as rightfully their own. It offers a repeating structure that models the pattern of how to handle the death of a parent—accept their passing and move on. Expect to earn a place in the new family, and do not expect unconditional acceptance from the new stand-in parents. But one can attain a sort of peace in knowing exactly what is expected of one from adult authority figures, and knowing what to expect from them. And as a tween, this is not a life sentence after all.

Conclusion

When Nina Auerbach says that "Each Generation gets the vampire it creates" (1), in some important ways, she is correct. The writer creates the vampires which act as the catalyst causing the human characters, both tween and adult, to react. The readers observe the interactions and construct their own ideas regarding the behaviors they read on the page. And on some level as they read, they are participating in a game of "what if." Tweens are being allowed to make vicarious choices without having to follow them through in reality, allowed perhaps to sublimate their own angst at having parents who one moment are telling them to grow up and offering them more agency, and at the next withdrawing that same agency and treating them like the child they were five years earlier. The parenting behavioral styles appearing on the pages, arguably, are those that concern adult writers enough to present them in the books they write for tweens.

This study looked at only four of many variations of parenting styles as they relate to the tween characters: the inattentive—overly busy—parent; the parent abandoned by the newly turned tween in order to save them; the heroic adult (parent or parental substitute); and the dead parent. Each of these parenting styles have different advantages for the plots of the narratives. The inattentive, overly busy parent allows the children almost free range in the story, while the parental character can be almost ignored. The abandoned parent flips the focus from the social problem of abused parents (parents abused by their children) to the heroism of the newly-turned, vampiric tween, painting the tween as a hero for recognizing the danger he or she now presents to their former family. This device also allows the story-line to move the tween character into an entirely new world, in which they usually acquire full agency, while having to comply with new rules and reach for new opportunities. The heroic adult figure appears in a world in which vampires are evil, and gives the tween the reassurance that there will be an adult figure—who might or might not be related to him or her—willing to stand with him or her to fight the vampire, willing to die for him or her if necessary. And finally, the very interesting "what-if" plot device of the dead parent[s]. It raises the question which most children ask at one time or another: what happens to me if my parents die? The answer offered in these is that often transitive or substitute parents are fostering or adopting the tween for reasons which might or might not offer the tween emotional anchoring. But that one can earn one's own home through friendliness and utilization of one's skills.

Asma stated that for Greeks and Romans, "Monsters were prodigies—warnings of impending calamity" ("Monsters on the Brain" n.p.). The calamity presented in tween vampire literature is not that the vampires might win and the world within the pages experience some sort of vampire apocalypse period. Rather the warning is that adulthood is fast approaching, the changes taking place in one's physical body are unstoppable, and parents—while often well intentioned—are not always the font of all answers. And it is up to the reading tween, with a little help from a vampire and a book, to negotiate that aging terrain.

Works Cited

Asma, Stephen T. "Monsters on the Brain." *Chronicle of Higher Education* 56.10 (2009). Academic Search Premier. http://www.colum.edu/academics/mind-science-culture/pdf/Monsters-on-the-Brain-Social-Research.pdf. Accessed 15 July 2016.
_____. *On Monsters: An Unnatural History of Our Worst Fears*. Oxford: Oxford University Press, 2009.
Auerbach, Nina. *Our Vampires Ourselves*. Chicago: University of Chicago Press, 1997.
Beir, William C. *The Adolescent: His Search For Understanding*. New York: Fordham University Press, 1963.
Benson-Allot, Caetlin T. "Paradoxes of the Heart: The Philosophy of Horror Twenty-Five Years Later: An Interview by Caetlin Benson-Allot." *Journal of Visual Culture* 14.3 (2015): 336–343.
Bodart, Joni R. *They Suck, They Bite, They Eat, They Kill: The Psychological Meaning of Supernatural Monsters in Young Adult Fiction*. Lanham, MD: Scarecrow Press, 2012.
Bumpus, Matthew F., Ann C. Crouter, and Susan M. McHale. "Linkages Between Negative Work-to-Family Spillover and Mothers and Fathers Knowledge of Their Young Adolescents' Daily Lives." *Journal of Early Adolescence* 26 (2006): 36–59.
Carroll, Noel. *The Philosophy of Horror: Or, Paradoxes of the Heart*. London: Routledge, 1990.
Griffen, Adele. *Vampire Island*. New York: Scholastic. 2007.
Haine, Rachel A., Tim S. Ayers, Irwin N. Sandler, and Sharlene A. Wolchik. "Evidence-Based Practices for Parentally Bereaved Children." *Professional Psychology: Research and Practice* 39.2 (2008): 113–121.
Lintner, Timothy. "Using 'Exceptional' Children's Literature to Promote Character Education In Elementary Social Studies Classrooms." *Social Studies* 102.5 (2011): 200–203.
Martarelli, Corinna S., Lilla M. Gurtner, and Fred W. Mast. "School-Age Children Show a Bias Toward Fantasy Classifications after Playing Platform Games." *Psychology of Popular Media Culture*. 20 November 2014. https://www.researchgate.net/publication/2670353

95_School-Age_Children_Show_a_Bias_Toward_Fantasy_Classifications_After_Play ing_a_Platform_Game. Accessed 1 September 2016.
McNamee, Sharie, and Faith Wesolik. "Brief Report: Heroic Behavior of Carnegie Medal Heroes: Parental Influence and Expectations." *Peace and Conflict: Journal of Peach Psychology* 20.2 (2014): 171–173.
Overstreet, Deborah W. *Not Your Mother's Vampire: Vampires in Young Adult Fiction*. Lanham, MD: Scarecrow Press, 2006.
Paterson, Gerald R. and Marion S. Forgatch. *Parents and Adolescents Living Together: Part 1: The Basics*. Eugene, OR: Castalia Publishing, 1987.
Powell, Katrina M. "Rhetorics of Displacement: Constructing Identities in Forced Relocations." *College English* 74.4 (2012): 299–324.
Rook, Sebastian. *Vampire Plagues: London, 1850*. New York: Scholastic. 2004.
_____. *The Vampire Plagues II: Paris, 1850*. New York: Scholastic. 2004.
Shan, Darren. *Cirque du Freak #1: A Living Nightmare: Book 1 in the Saga of Daren Shawn*. New York: Hachette Book Group. 2001. Kindle. 21 December 2007.
Spillane-Grieco, Eileen. "Feelings and Perceptions of Parents of Runaways." *Child Welfare* LX111.2 (1984): 159–166.
Staub, Ervin. *The Psychology of Good and Evil: Why Children, Adults, and Groups Help and Harm Others*. Cambridge: Cambridge University Press, 2003.
Stomper, Justine. *Vampirates Book 1: Demons of the Ocean*. New York: Little, Brown, 2005.
Summer, Montague. *The Vampire: His Kith and Kin*. New Hyde Park, NY: University Books, 1960.

SECTION THREE: SYMBOLISM, MEANINGS AND INTERPRETATIONS

Dick and Jane and Vampires
The Interstitial Bridge Between Social Imaginary and Spirituality

PHIL FITZSIMMONS

Introductory Overview: From Personal Reaction to Frames of Meaning

Acknowledging the peculiar "location of meaning" (Turner 19) that characterizes an Australasian approach to text analysis, the aim of this essay is to unpack the findings and evidentiary warrant in regards to the transtextual visual analysis of the children's "mash up" text, *Dick and Jane and Vampires*. This analysis was comprised of a digging into the text through a process that Ellis and Bochner have termed "spiraling refinement" (387). This spiral of transtextual reactions frames the following organizational structure of this essay.

Genets defines transtextuality as "textual transcendence of text" (82). As summarized in Appendix B, he also believes transtextuality is comprised of five processes "that sets the text in relationship, whether obvious or concealed, with other texts" (82). To paraphrase Fetterman the use of transtextuality reveals the subjective possibilities in the visual images that act as "can openers of meaning" (41). As Foucault also notes, "a book ... is caught up in a system of references to other books, other texts, other sentences: it is a node within a network.... The book is not simply the object that one holds in one's hands ... its unity is variable and relative" (23).

The *Dick and Jane* books commonly trigger some form of emotional "can opener" of transtextual memory in children and adults ranging from nostalgic longing (Victoria Public Record Office) through to loathing (Bloomfield). While some adults often have a deep sentimental yearning regarding these books, which are still found in homes across America and Australia, *Dick and Jane* have been blamed for the poor reading scores in the United States (Toppo) and disappeared from most classrooms in Australia decades ago. Indeed, along with two other colleagues I had railed against these kinds of sugar coated basal texts and "the faulty psychological model of reading" (Geekie, Cambourne and Fitzsimmons 2) on which they were based. The faulty ideological approach to how children's books should be constructed was not the only reason for opposition to these books, because as Anderson states, "Our own heritage of primers and abecedaria embarrasses us. We all fear Dick and Jane. We cringe at their knee-socks and the plasticine sheen of their cheeks. Confronted with their image, we want to dis-avow the vacuous sweetness of their moral world" (Anderson 372).

Half-jokingly but still pejoratively, I had often referred to all the *Dick and Jane* texts in particular as "phonication" with their over reliance on grapho-phonics and stunted use of grammar, but more importantly I, like many others, baulked at their idealized emblems of American childhood, "Stepford"[1] like illustrations and markers of 1950s cultural capital. While it has been my experience that the overwhelming majority of Australian educators and researchers would also see little value in these texts, it is the overt transtextual connection to what Australians see as a "nightmare rerun of the American dream" (Wark 256) that causes concern. While embracing many things American in the Australian way of life, the cover of this book also immediately sets in train for Australian eyes negative echoes of the perceived "coca-colonization" (Scheckter 6) evident in much of American television "Stepford-like" sit coms. While the term Stepford typically applies in a generic sense to the feminist movement, and specifically to the way American woman can be often portrayed as "placid and docile submissiveness and seem unwilling or unable to express any thoughts or opinions that diverge from those of the men" (Schweishelm 109), in Australia it can have a broader association. While the Australian ideological mainspring regarding this term is similar to the previous definition, Australian researchers have tended to label any singular textual or visual 1950s reference in a negative light, and as being Stepford.

It has taken me some time to resist my misgivings and revisit *Dick and Jane* in the awareness that while all texts are "culturally derived and bound" (Harris et al. 6), Australians often read any references to the family as dystopic. More importantly, as Scheckter (58) emphasizes, because of the cultural sense of being criminal outcasts of "Mother England" the Australian social imaginary views references to the family from within a "mythic lens of the lost child." This perspective of loss due to the death of children wreaked by the landscape itself "acknowledges a sense of imperfection within attempts at self-definition and ontological uncertainty" (58). In discussing this point, and the ways in which white Australians are contrasted with the indigenous people and their sense of land, Rolls claims that Australian narrative reveals white Australia as being "alienated from the land they inhabit and are hence spiritually unhomed" (108). This is perhaps one of the few key overlaps with American children's narrative.

Children's minds are not unhomed, and nor are they *tabula rasa*. Like all child readers Australian children become embedded in a cultural memory and deep insight (Bhabha). Visual elements are sublimated by children at both the conscious and unconscious levels (Bettelheim), and are the pictorial spaces where intuition and ideas interact "encompassing all the curiosities of the world" (Jeffers 13). Children are not vessels to be filled by adult carers and authors, who in some instances often see their role as shaping children's minds in regard to sameness and difference (Edwards 25), as research has shown that young children do take responsibility for their reflective thinking. More importantly, they use literature "as a means of organizing a representation of the world—each for them self—and that the representation so created constitutes the world we operate in, the basis of all our predictions by which we set the course of our lives" (Britton 31). Even seemingly fatuous texts have a role in this process, and especially "something which is familiar and trusted is suddenly made strange and disturbing" (Thomson 58). As Bradford states, this is the ultimate purpose of children's literature, to "unsettle distinctions between fiction, autobiography, and history, foregrounding the interplay of memory and narrative" (Bradford 102).

Although on one level *Dick and Jane* appears to be "ultimately sterile" (Van Manen 125) the inclusion of both the Stepford and vampire motifs on the cover sets in train two key intertwined "can opener" motifs of immediacy that reveal a different perspective. As stated previously, from a purely Australian literary perspective with its "entrenched suspicion of authority" (Foster, Finnis and Nimon 15) and reluctance to engage in any sense of nostalgia in general, there is always a suspicion of familial Stepford aspects in particular. As Scutter sees it, these aspects are related too, and are coded as the feminine through the notion of the "monstrous mother" (201). However, these images are prone to meaning "inversion" (262). In an Australian children's literature context, the mother may appear as corporeal and spiritual, with "softer albeit sinister overtones." Along with the concept of the 'lost child' she further believes these texts often detail "a fake yearning for an absent mother" (127). The entire web of imagery in these text types set in train and reveals, "a manipulative nostalgia: a reconstruction of memory divorced from any reality; a strategy of using the past to deal with the present; connected with a desire that is irretrievably lost" (108). For Scutter, Zornado and Finnis et al., these text types are always blurry in regard to specific relational connectivity with ragged edges of uncertain socio-familial meaning "since the object can never be imagined" (108). As well, the endings of these Stepford or sentimental texts always "leak, when the happy ending wins out over reality" (108).

As will be unpacked in the next section of this essay, the second underpinning and conjoined paratextual framework related to the *Dick and Jane* text is, of course, the vampire motif. While the vampire as per the image in *Dick and Jane* has never taken a firm foothold in Australian literature, and in fact "has been unsuccessful" (Moran and Vieth 112). However, the sense of a Gothic vampiric monstrous has become an entrenched indigenous form as seen in Mudrooroo Nyoongah's narrative *The Undying*. As Clark suggests is the case for all Gothic vampire and monstrous references in Australian children's literature, this creature is also coded as female: "Her horrendous acts of penetration and murder can be read as cruel metaphors for indigenous dispossession, displacement and imposed cultural enfeeblement that are the hallmarks of the colonial enterprise" (121). Hence, in the Australian context the image of the vampire is still typically seen as an inclusion of a "difficulty," which for children "no one dares to speak" (Rose 10). The apparent simplicity of *Dick and Jane* brings to the fore this 'difficulty' locating the vampire motif and children on the cover. This appears to speak to the notion that "the line between human and monster is precariously permeable" (Kavaldo 60).

Immediately recognizable to readers of all ages, the visual referent to a vampire is a "a node within a network" providing an insight into the "deformed discourse" (Fitzsimmons 18) that resides as textual immediacy within us all and constantly surfaces in the first glance at all forms of popular culture. Deformed discourse, or the textual aspects that gives sudden voice to "harbingers of anarchy, chaos, death and hell" (Deardorff 131), is found in the "difficult stories" (Niemi and Ellis 2) of children's literature and is characterized by "heavy words lightly thrown" (Roberts 1). For the images in children's literature these are visual threads that "are designed to unsettle the reader-viewer" (Fitzsimmons and Reynaud 189). These texts reflect a visual sequence that reflects "category crisis, resistance to change and growth, a policing of the border, the desire of forbidden practices and the revealing of the monster in self" (Fitzsimmons 21). In particular, the visual aspects of deformed discourse often disengage with the actual written text, bending or subverting the meaning of the text as a whole to reveal more than a literal meaning in order to produce new and richer connections to our often unspoken fears. In children's literature, especially those texts which touch elements of the "other within," the visual aspects of deformity, otherness and the abject are often introduced as being discursively proximal. In the smallest of spaces, the illustrations allow the monstrous to be either intertwined or suspended with the human, becoming a co-signifier. Daniel Deardorff suggests that this boundary crossing ability is a key role of the monster, as "deformity makes its victim the benign or the malign intercessor between the known and the unknown, the dark and the light and the bright side of nature, this world and the beyond" (3).

It is through touching the "dark side" of texts often contained in the pictorial elements that children not only gain a deep sense of enjoyment but are able to develop an appreciation of self and aid their developing imagination (Howarth). Rather than "transgressing the boundaries and norms of childhood innocence" (Rose 183) through the tools of visual literacy (Appendix A) and the use overarching aspects of transtextuality the seemingly dark aspects of children's literature can become reflective bridges "reaching children's hearts and minds and helps them understand themselves and the world in which they live" (Feeney and Moravcik 21). As stated previously, the psycho-socio-emotionally touching of the "dark side" is perhaps best achieved by reading through the critical literacy lens of transtextuality (Appendix B), which even for young children "knowing about networks of relationships among texts not only equips readers with tools of interpretation, but also gives them the courage of their own convictions when exploring their own interpretations" (Harris and McKenzie 36). Using the entwined notions of the Stepford, the tropes of the vampire, the elements of transtextuality and tools of visual literacy the following sections reveal specific facets of how the illustrative marker of the "archetype of vampire literature" (Hirschmann 21) have become enmeshed in a children's text and touch a core aspect of human meaning.

Visual Markers of the Vampire: Transtextual Frames of Meaning

The Paratext of *Dick and Jane*

As stated previously, the text in focus is based on the children's primer of *Dick and Jane* found in most kindergarten rooms in Australia and the United States in the 1950s. At first glance the vampire version looks and reads like these texts. On a visual level, the inclusion of a vampire simply appears to be a somewhat superficial transtextual inclusion, especially in an age where the vampire motif has entered an apparent global social imaginary in texts ranging from horror movies, adolescent fiction, children's television cartoons and cereal boxes. While it would be relatively easy to dismiss the inclusion of a vampire into a *Dick and Jane* text as a poor attempt at commodification, and relatively thoughtless means of inserting the vampire as crudely constructed palimpsest, further investigation reveals otherwise. In fact such are the number of threads, editorial space and word limits precludes an unpacking of all of those contained in this text. Hence only the salient elements will be discussed.

From the outset the visual paratextual facets of this text act as an initial bundled icon or metaphor of the vampire, which in turn then becomes a "read thread" through the entire text. This bundle acts an iconic threshold concept, inviting the reader to cross a threshold of possibilities and move on to following pages (Genette). While paratext is always "a treasure trove of questions without answers" (Genette 4), it also the mechanism through which we can reflectively explore what Sarbin (15) calls our "believed in imaginings." The first visual fiber in the paratextual bundle is the use of the same set of images on both the front cover and title page which shows the typical depiction of Dick and Jane running happily, with a vampire behind them with his arms outstretched in an apparent attempt to grab them. The Count in these "images as icons" is revealed with what has now become the eponymous representation with the "widow's peak and the cape" that has "become so closely associated with the vampire that they can be set onto a purple puppet (The Count, *Sesame Street*) or a green cartoon duck (*Count Duckula*)" (Stuart 181). Even at first glance, this centrally aligned representation of the Count is one of uncertainty. While there is the symbolism of menace and consumption, Dracula appears to act as a being that seeks to gather in and save. With the majority of his body illustrated in the top half of the page denoting happiness and spirituality (Bang), this illustration is also unstable in nature. Not only has the vampiric visual been placed in the center of the framed page denoting stasis and permanence, but his feet have been drawn below the ground surface also typically suggesting instability and lacking grounding (Strube) or sadness (Bang). This spatial location of uncertainty, motion to make contact with the children and apparent motifs of instability entangled with a marker of stasis suggests the notion of contagion.

The vampire has become emblematic of a range of current contagion issues such as viral contamination (Stephanou), capitalism (Fisher) and terrorism (J. Edwards), with the single thread connecting these representations being the notion that a single point of contact corrupts. As Fisher states, the monstrous of any kind is "an infinitely plastic entity, capable of metabolizing and absorbing anything with which it comes into contact ... a strange hybrid of the ultra-modern and the archaic" (12). However, the vampire is more than just contagion by the slightest touch, because as Douglas suggests, its symbolic role has always been to represent that which "order to disorder, being to non-being, form to formlessness, life to death" (5). For Abbott, this is a critical aspect of the vampire, in that it is "eternally able to reshape and resurrect itself" (Abbott 209). Thus, this paratext has perhaps begun to suggest the shift out of more recent vampiric symbolism into a linkage between immortality and technology, to a current awareness that the vampire has begun to be a marker of technology, which has increasingly enabled suspension of both life and death through cryonics (Stephanou), or the relatively recent practice of induced coma.

It is in reference to this interspace or interstitial interval between life to death and form to formless that would appear to be a small semantic leap, but as Deardorff suggests, is vital aspect of both human evolution and the role of the vampire in its symbolic forms. As Deardorff understands the human condition, one of the key transformative developments is the "spiral dance of the spirit" (171) in which authentic human growth or genuine "ways of knowing" (171) requires a breaking down, deformation and wounding of the collective soul formation in order to create a new imagination of being and belonging. In his work on religious and spiritual movements across the globe, Partridge is of a similar opinion in that there is a current uncertainty and sense of "life and death betweeness," which is directly related to a worldwide surfacing of vampire symbology. As he sees it is the surfacing of all things vampiric is related to the global desire for young people to be more spiritually connected given "their sense of disenfranchisement with established religion and rampant consumerism" (Stephanou 167).

In the second paratextual configuration of the "gaze," only the vampire is looking directly at the reader with the children's eyes focused off the page and the right. As shown in the appendices, the direct "gaze" acts as an engagement facet demanding attention. Typical of the cinematic gaze of vampires with their demands used "to emphasize both their power over their victims and their desire for blood" (94), there is another visual intertwining in this text which suggests a shift in this text to a symbolic act of surveillance and protection. The eyes of the vampire in this text are never menacing but much more open than in other textual forms, which in children's literature tends to suggest an awakening from a dream or dream like state. This gaze occurs as suggestion that there is both a cultural and personal void, a liminal state related to authenticity of self, with the visual implication that the viewer must awaken to a new understanding. In discussing this notion, and its role in text, Blanchott believes that this focus reveals that in engaging with the visual "we find ourselves in the situation of strangers; and we are strangers precisely because the dreamer's self lacks any sense of true self. One could almost say that there is nobody in the dream and therefore, in a certain fashion, that there is nobody to dream it" (xxiv–xv). Clearly, this gaze is emblematic of the vampire being the ultimate liminal stranger. The gaze of the vampire is never a one focused viewpoint, but emblematic of the relationship it has with the human condition. In other words, while in narrative even though the gaze is often out of frame or out of the page, representing the "life that is" but also "is not," the vampiric gaze has changed. As Abbott notes;

> The vampire in the 1970s must work hard to conceal his existence from modern surveillance and he does it by becoming the surveyor ... the automated quality of his surveillance, as his gaze demonstrates none of the bloodlust of his vampire predecessors. His stare is neutral and everything around him is given equal attention [95].

The vampiric gaze is always relational, and while in the past the gaze has been directed at specific humans and human conditions, the new vampiric gaze is directed to all. To some degree the cover on Dick and Jane possibly exemplifies this. While the children are refusing are looking away in ignorance, they are reflecting Deardorff's notion that the emblematic reference to the children is the current need to "prize open the oppression of history's monumental closure" (177). For Thomassen, whether we know it or not, or see it or not, the role of the monster has always been to bring us into the liminal experience they inhabit to turn us from "that which characterizes cultural life in our contemporary context" (2).

It seems that *Dick and Jane* have perhaps become a component of the entire visual vampiric narrative that have also come to represent not only rampant consumerism but a lack of authentic relationships. In regard to the latter, this not encompasses one to one relationships and familial ties, but also the lack of connectivity with those who are not white or middle class (Arrow). Indeed, there has been a persistent string of researchers such as Sidney Matrix and Michelle Arrow who believe that the visual emotional inability represents the setting up walls and barriers to the outside world as a whole, and the dystopic nature of the feminine within American culture. To return to the Australian context, Scutter believes much the same as the previous researchers, sensing there is shift towards a "monstrous paradigm" in antipodean children's literature. In this paradigm shift of textual superficiality, she believes the related subtext of the absent mother in general and the concept of authentic family relationships in particular are being "pushed to the margins" (Scutter 201). The lack of ability of the Stepford female or Stepford family in text represents the creation of psycho-emotional walls for the children in these families both real and imagined, thus creating an inability to attach emotionally or be affected emotionally (Silver). Interestingly, Phillips comments that this lack or inability "will often graft its affects onto the self in a manner that may be at once paralyzing and quantitatively monster producing" (187). It is the familial setting of *Dick and Jane* that the monster appears with its paucity of affection, that the children are gazing into the unknown, looking for the impossible to find the essence of the material culture that is "the construction of the American counterfeit" (Balkun 28). While children's literature often suggests that sameness and "familiar old home is best" (Wu, Mallan and McGillis 50), this text suggests otherwise. Is it any wonder that the archetypal monster appears in this version of *Dick and Jane*, representing both the benevolent and the beast, and that which was lost and that which needs to resurface.

It is in these two visual facets the reader is introduced to the hybridity of the vampire and all monsters. Stallybrass and White believe that is always the nature of the monstrous which is "a boundary phenomenon of hybridization or inmixing in which self and other become enmeshed in an inclusive, heterogeneous, dangerously unstable zone" (193). In what should be the most stable and supportive of fields, this simple children's text actually reveals chronic cultural issues around abandonment and detachment and childhood, which as Doonan suggests is revealed in many texts for children. The current trans-national narrative as a whole and especially as it relates to children, has seen Dracula become both monster and almost motherly in appearance. This spectrum lies at the heart of who the vampire actually is. This visual representation as a whole and as seen in *Dick and Jane and Vampires,* has morphed into an almost universal string of mythic imagination representing either evil and uncertainty, or a benign friend of children. This spectrum as a whole and not the image of evil alone is the most dangerous aspect of the monster. When it achieves actuality through human agency it achieves an inexplicable power: a "conflictual doubling, and at times [through] the possibility of a hybridity that might transform conflict into a disquieting, risky merger, whose results are unpredictable" (Riquelme 10). Indeed, further unpacking of the text reveals that indeed this paratextual inference is a precursory marker of the hybridity of childhood and the cultural narratives of Western cultures that have created a situation in which childhood growth and development is viewed as both a "risky business" and the realm of the monstrous. Dracula, denoting all monsters, is "no longer shut away and made safe" (Cohen 256), but as inferred in this instance of paratext, free to engage in and become a part of a much more universal "myth of idyllic childhood" (Brewer 23). In more culturally specific sense of Americana, Coontz suggests, this is "the way we never were" (xxxiv).

Further extending the notion of a safe and idyllic childhood, a critical paratextual clue lies in the title of the book in which the vampire is named in the plural form. Throughout the majority of the text there is only a singular representation of the vampire until the final pages where he is framed as heterosexual having found a female companion, who also appears as a vampiric image. This simple use of a plural form of language gives voice to the ideal that Dracula has long entered the realm of hyper-reality in that what was once entirely symbolic has become so universally simulated and circulated to the point where the symbolism of it means to be a vampire is uncertain. As Stephanou states, the current vampire myth is "caught in the tendrils of bio-political production, hybridity and new identities are not only promoted and celebrated, but also become increasingly ordinary and assimilated within a system that devours and corporatizes difference" (116–117). This single use of language turns the symbolism of the vampire from a noun to a gerund, and in one linguistic turn summarizes Strobe's assertion that "there is no such creature as 'the Vampire'; there are only vampires" (135).

However, with the vast Dracula amount of adaptations consuming the cultural memories of the archetypal "drinker of blood" across the globe, Ellis' comment that this hybridity is actually "aiming to efface itself with the presence of its own images" (3) seems more apt. The plural naming of the vampire on this front cover with its obvious linkage via the children to a nostalgic past could also symbolically coagulate the reflective paratextual possibility that the plurality of the vampire is seeking to devour itself. Without any presence of blood in any of the visual aspects, could this simply paratext suggest the need to "open new veins of signification in the otherwise exhausted and dry landscape of vampire scholarship" (Stephanou 1). In this instance the reader is asked to perhaps consider the possibility that while there a sense of security in the old these belief structures need to be swept away, and that the truth of human stasis actually lies in the symbolism of the vampire without any of the spiritual associations to the partaking of blood. Instead, as Partridge believes, the vampire generation is indeed "in search of spirituality, in search of that which transcends history" (143). He further writes that the current fascination with the vampire "represents a protest against the authority of any particular religion and its claims of truth in a religiously pluralistic world" (130).

The Metatextual and Intertextual Linkages in *Dick and Jane*

Following on from the paratextual inferences, a simplistic set of linked images flows through the ensuing pages, which belies a complex web of metaphoric and metonymic interplays. In the ensuing pages and images the shift from the vampiric hint of malevolence combined with the maternal shifts even further into transtextual inferences of the archetypal images of the vampire continue with related culturally out of date images of the children and family life, with the children gradually engaging with the vampire in their daily activities, and actually engaging through a direct gaze.

The first key metatextual link is in the image of the Count as a bat. The father of the family, without any pictorial presence of the mother, implores the children to "come and see" a bat. Both Dick and Jane question their father as to what the thing is with language reminiscent of the introduction to the 1950s Superman television program: "Look, up in the sky." Saunders believes that this sentence still "evokes the character in the minds of millions" (21). Just as the vampire represents a challenge to the status quo, so too the very image of Superman and his superpowers present such a powerful challenge to conservative elements in America during the 1950s both the comic book series and television programs "were forced to take him in a less radical direction" (21). Thus, the vampire symbol is metatextually equated with the superhero most equated with representing the state, the American way and conservatism (Tye), and the absent nature of the Stepford wife. All of these conjoined aspects represent the shallow and superfluous nature of conservative America, and their continued representation in all forms of media and popular culture (Vint). The textual thread of absence and lack of emotional attachment continues in the exhortation of the father "to come and see," but when they look over the fence the bat is not shown. Blindness to what is actually over the metaphoric fence of exclusion is further embellished when in the next section Spot the dog can sense that something is hiding in a bush, but both the animal and the children are unable to see the head of the Count is peering out. The dog runs away when the vampire as a bat emerges, and still the children are unable to see the image of the bat.

The inability to see the vampire, again portrayed in a benevolent form, is indicative of not so much the current nostalgic view of American childhood, but one of entrapment of in supposed innocence. In this perspective, there can be no difference; just the ongoing enforcement of heterosexuality, Christian norms and gender divides. Just as the children peer over the fence that actually has them trapped, and into the small bush, but unable to see the reality in front of them so too in this unknowing landscape precludes children from any understanding of the adult world they are encased in, or any chance of change. In this sequence the act of simply seeing reflects the emergence of the vampire as the means of liberation to the point of being messianic in nature: the freedom to emerge from the established borders, boundaries, false ordering and prohibition. One of the roles of the monstrous in general, and the symbolism of the vampire in particular has always been to liberate, and in this instance the children are exemplars of the possibility of actually living in the world, rather than being cardboard and fatuous actors they are superficially cast as in the surface level reading of this text. The monstrous in fairy tales has always been to allow children to engage with the darker issues of life and thus gain emotional and cognitive control over their sensory reaction to the world they live. The Disneyfication and Stepfordication of popular culture related to children do not allow for this, and so children are trapped in "fenced in cultural narratives." "To live such a life is to isolate ourselves from family and friends, impeding our own identity formations and damaging the growth and development of not only our personalities, but also our future and all its possibilities" (Howarth 52).

Numerous researchers have made the intertextual connection between the particular cultural form of ongoing American humor in an array of texts that include *Dick and Jane*, children's magazines and television, all of which serve "to invoke the 1950s-style suburban situation comedy as a metaphor for exploring the repressions and assorted neuroses of contemporary American suburbia" (Beuka 228). Indeed, Postman believes that the 1950s advent of television, in American households heralded the end of authentic childhood.

This medium requires no genuine "seeing" or reflection, and became the grand master of socializing all who watched it, transforming the American culture into pure consumerism. The language and visual elements shared by adults and children simply became the enabler of entrapment in, or behind a metaphorical fence of "unknowing" and "unbeing." As Postman further states "all assumptions of coherence have vanished. And so, perforce, has contradiction. In the context of no context, so to speak, it simply disappears" (10). In a similar sense, just as the vampire contains two opposing states within one body (life and death), so too the vampire in this text represents the disembodied state of childhood. As stated previously, "deformed discourse" resides in all of us but particularly in childhood with its often incoherent or discordant emotions related to death, sexuality and sense of place in the world (Howarth 2014). Just as the monster "arises at times of category crisis" (Cohen 6) so to Dracula appears in this text as the constant reminder that within the Western social imaginary children are still part of the dead space of liminal exclusion which Uebel has termed the "unthought" (264). The vampire representations in this particular text reveals that the cultural and deeply personal sense of self for children has "exteriorized and shut away."

Another ensuing intertextual and hypertextual linkage is the morphing of the vampire in this particular text into a double binary representation. The next definitive appearance of the vampire is in the form of a shadow radiating from Jane. Linking the time setting of this children's book and cinematic period, this obviously demonic form is almost an exact replica of the staircase shadow of the vampire in Murnau's film, *Nosferatu: A Symphony of Terror*. In a generic narrative sense, the vampiric essence of this shadow represents the captivity of the vampire and the related captivity of "humans, who are imprisoned in shadows, are eventually led into the light (the Undead Presence) where they then recognize the truth of their world (Vampiric control)" (Temple of the Vampire 3). While the vampire representations can typically be seen as a process that moves from captivity to agency "through these inbetween spaces of matrial folds" (Stephanou 47), the shadow related to a vampiric aspect in the Australian context is often seen to represent an emblem of being a "guilt inducing shadow of real mother's lives" (Thurer 97). With only the male child able to see the actual shadow, the message is somewhat unambiguous, but when viewed through the lens of the feminine is somewhat different. In specific terms, this shadow's linkage to the feminine is a typical reference to the enslavement of the feminine, or the degrading of the feminist movement (Peruccio).

In more general terms related to the social incarceration of woman is the overarching metaphoric meaning often referred to as the current "entrapment of global capitalism" (Stephanou 120). While concurring with this this relationship, Lott believes this understanding and application has deeper roots, which "signify the shadows of white American life in the 1940s" (85). While there is a cultural linkage with these ideals, the reversal in *Dick and Jane* of the entire notion of the vampire unable to exist in sunlight, the vampiric order sets in train a new metaphoric concept. In other words, the old American conservative order needs to be broken, with its seemingly unrelenting control over "gender, race, ethnicity, history power and religion" (Mutch 9). However, Mutch digs deeper into the trope and the application to its concurrent realization, believing that at the heart of all these divides is the concept of spirituality, which is embedded in all aspects of *Noir*: "*Noir* specifically spoke to what was perceived as a spiritual divide within American society where 'White' is necessarily seen as good and 'Black' is evil or ungodly" (116) As noted by Abbott, "*Nosferatu* similarly uses the image of the shadow to equate the vampire to a shadow of humanity" (52) which is carried forward in *Dick and Jane* in that the Nosferatu image is linked to Jane's feet. The theme of the vampire being coded as feminine has continued throughout this text with the implication that "here is a cartographic grid map of a disturbed psyche going on" (Scutter 243). Heather Scutter brings this metaphor back to an Australian perspective when she qualifies the incongruity of this disturbed textual mindset, stating that it is "sort of redneck Queensland meets Dracula" (243).

While a reader-viewer was invited to look closely at the vampire in the paratextual sequences, there are no eyes in this Nosferatu like portrayal of the shadow. At the most simplistic level of polyvalent meaning, this shadow with no eyes is unable to attract attention, and is clearly caught in a state of liminality between human and non-human. While continuing on the theme of connecting the feminine to the monstrous in vampire texts in the frame of this child-like narrative, only Dick can see the monstrous shadow. As with all monstrous states, there is also a disruption of the social order, and so in a following page the shadow has departed, Jane has lost her shoe and so is now free to act on her own. An apparent fundamental concern of our current age has become a free agent through the dislodgement of an unseeing authority. As revealed in the previous images and in this text as a whole, the constant morphing of the vampire images speaks to the possibility of a new mindset in an emerging generation that in actuality is suspended between multiple forms and identities, and threatens to shatter all cultural distinctions. While not yet realized, perhaps there will arise a generation who accept the "dichotomy between the base elements of the mind, the impulses and consciousness, whose role is to control the mind" (Cohen 215). As per the children in this text, the more closely the Stepford influence seeks to rope children into "conformity and rigidity" and ensuing "stress and incoherence" (Maden 83), the more likely it is they will eventually become the emancipatory vampire and the disturbing hybrids "collapsing the differences between "Self" and "Other" (Gelder 43).

Conclusion: A Dead End?

To reiterate and summarize, like childhood itself the notion of what constitutes quality children's literature is a contested space. While never going to win literature awards and however seemingly vacuous, the *Dick and Jane and Vampires* text appears its use of the vampire image as a carrier of deep socio-cultural characteristics, and clearly incorporates personal issues and cultural concerns related to the need for change and social shifts. It is these spaces of vampiric insertion that literature allows children to grow into an understanding of self and out of childhood. While young children may not be able to read per se they are able to absorb and infer possible meanings, with the visual elements of text generating emotional contacts that "reflect the world and construct possible models of the world" (Wu, Mallan and McGillis 4). For C.S. Lewis the narratives that engender these possibilities "are spiritual explorations, and the most life like since they reveal human life as seen, or felt, or divined from the inside" (Bettelheim 24).

This simplicity of the spiritual message of *Dick and Jane* in this instance is the vampiric reply to the debilitating incursion and saturation of sameness into the reality of everyday life: these "in-between" spaces provide the terrain for elaborating strategies of selfhood singular or communal—that initiate new signs of identity, and innovative sites of collaboration, and contestation, in the act of defining the idea of society itself (Bhabha 2).

Appendix A

Visual Literacy Tools	*Characteristics*
Tool 1—Actions and Vectors	Within each illustration the focus is what is happening within the image itself. Usually, there is some type of ACTION going on. Within the image there are lines that lead the eye towards this action. These lines are known as VECTORS and can be thick or thin, light or dark and serve to lead the eye towards this action. Lines are used to suggest direction, show movement, create energy or establish a mood.
Tool 2—Concept	Iconic in nature, images are created to indicate a holistic CONCEPT rather than an action.

Visual Literacy Tools	Characteristics
Tool 3—Angles	Also linked with height, angles enable the reader to gain a sense of power, position, vulnerability, movement, direction and emotion.
Tool 4—Framing or Cropping	Framing limits the amount of information available to the viewer as well as signaling some type of social relationship with reader. Long Shots: Are those that show the subject in full figure and at a distance from the viewer, these type of shots give the perception of a more public type of distance. Medium Shots: These are shots that frame the upper half of the body. These type of shots show a more social type of distance. Close Up Shots: These type of shots are usually head and shoulders and suggest a much more intimate and personal relationship to the viewer.
Tool 5—Demands and Offers	The composition of an image affects the viewer in several ways. Images that appear to be making eye contact with the viewer are said to be making a demand for your attention. When the eyes in the image look elsewhere, or when there are no creatures or people in the image this is termed an offer. Here the viewer feels free to look at a range of other elements first.

Appendix B

Intertextual Category	Reflective Linkage
Paratextual Suggestive and interpretative aspects of visual or written text on the title pages and end pages	Book Covers/Title Page serving as points of reflection What do the illustrations, images and text suggest? What aspects appear out of the frame or page? What are the key themes? How is the reader invited to participate in the text?
Metatextual Linkages of meaning or comment within a text	Relationships between the written language, the written language and illustrations and strings of illustrations What strings of meaning appear or are created throughout the text? Does the written text match the illustrations?

Intertextual Category	Reflective Linkage
	What are the layers of meaning? What is the relationship between the paratext and the strings of text/illustrations in the text?
Intertextuality	Relationships between the written language, the written language and illustrations in two or more texts
Linkages of meaning between a text and other texts	How does the language and illustrations in one text draw on and then compare, share, contrast and shape meaning? What are the layers of meaning in one text as alluded to in others?
Archtextual Linkages of meaning between single texts and other genres	Relationships between various genres that develop a macrogenre, establishing purpose(s) How have other genres contributed to meaning? How do illustrations in other genres shape a larger meaning and text type?
Hypotextual Linkages between a text or genre that then transforms or transliterates it	Relationships between one text and others that blend or form a pastiche, blurs boundaries that are seamlessly combined What aspects of text or illustrations reflect, echo and/or combine into a new text, or translate existing tropes into a new metanarrative?

Tools of Transtextuality and the Means of Forging Connective Meanings (Adapted from Gerard [1992]).

Note

1. The overarching term "Stepford" entered the language of film and literature as a trope of feminine submission soon after the release of the remake of the original film in 2004 (Short). For researchers in the Australian field of children's literature the term tends to encompass any and all glorification or representations of the narrow familial conservative views of the "nostalgic 1950's" (Martin 134).

Works Cited

Abbott, Stacey. *Celluloid Vampires: Life After Death in the Modern World.* Austin: University of Texas, 2007.

Anderson, M.T. "Point of Departure." *Handbook of Children's and Young Adult Literature.* Ed. Shelby Wolf, Karen Coats, Patricia Enciso, and Christine Jenkins. London: Routledge, 2010. 372–374.

Arrow, Michelle. *What Happened to the Revolution? Seventies Culture of Crisis.* Sydney: Macquarie University, 2013.

Balkun, Mary. *The American Counterfeit: Authenticity and Identity in American Literature and Culture.* Tuscaloosa: University of Alabama Press, 2006.

Bang, Molly. *Picture This: Perception & Composition.* Boston: Little Brown, 1991.

Bettelheim, Bruno. *The Use of Enchantment: The Meaning and Importance of Fairy Tales.* New York: Vintage, 1976.
Beuka, Robert. *SuburbiaNation: Reading Suburban Landscape in Twentieth-Century American Fiction and Film.* New York: Palgrave Macmillan, 2004.
Bhabha, Homi K. *The Location of Culture.* London: Routledge, 1994.
Blanchot, Maurice. "Dreaming, Writing." *Nights as Day, Days as Night.* Ed. Michel Leiris. Trans. Richard Sieburth. Italy: Eridanos Press, 1987. xix–xxviii.
Blumenfeld, Samuel. *The Victims of Dick and Jane and Other Essays.* Valecito, CA: Chalcedon, 2003.
Born, Thomassen. *Liminality and the Modern: Living Through the Inbetween.* Surrey, England: Ashgate, 2014.
Bradford, Clare. *Unsettling Narrative: Postcolonial Readings of Children's Literature.* Waterloo, Ontario: Wilfrid Laurier University Press, 2007.
Brewer, Elizabeth. *T.H. White's The Once and Future King.* Cambridge: D.S. Brewer, 1993.
Britton, James. *Language and Learning,* 2nd edition. Portsmouth: Boynton-Cook, 1993.
Clark, Maureen. "Postcolonial Vampires in the Indigenous Imagination: Philip McLaren and Drew Hayden Taylor." *Transnational and Postcolonial Vampires: Dark Blood.* Ed. Tabish Khair and Johan Hoglund. London: Palgrave Macmillan, 2013. 121–137.
Cohen, Jeffrey. *Monster Theory: Reading Culture.* Minneapolis: University of Minnesota Press.
Coontz, Stephanie. *The Way We Never Were: American Families and the Nostalgia Trap.* New York: Basic Books, 2000.
Deardorff, Daniel. *The Other Within: The Genius of Deformity in Myth, Culture and Psyche.* Berkeley, CA: North Atlantic Books, 2008.
DeMause, Lloyd. *The History of Childhood: The Evolution of Parent-Child Relationships as a Factor in History.* London: Souvenir Press, 1974.
Doonan, Jane. "Into the Dangerous World: We Are All in the Dumps with Jack and Guy." *Signal* 75. (1994). 155–171.
Douglas, Mary. *Purity and Danger: An Analysis of Concepts of Pollution and Taboo.* London: Routledge, 1966.
Edwards, Gail. "Reading Canadian: Children and National Literature in the 1920's." *Children and Cultural Memory in Texts of Childhood.* Ed. Heather Snell and Lorna Hutchinson. London: Routledge, 2013. 15–32.
Edwards, Justin. "Canada, Quebec and David Cronebeberg's Terrorist-Vampires." *Transnational and Postcolonial Vampires: Dark Blood.* Ed. Tablish Khair and Johan Hoglund. New York: Palgrave Macmillan, 2013. 67–80.
Ellis, Carolyn, and Arthur Bochner. "Analyzing Analytic Autoethnography: An Autopsy." *Journal of Contemporary Ethnography* 35 (2006): 429–449.
Ellis, John. "The Literary Adaptation: An Introduction." *Screen* 23.1 (1982): 3–5.
Feeney, Stephanie, and Eva Moravcik. "Children's Literature." *Young Children* 60.5 (2005): 20–28.
Fetterman, David. *Ethnography Step by Step.* Thousand Oaks, CA: SAGE, 2009.
Fisher, Mark. *Capitalist Realism: Is There No Alternative?* Hampshire, Winchester: Zero Books, 2009.
Fitzsimmons, Phil. "What Adolescents Are Reading and What Their Teachers Are Not: Between the Deformed Discourse and the Disdain of the Graphic Novel." *Literacy in the Middle Years* 15.2 (2007): 18–22.
Foster, John, Ern Finnis, and Maureen Nimon. *Bush, City, Cyberspace: The Development of Australian Children's Literature into the Twenty-First Century.* Wagga Wagga, Australia: Charles Sturt University Press, 2005.
Foucault, Michael. *The Archaeology of Knowledge.* London: Tavistock, 1974.
Geekie, Peter, Brian Cambourne, and Phil Fitzsimmons. *Understanding Literacy Development.* London: Trentham, 1999.
Gelder, Ken. *Reading the Vampire.* London: Routledge, 1994.
Genette, Gérard. *The Architext: An Introduction.* Berkeley: University of California Press, 1992.

Harris, Pauline, and Barbra McKenzie. "Networking Around the Waterhole and Other Tales: The Importance of Relationships Among Texts for Reading and Related Instruction." *Literacy* 39.1 (2005): 31–37.

Hirschmann, Chris. *Vampires in Literature*. Mankato: Capstone, 2011.

Howarth, Michael. *Under the Bed, Creeping: Psychoanalyzing the Gothic in Children's Literature*. Jefferson, NC: McFarland, 2014.

Jeffers, Oliver. *The Heart and the Bottle*. New York: HarperCollins, 2010.

Johnston, Jessica, and Cornelia Sears. "The Stepford Wives and the Technoscientific Imaginary." *Extrapolation* 52.1 (2011): 75–93.

Kavaldo, Jesse. *American Popular Culture in the Era of Terror: Falling Skies, Dark Knights Rising and Collapsing Cultures*. Santa Barbara: Praeger, 2015.

Lewis, Clive S. *The Allegory of Love*. Oxford: Oxford University Press, 1936. Cited Bruno Bettelheim. *The Use of Enchantment: The Meaning and Importance of Fairy Tales*. New York: Vintage, 1976.

Lott, Eric. "The Whiteness of Film Noir." *Whiteness: A Critical Reader*. Ed. Mike Hill. New York: New York University Press, 1997. 81–101.

Maden, Michael. "The Challenge of Children in the Education System." *Children and the State: Whose Problem?* Ed. Jane Tunstill. London: Cassell, 1999.

Marchesani, Laura. *Dick and Jane and Vampires*. New York: Grosset and Dunlap, 2010.

Martin, Linda Wagner. *A History of American Literature*. Oxford: Blackwell Wiley, 2012.

Matrix, Sidney. "'Behind the Idyllic Façade, a Terrible Secret': Technologies of Gender and Discourses of Domesticity in 'The Stepford Wives.'" *Storytelling* 6.2 (2007): 109–119.

Moran, Albert, and Errol Vieth. *Film in Australia: An Introduction*. Cambridge: Cambridge University Press, 2006.

Mutch, Deborah, ed. *The Modern Vampire and Human Identity*. New York: Palgrave Macmillan, 2013.

Niemi, Loren, and Elisabeth Ellis. *Inviting the Wolf In: Thinking About Difficult Stories*. Atlanta: August House, 2000.

Nyoongah, Mudrooroo. *The Undying*. Sydney, Australia: Angus & Robertson, 1988.

Partridge, Christopher. *The Re-Enchantment of the West, Vol. II*. London: T&T Clark, 2005.

Peruccio, Kara. "Big Screen, Little Boxes: Hollywood Representations of the Suburban Housewife, 1960–1975." *History Matters* (2011): 54–94.

Phillips, Thomas. *Liminal Fictions in Postmodern Culture: The Politics of Self-Development*. New York: Macmillan, 2015.

Postman, Neil. *Amusing Ourselves to Death—Public Discourse in the Age of Show Business*. London: Heinemann, 1986.

Riquelme, John-Paul. "Dark Modernity from Mary Shelley to Samuel Beckett: Gothic History, the Gothic Tradition, and Modernism." *Gothic and Modernism: Essaying Dark Literary Modernity*. Ed. John-Paul Riquelme. Baltimore: Johns Hopkins University Press, 2008 8–28.

Roberts, Chris. *Heavy Words Lightly Thrown: The Reason Behind the Rhyme*. New York: Gotham, 2006.

Rolls, Mitchell. "The Green Thumb of Appropriation." *The Littoral Zone: Australian Contexts and Their Writers*. Ed. Cranston Zeller and Robert Zeller. Amsterdam: Rodopi, 2007. 93–122.

Rose, Jacqueline, *The Case of Peter Pan or the Impossibility of Children's Fiction*. Philadelphia: University of Philadelphia Press, 1993.

Sarbin, Theodore. *Believed-In Imaginings: The Narrative Construction of Reality*. Washington, DC: American Psychological Association, 1988.

Saunders, Ben. *Do the Gods Wear Capes? Spirituality, Fantasy and Superheroes*. New York: Continuum, 2011.

Scheckter, John. *The Australian Novel 1830–1980: A Thematic Introduction*. New York: Peter Lang Publishing, 1998.

Schweishelm, Kathryn. "Remaking the Stepford Wives, Remodeling Feminism." *Film Remakes, Adaptations and Fan Productions: Remake/Remodel*. Ed. Kathleen Loock and Constantine Verevis. New York: Palgrave Macmillan, 2012. 107–121.

Scutter, Barbara. *Displaced Fictions*. Melbourne: Melbourne University Press, 1999.
Short, Sue. *Cyborg Cinema and Contemporary Subjectivity*. New York: Palgrave Macmillan, 2005.
Stallybrass, Peter, and Allen White. *The Politics and Poetics of Transgression*. Ithaca, NY: Cornell University Press, 1986.
Stephanou, Aspasia. *Reading the Vampire Through Blood*. New York: Palgrave McMillan, 2014.
Strübe, Katrin. *After Nightfall*. Marburg: Tectum Verlag, 2006.
Stuart, Roxana. *Stage Blood: Vampires of the 19th-Century Stage*. Bowling Green, OH: Bowling Green State University Popular Press, 1994.
Temple of the Vampire. *The Vampire Bible*. Lacey, WA: Temple of the Vampire, 1989.
Thomson, Philip. *The Grotesque*. London: Methuen, 1972.
Thurer, Shari L. *The Myths of Motherhood: How Culture Reinvents the Good Mother*. New York: Penguin, 1994.
Toppo, Gregg. *USA Today*, 2 June 2004. http://usatoday30.usatoday.com/life/books/news/2004-02-25-dick-and-jane-main_x.htm. Accessed 2 September 2015.
Turner, Graeme. *National Fictions: Literature, Film, and the Construction of Australian Narrative*. Sydney: Allen and Unwin, 1986.
Tye, Larry. *Superman: The High-Flying History of America's Most Enduring Hero*. New York: Random House, 2012.
Uebel, Michael. "Unthinking the Monster: Twelfth Century Response to Saracen Alterity." *Monster Theory: Reading Culture*. Ed. Jeffrey Cohen. Minneapolis: University of Minnesota Press, 1996. 264–291.
Van Manen, Max. *Researching Lived Experience: Human Science for an Action Sensitive Pedagogy*. Albany: State University of New York Press, 1990.
Victoria State Government. Public Record Office. Victoria. *Fun with Dick and Jane Readers*. Melbourne: Victorian Archives, 2 May 2012. readershttp://prov.vic.gov.au/blog-only/fun-with-dick-and-jane-readers. Accessed 2 September 2015.
Vint, Sherryl. "The New Backlash: Popular Culture's 'Marriage' with Feminism, or Love Is All You Need." *Journal of Popular Film and Television* 34.4 (2007): 160–169.
Wark, McKenzie. "Virtual Empire." *Americanization and Australia*. Ed. Phillip Bell and Roger Bell. Sydney: University of New South Wales Press, 1998. 261–276.
Wu, Yan., Kerry Mallan, and Roderick McGillis. "The World Is Never Too Much for Us": *(Re)Imagining the World Children's Literature's Response to Changing Times*. London: Springer, 2013.
Zornado, Joseph. *Inventing the Child: Culture, Ideology and the Story of Childhood*. London: Garland Publishing, 2000.

The Dhampir Gets His Fangs
Miscegenation and Exogamy in the Hotel Transylvania Film Franchise

Mark Chekares

Introduction: Cultural Dominance from California to the Carpathians

Despite uneven and divisive critical reviews, Sony Animation Studio's *Hotel Transylvania* franchise has raked in a monstrous $320 million dollars at the domestic box office, and nearly half a billion dollars worldwide.[1] Those are some scarily good numbers for two animated children's films that are heavy on monster puns, cartoon slapstick, and toilet humor that Adam Sandler is so famous for. Sandler voices the iconic vampire Count Dracula in the films, who is less a bloodsucking threat, and more of a creepy overprotective and domineering father to his vampire daughter Mavis (Selena Gomez). Not so thinly veiled in these films is an iconological pedagogy, one that is often difficult to analyze and disseminate. As J. Zornado notes, children's animated films always contain a symbolic meaning toward a larger pedagogical intension by the dominant culture. He argues that "iconology understands the animated feature as a perfect merging of ideology and pedagogy both in the way the animated feature represents pedagogy in terms of narrative while enacting pedagogy in terms of the positioning of the spectator as one in a community of passive recipients of the film screen's action" (2). In other words what hidden pedagogy does the film relay to its target audience, children? Iconography is a broad way to analyze an animated film, but in the HTF, the dialogue implies that there is fear of miscegenation between Johnny and Mavis, trepidation toward their child Dennis (Asher Blinkoff) appropriating important characteristics of cultural hybridity (in this case, human vs. monstrous traits), and in HT2 specifically, an implication that exogamy (marrying outside of one's "tribe") exists between the monsters and the humans in the form of anti-Semitic imagery and a use of stereotypical Yiddish accents.

It is important to note moving forward that there is a convoluted racial and cultural coding in these films. It is clearly demarcated that monsters and humans are of different cultures, and the subject is discussed in almost every line of Sandler's dialogue throughout the films. What may confuse viewers is which race the filmmakers are pushing to represent the dominant culture. The audience is human, but the protagonists are monsters. Which culture do we identify with? In narrative myth, humans have created monsters to warn of some unseen dangers, and more often than not, monstrous characters are othered by race, gender, religion, or sexuality, a trope that has continued throughout literary and cinematic history. As Dale Hudson notes,

> Vampires, werewolves, and other movie monsters serve as a means of acknowledging social difference without addressing it directly. Whether comedy or horror, relationships between humans and supernatural species offer ways to negotiate—and even contest—naturalized social inequalities, yet they can also serve as a way to ignore discursive and material legacies of these inequalities [66].

When Johnny marries and "earns" his monstrousness, does that designate humans as the dominant culture once again? If Dennis, his son, does not become a monster, have the monsters failed at preserving cultural dominance as the film (inconsistently) suggests? Curiously, in the HTF, Dracula is the one that casts aspersions on humanity throughout most of the narrative, initially isolating himself and Mavis in the hotel. With his daughter, he consistently reinforces the ideological assertion that monsters are a dominant race and it is the humans that are not equal. Dracula is distrustful of humans because his wife Martha was murdered by an angry mob of villagers for being a vampire. Subsequently, Dracula isolates himself from humanity and transforms his castle into a hotel for weary monsters to escape the daily grind of interacting with humans. In other words, the film is saying, the monsters have become more scared of the humans, than the humans are of the monsters. Fear in this movie franchise is best represented by Drac's xenophobic intolerance of humans. Surfer dude, Johnny, poses no actual threat to the hotel or Mavis; he is simply feared because he is different. Ultimately, it matters not whether monster culture or human culture is the dominant "race." Positions of power are fluid and change throughout the films. There are even social hierarchies within the monster race. Vampires sit atop (Dracula owns the hotel), while the drooling, grunting zombies make up the hotel staff and maintenance workers. What is important about these films is the constant tension between monsters and humans and what lessons kids may learn from these conflicts.

Fears in the Hotel: Monsters and Humans or Miscegenation and Exogamy?

Despite his attempts to cloister Mavis inside the hotel, she yearns to break free from Drac's parental clutches and interact with the human world. When Johnny inexplicably avoids all of Drac's trappings and stumbles into the hotel, Dracula quickly disguises him as one of the Frankensteins to conceal his identity. He later banishes him from the property to avoid the risk of the other monsters realizing there is a human guest amongst them. However, he and Mavis experience a "zing" (love at first sight) despite her father's glowering disapproval. This *Romeo and Juliet* trope, which the vampiric *Twilight* series also follows, leads to Drac desperately trying to rid himself of Johnny and "protect" his daughter. But eventually, he recognizes their love for one another. Despite the notion in the first film that Drac has learned his lesson and accepts humans, he exposes his grandson to dangerous and traumatic situations attempting to "force out" his vampirism, even though Dennis shows no signs of being a monster. He is the spitting image of his father, Johnny; a ruddy complexion, be-freckled, with a healthy tuft of orange hair. But if Dennis does not "get his fangs" by his fifth birthday, Drac will be stuck with a human grandchild, a reality which clearly bothers him. To complicate matters further, Drac's father Vlad (Mel Brooks) still retains an unhealthy hatred of humans which will be problematic for the family if he finds out that his grandson is not a vampire. In *HT2*, Johnny's human family, a WASPy clan of upper-middle class Californians attempt to embrace monster culture, but essentially they fall victim to their prejudices and aforementioned preconceived notions of what makes the other, monstrous.

By the end of *HT2*, we finally meet Grampa Vlad, a monster who would not tolerate the miscegenation that has occurred between Johnny and Mavis. However, Mavis desperately wants him to meet his great grandson, fangs or not. He receives Mavis' invitation and decides he will go to the hotel to meet Dennis. Voiced by Mel Brooks in his usual thick Yiddish accent, Vlad carries an enormously grotesque nose, and disproportionate chin; his skin has a feint purplish tint. It is implied that he has a foul odor about him. He is a quintessential Jewish stereotype. Vlad, much like his son the Count in *HT*, does not belong to the society he threatens (or in the case of the confusing dominant culture quagmire in the HTF, the culture he is threatened by). He represents an outsider even to monster culture, choosing to live in a cave around sycophantic bat-creatures, including henchman Bela (Rob Riggle), rather than interact with his son at the hotel. Brooks plays on the Jewish parents' penchant for disappointment in their children, commenting that Drac was "once the prince of darkness, now the king of room service." This outsider status, mixed with his cartoonishly exaggerated Jewish appearance and accent, place him directly within a stereotype of the Eastern European Jew. This is connect to a longstanding tradition in Victorian England and 19th-century Europe to link Jews with vampirism both iconographically and historically. At the time Bram Stoker wrote *Dracula*, no other demon was so prevalent in the collective imaginations of Britons than the vampire. Dracula became a metaphor for anti–Semitic anxieties and fears at the turn of the twentieth century (Libby-Robinson 16). And according to Peter Dan, "The eternal Jew and the vampire represent different forms of immortality: the Jews are virtually unchanged since the beginning of time and vampires cannot die on their own. They have certain physical characteristics in common: pallor and general unhealthy aspect, they wear black clothes and loathe the cross, holy water, and other symbols of Christianity" (1).

Historically, the correlation between Jews and early revenants can be traced to their symbolic connection with blood. Firstly fallacies about blood and blood type were perpetuated by Western European scientists who claimed that blood type dictated everything from physical appearance and features to personality types, proclivity for criminal behavior, and ability to form moral judgments (Libby-Robinson 23). They believed that blood types made it impossible to escape one's social caste, or to break a cycle of familial criminal activity or moral degradation. Peter Dan then notes that in this clear misunderstanding, "physical degradation always follows moral degradation even more so in the case of the Jews." Blood was seen as the "locus of heredity and race, the mixing of the inferior, Jewish blood with that of the superior blood of the host nation was seen as necessarily resulting in degeneracy" (6). Just as the vampire's bite transform the victim with its contagions, so the Jew's blood contaminates the Christian nation's blood, thus establishing the parallel between the monster and the Jew.[2]

In the HTF, the victims of the Count are predominantly young people, first Mavis as a young woman trapped in her own home, and later Dennis as a victim of his grandfather's social pressures. Libby-Robinson argues whereas Christian iconography in vampire fiction did not figure prominently in early nineteenth-century vampire lore, images of holy water, communion wafers, and crucifixes rose exponentially within the genre by the end of the century as an influx of Jewish immigrants began to inhabit Western Europe (24). Even though the HTF does not delve into the vampire's aversion to the cross to avoid any unwanted religious controversy from an animated children's film, the interactions between the Laughlans and the Draculas can be seen as contentious misunderstandings between gentile and Jew. When Vlad first meets Johnny's parents, he sniffs them, noting that they "smell funny." Linda replies—"oh, you're European ... it's called deodorant." Grampa Mike reprimands her for this, saying, "Nothing like insulting an entire continent Linda."

Worthy to note is that Linda is not in London or Paris, but in Eastern Europe, whose people and their migration to Western Europe were historically seen as threatening, and is one of the major symbolic motifs in Stoker's novel. Establishing that Vlad is an Eastern European Jew helps to dissect all the new culturally insensitive dialogue Sandler introduces, and read the Draculas as not a particular race per se, but as a different "tribe" of people. So this begs the question, do the Dracula's trepidations regarding Mavis and Johnny's marital and physical union represent deep rooted prejudice around miscegenation, where the monstrous "other" is a race, or does the coding of the Draculas as Jewish suggest that they are of the same "race," but exist in inherently different tribes with widely variant social norms and values? When Drac offers Mavis some "monster ball soup," does it represent a clever pun, or a culinary cultural tradition that demarcates the Draculas from the Laughlans? I argue it is the later, especially in regards to young Dennis' monstrous childhood development.

"New Vampirism": Dracula as Metaphorical Parasite

In order to investigate the complicated and problematic relationships between the vampires and humans, this study will investigate what kind of vampire Dracula and Mavis represent, because recently vampires have experienced a dramatic cultural makeover from both their mythical roots, and early literary popularity. Veronica Hollinger argues that the vampire has made the transition from the horror genre and entered the realm of Sci-Fi, but also genres of Romance, and in this case, Animated Comedy. This is impressive for a creature she compares to the devil, in regards to its popularity in mythos and literature as well as prominence in iconographical studies. She notes that "The Vampire, a less grandiose (than the devil) but equally horrific archetype, is one satanic figure which is currently enjoying a resurgence of literary and critical popularity, (the vampire) has occasionally crossed the border from fantasy to Sci-Fi, undergoing varieties of domestication..." (146). Certainly, most of the conflicts in the HTF are domestic in nature, so it is important to briefly track how vampires ceased to be agents of fear, and became loveable protagonists.

The scope of analyzing substantial literary descriptions of vampires is too broad for this study, but a lead up to Bram Stoker's description in his seminal novel is worth looking at, and informs the cultural relevance of the HTF's Draculas, the Count, Mavis and Vlad. John Polidori's "The Vampyre," widely considered to be the main inspiration for Stoker's tale, is one of the first vampire narratives. Polidori's Lord Ruthven is described as a nobleman who had a "dead grey eye" which "at one glance (pierced) through to the inward workings of the heart." He was a man who "had a deadly hue of his face, which never gave a warmer tint" (7). His appearance is later described as being "supernatural." Ruthven also possesses "evil power(s)" and had "irresistible powers of seduction" and "licentious habits" which Polidori concludes were "dangerous to society" (10). *Varney the Vampyre* by James Malcolm Rymer describes the titular character as "perfectly white—perfectly bloodless. The eyes look like polished tin; the lips are drawn back and the principal feature next to those dreadful eyes is the teeth—the fearful looking teeth—projecting like those of some wild animal, hideously glaringly white, and fang like" (29).

These descriptions of course lead to Bram Stoker's *Dracula*, a character who still haunts literature, film, and pop culture of today: "Within, stood a tall old man, clean shaven save for a long white moustache, and clad in black from head to foot, without a single speck of colour about him anywhere" (46). Stoker continues to shape the popular iconography as Jonathan Harker becomes more acquainted with his host, a host he initially believed to be warm and charming:

> His face was a strong, a very strong, aquiline, with high bridge of the thin nose and peculiarly arched nostrils, with lofty domed forehead, and hair growing scantily round the temples but profusely elsewhere. His eyebrows were very massive, almost meeting over the nose, and with bushy hair that seemed to curl in its own profusion. The mouth, so far as I could see it under the heavy moustache, was fixed and rather cruel-looking, with peculiarly sharp white teeth. These protruded over the lips, whose remarkable ruddiness showed astonishing vitality in a man of his years. For the rest, his ears were pale, and at the tops extremely pointed. The chin was broad and strong, and the cheeks firm though thin. The general effect was one of extraordinary pallor [Stoker 48].

This description of the pointed ears and protruding teeth made way for film vampires such as in the film *Nosferatu: A Symphony of Terror*, and later Universal's *Dracula*, which brought to the masses the Count's current iconography. The HTF Dracula is essentially Bela Lugosi in animated form. Noel Carroll adds to this iconological approach to the historical vampire by specifying where Count Dracula the character fits into the general category:

> The vampire of lore and the Dracula figure of stage and screen have several points of tangency, but Dracula also has a number of distinctive attributes. Of necessity, Dracula is Count Dracula. He is an aristocrat; his bearing is noble; and of course through hypnosis he is a paradigmatic authority figure. He is commanding in both senses of the word. Above all Dracula demands obedience of his minions and mistresses. He is extremely old-associated with ancient castles-and possessed of incontestable strength. Dracula cannot be overcome by force-he can only be outsmarted or outmaneuvered; humans are typically described as puny compared to him. At times, Dracula is invested with omniscience, observing from afar the measures taken against him [20].

Certainly all of these attributes are frightening within the genres of folklore and horror, but as Angela Tenga argues, if the motive of horror fiction is showing the audience things they have avoided seeing, "we would likely classify much of today's popular vampire fiction elsewhere" (77). This is true especially within the genre of the animated feature film, where monsters cease to be frightening, and become sympathetic, supporting, caring, and comedic. Mavis and Dracula both share mostly all of the traditional vampire qualities, but we view Mavis as a tolerant, caring daughter and mother, not a highly sexualized human bloodsucker. The same is true for Dracula, who is clearly the butt of many a joke in the HTF.

Tenga also contends that vampires like the Draculas in the HTF should be categorized as "New Vampires." Whereas Dracula was once viewed as a threat to staunch Victorian values in regards to repressed sexuality and xenophobic ideology, the New Vampire "obeys human laws, respects Western society's norms, and shares its values" in a case of "vampiric reform" (77). One of her main points, and one that I would like to emphasize here, is that "vampires have lost much of the edge that once defined their monstrosity; no longer terrifyingly parasitic, vampires are often (sym)pathetic or even palliative" (76). There is an interesting dynamic between humans and all the monsters in the HTF. Specifically, the humans in HTF are not scared of the monsters as they once were. In *HT* humans hold a monster festival to celebrate monster culture, adoring their ghoulish neighbors, and aid Dracula in his quest to find Johnny and reunite him with Mavis. They lift their capes to protect Drac from the sun, as he chases after Johnny's departing flight from Transylvania. In *HT2*, humans can now stay at Drac's hotel. And the human/monster integration does not exist solely in Transylvania. When Mavis and Johnny visit Johnny's family in Santa Cruz, Johnny's naïve mother Linda (Megan Mullally) explains to Mavis that they have a couple of "Mixed Families in the neighborhood" that she invited over to persuade the young couple to relocate to sunny California. When Karen and Pangrigora, a squid-like monster, arrive, they explain, "people are totally cool with (their) lifestyle choice." Karen mentions that the kids get picked on a little, but it "toughens them up," which is exactly what Drac attempts to do to elicit the fangs from Dennis' gums.

Analyzing our Draculas within the "New Vampire" paradigm, we see that although Drac has a lingering aversion and distrust of humans throughout the entire HTF, his most problematic relationships are with his own family. In his study of parent/teen relationships in horror films, Pat Gill notes that most children who go on to become monstrous in horror and slasher films tend to have deep rooted dissatisfactions with their parents. Conversely, the monstrous parents in these films are in a "hideous hunt" or search for "ghastly revenge" for lost children or spouses (17). Drac has already lost his wife, and will be double damned if he loses his daughter too. Gill goes onto recount that it is often the parents who have created the monster. Mavis is fairly well adjusted in these films, but her moral integrity and social acceptance sets her apart from the majority of her monster companions, despite her confinement to the castle by her father. Saying that Drac is overprotective of Mavis is a gross understatement, and his subversive, manipulative behavior in regards to her sexuality and life choices are arguably the creepiest, most disturbingly frightening thing about him. His shortcomings certainly will resonate with human audience who will relate to Mavis' predicament. The threat Drac presents is not literal blood sucking but his parasitic behavior takes its form in parental (and later grandparental) control. He is an emotional parasite.

In *HT*, Sandler establishes that Drac is overprotective of Mavis from the beginning, especially during her "growing up" montage. Drac has her wear a bike helmet as she learns how to transform into a bat and fly. He pulls her away from a sunlit open door exclaiming, "We never go out there.... EVER." "Out there," of course, is code for the human world. He reads Mavis stories from "Tales of Humans" about Harry the Human who hunts and kills monsters. Mavis is clearly scared, but Drac assures her, "Don't be scared.... I promised your mommy I would protect you FOREVER." Drac sings to her that, "humans are nasty, so with me you will stay." Unfortunately for Mavis, he means that quite literally. The prime example of Drac's control over Mavis happens on Mavis' 118th birthday, a monster's rite of passage into adulthood. Dracula has a whole day planned for just the two of them catching scorpions, but Mavis longs to go out into the world. She wants to "see new things" and "meet someone (her) own age" (in this case, since monsters are immortal, we're going to assume it's a young adult-type character). Dracula agrees telling Mavis that she is old enough to make her own choices, and we begin to feel as if he may be relinquishing control over his daughter (who has never left the castle!) but Dracula's deception becomes clear. Mavis flies to the nearest human village and attempts to interact with the locals. Little does she know Dracula has built the simulacra village. The buildings are merely facades. The human inhabitants are zombies in human masks, ordered to attack Mavis when she arrives. They carry pitchforks and torches. Mavis is clearly spooked and flies away. Later she explains to her father, "Dad ... you were right ... humans are awful." When Mavis whimpers that she "will never leave here again." Drac smiles wryly. His plan has worked.

It should come as no surprise that when Johnny and Mavis finally do marry, Drac will be the same meddling force he has been throughout Mavis' childhood and early adult years. Drac's aggressive and subversive interference casts him as more of a metaphorical vampire, sucking the freedom and energy from the young couple, and forcing his will upon them and their son. The wedding scene also highlights the awkward tension between the two families, as we finally meet Johnny's side. When the Laughrans enter the hotel, they are immediately othered by the monster community. As they are announced by the bodiless suit of armor, the monster pause glaring judgmentally at the "hideous creatures" who have infiltrated their turf. The music stops, and the monsters stare in disbelief. Johnny's sister struggles to free herself from a monster attempting to eat her flowered headband. During the ceremony, Johnny's winsome brother puts on his best fake smile, but is clearly uncomfortable walking a big busted, purple octopus creature down the aisle. But as uncomfortable as *he* is, she turns to her friend and sticks a tentacle in her mouth, faking like she is going to vomit. She is just as disgusted with him as he is with her. The rest of the family is disgusted with the "Scream cheese" frosting cake, and Johnny's parents generally glare at each other anytime something monstrous happens. When The Glob, a green, gelatinous character asks Johnny's mom to dance, she hesitantly glares at him and says, "Oh … look at you" in a sarcastic way. Then the blob man puts her inside his body instead of dancing with her. Johnny has to come and pull her out. Bigfoot drops a gigantic tear on Johnny's mother after the ceremony ruining her dress. They are clearly horrified to be there. But they are not horrified because they fear for their lives. They are horrified because of the cultural disparities between the human and monster cultures.

At the wedding, Mavis-clad in a sexy black form fitting wedding dress and spider web veil-walks, toward the altar. Drac imagines her as he wishes she still was; a little girl. He then sabotages the couple's first kiss. After Johnny places the ring on Mavis' hand, they lean into one another and Drac uses magic to send a shrunken-head monster in-between the couple's smooch. When the newlyweds glare at him for his meddling. Drac closes his index finger and thumb, signifying he wants to see just a little peck. The couple quickly pecks each other on the lips, and Drac stands and applauds. Drac serenades the couple with a ukulele claiming that Mavis is "now Johnny's girl." Before we can even see Johnny and Mavis share their first dance as husband and wife, Drac cuts in for a daddy-daughter dance. Is Drac reluctant to let go of his little girl, or is this a subconscious move because deep down in his dark place he still does not approve of the human/monster union? Either way, his metaphorical vampirism is set to cause the couple problems in the sequel, just like it did in the original movie. During the dance scene, we also learn that Mavis' grampa Vlad is not present at the wedding, because as Drac explains, "he would not have approved of this. He's old school." When Mavis protests that "If he could just meet Johnny" Dracula interrupts and concludes, "he would have eaten him." Drac then claims he's "not as enlightened as your hip father." If Grampa Vlad is Old School, then what was Drac a mere year ago when Mavis and Johnny first met? Mavis asks if he is sure that he is OK with Johnny not being a monster to which he replies, "human, monster, unicorn ... as long as you are happy." These words are of course, disingenuous, because Drac respects none of Mavis' decisions moving forward.

Dennis the Dhampir: Cultural Hybridity and "Getting Fangs"

A year after the wedding, Mavis is pregnant. Interestingly, she chooses to reveal this information to her father alone, without Johnny. The two morph into their bat-form, and fly amongst the night clouds as Mavis reveals her swollen bat-belly to Drac. In both films, the two vampires flying around as bats functions as bonding scenes between father and daughter. This scene is interesting because in her previous human form, Mavis does not appear to be noticeably pregnant. Drac, of course, is thrilled, but that once tolerant-of-humans rhetoric which he displays at the end of *HT* and at the beginning of *HT2* comes into question. Mavis and Johnny lie in bed as Johnny sings to the baby in utero. It is an intimate moment for two expecting parents, but Drac never ceases to interfere. Mavis is having some pregnancy cravings and asks Johnny to get her some ice cream and anchovies. Drac flies in through their window criticizing her diet and explaining she must eat more spiders for the baby's health. He consults a book entitled, "*What to Expect When You're Expecting a Vampire.*" Mavis reminds him that they "don't even know if the kid's going to be a vampire. I'd be thrilled if the baby is humany just like Johnny." "Humany, with thousands of years of Dracula genes? Not gonna happen." Drac may have tried to convince himself that he is hip by letting Johnny and Mavis marry, but clearly he wants his grandchild to be like him.

He maintains his overprotective and intrusive ways when he attempts to enter the delivery room, but is told that only the father is allowed in. Drac responds, "Really? OK ... he's the family.... I guess." Drac slinks away and we know he is up to no good. Shortly after the doctor delivers Dennis, he is snatched away by a suspicious looking nurse with large breasts and a blonde wig. Sure enough, Drac goes undercover nurse to ensure he is not only in the delivery room with Mavis, but is the first to hold his grandson. He shouts, "The Dracula blood line carries on." And then assures his grandson, "No one will ever harm you as long as I'm here my little devil dog." Drac now has new child to keep watch over, but he still does not relent on protecting Mavis. Dennis is the spitting image of Johnny and his physical image and iconography builds on the conflict of the film of whether or not Dennis is human or monster.

Dennis' identity as either a human or a monster defines the central conflict of *HT2*. Interestingly, the film designates his hybridity as an "either/or" situation, as in will he be a human, or a monster. Both families attempt to claim his as their own, with Johnny's mother Linda being the passively aggressive human counterpart to Dracula. If the initial racial codings in the HTF hold true this becomes problematic, just from the very nature of hybridity and bi-raciality in general. Dennis clearly suffers trauma in trying to please both sides of his family with an identity he is too young to understand. At Dennis' first birthday party, Dracula calls Dennis, Denisovich, and Johnny's father, Grampa Mike (Ron Swanson) angrily reminds him that, "his name is *Dennis*, named after my father." Drac quickly replies, "That's not his Vampire name." Grandma Linda gives her trademark saccharine coated response to Drac: "Huh … are we sure that he's a vampire? Not that that is a bad thing. Shouldn't he have fangs and that pasty skin…?"

Perhaps the most intriguing discussion of where the Draculas (Dennis included) are placed within vampire mythos revolves around their fangs. Drac and Mavis both have noticeable fangs, but within the narrative of the films, they seem useless. Dracula mentions on several occasions that he and Mavis do not drink human blood. When Mavis is a baby, Drac sings her a lullaby where he croons, "Hush little vampire don't say a word, papa's going to bite the head of a bird" to feed her. Later in the film, Mavis reminds Dracula of his promise to let her leave the hotel to explore the human world while they were "eating mice." When Johnny first realizes the castle he has entered is actually a hotel for monsters he is clearly fearful. He asks Dracula is he is going to eat him, but Drac explains to Johnny that human blood is too fatty and he uses a "blood substitute." In *HT2* we see him drinking blood from a wine glass (presumably his blood substitute) but there is no fang-on-neck penetration anywhere in these films. The closest we get to any threat of monster/vampire violence is when Johnny refuses to leave Mavis in the first film despite Drac's overprotective threats. Drac warns:

> Listen to me. You are never to return here. You are to stay away and never tell humans about this place, or I will track you down and suck every ounce of blood from your body, until you look like a deflated whoopee cushion!

This seems like an empty threat, considering Dracula and Jonathan have shared laughs together in what reads as a human/monster buddy comedy. Dracula and Mavis are "monsters" only because of their supernatural abilities and liabilities, and less for their actions or motives toward the dominant culture of humanity.

There is no better example of this as when Mavis visits Johnny's hometown in California. The couple scope out Southern California because if Dennis is not a monster, they plan on moving there to be with people like him (read humans). In these scenes, Mavis questions her own monstrosity and otherness, and questioning whether she is a "freak" or not. In the least surprising revelation, Dracula enlists Johnny using threats and manipulation to make Mavis' trip to California miserable and unhappy, much like he did with the zombie village in *HT*. Mavis, ever the optimist loves So-Cal, despite the glaring sun and cultural differences. She participates in local skateboarding culture, enjoys the stunning landscape, and even marvels at the flavor selection of Slurpees at the local mini-mart. Mavis not only accepts Johnny's culture, but also plans to relocate their family to the sunny surfside community, a stark contrast from the dank, misty confines of the hotel, where she has essentially been her father's prisoner for over 120 years. Her ambition to carve her own niche for herself and her family is in constant opposition to her father's wishes, but as Tenga explains, "today's vampires offer a romanticized view of monstrosity in which the Self transcends death and people are eternally unique" (80). Mavis' struggles mightily to locate her uniqueness amongst the monsters she has been forced to live with for her entire life. Marrying Johnny and having Dennis suggests that her quest for self exists outside of the confines of the castle and rigid racial barriers that monsters and humans have adhered to over the centuries.

If the Dracula's fangs are unthreatening to humans, why all the concern with whether Dennis gets them or not? Mavis is already feeding Dennis trendy health conscious human food (he loves avocados) not spiders, mice, or snakes. It is presumed that if Dennis gets his fangs he will only be drinking animal blood out of a glass like his mother and grandfather. However the fangs in the HTF are an extremely important symbol of racial identity in the second film. Since a motif of exogamy has emerged in the HTF, and since Dracula's questionable parenting has been established to try and preserve his tribe, the discussion now leads specifically to Dennis, a half human, half vampire hybrid known as a dhampir in folklore. The genesis of the term began with Slavonic gypsies. According to myth, dhampirs traditionally are the offspring of male vampires and female humans, mainly because it is recognized in vampiric lore that the male vampire is a suave seducer of young women. Some cultures however include female vampires and male humans (in the case of Mavis and Johnny) as viable parents of the dhampir. They may possess all of a vampire's powers and none of their weaknesses, or degrees of both. dhampirs are usually tormented with an uneasy childhood because of ostracization from their peers, or because they're hybrids exposed to bigotry, or because their monster half is by humans (vampires.com).

The finale scenes of *HT2* reveal whether or not Dennis is human, and the family being forced to move to California amongst the humans, or is a monster who feels more comfortable in the castle. Even this special segregation suggests to poor Dennis that if he genetically identifies with one culture, he cannot move fluidly within another. He is either surfing in the California sunshine, or catching spiders in Transylvania.

It is interesting to note that a whole other dynamic starts to emerge between humans and vampires. To Vlad and Drac, humans are "wimps" because they do not have the supernatural powers or unnerving presence to intimidate as vampires do. So if humans are wimps, then the vampire takes the role of the bully, a role that Drac seems to embrace through his manipulation of Johnny, Mavis, and Dennis throughout the HTF. This being said, it is important to mention that with the exception of Mavis, it is extremely challenging to analyze the HTF vampire tribe mainly because the characterization is inconsistent and contradictory. In other words, Drac and Vlad are intolerant of humans, or accepting and loving toward them depending on when the plot needs them to be. This in no way suggests the characters are complex, trying to learn about themselves and others in an attempt to bridge the gap of human-monster relations. It suggests that Sandler's dialogue is not exactly Oscar worthy, and whatever cultural stereotype the plot needs at any specific moment is what Sandler will throw in there, even if it is not consistent with the characters' past revelations or epiphanies. The final scene is a perfect showcase for these inconsistencies.

Dennis is set to enjoy his fifth birthday party at the castle. His parents have hired an actor to play Kakie, a cake loving Cookie Monster analogue, and Dennis' favorite children's TV personality. Having already failed at eliciting Dennis' fangs through fear and forced bat-morphing by throwing him off of a rickety wooden tower at vampire summer camp, Drac turns to human-hating Vlad to help him turn his grandson into a vampire. Vlad, still unaware his great-grandson is a Dhampir, suggests possessing Kakie's body to scare Dennis into getting his fangs. Johnny is hesitant to allow this because Dennis loves Kakie, but Drac insists that it is the only way that they will not have to leave the hotel (yet again imposing his will onto the family). Kakie is transformed from a fuzzy, rotund, lovable mascot into a muscular, threatening beast. Dennis is confused and petrified, so Drac stops the possession, much to the disgust of Vlad.

After this horrific scene, the adults begin to argue about what is best for Dennis. Mavis lets the proverbial "bat out of the bag" when she insists Dennis is not a monster but human. Drac is stubborn, and insists they stay at the castle. Linda Laughlan chimes in that she thinks that Dennis "just wants to be normal," a problematic label that Mavis immediately calls her on pleading, "can we stop using the word normal?" and adding, "he is who he is." Mavis quickly learns that both her father and her husband had contrived a plan to deceive her and trick her into staying at the hotel, and by this point, our sympathies lie with her because she is clearly the victim of an unbreakable patriarchal hierarchy that her husband is now a part of. Vlad is horrified at the revelation that the Laughlans are human, and places the blame squarely on his son's shoulders: "You let your daughter marry a human and have a human kid?" Replace "human" with any other racial, cultural, or tribal signifier or slur and it becomes extremely problematic, and this is why the cultural coding in these films is so vitally important.

When Vlad's Man-Bat henchman, Bela learns that Dennis is not human he vows death to the child. Simultaneously, Dennis and best friend Whinnie the Werewolf (Sadie Sandler) exit the party to escape his bickering family. Dennis feels truly misplaced. He does not know where he belongs and flees into the haunted forest to escape the onslaught of adult ideology. Bela eventually hunts them down, and hurls Whinnie across the forest injuring her. The camera pans on Dennis' face; his eyes redden; his canine teeth pop out, and we can guess what happens next. Dennis finally gets his fangs. Interestingly, Drac and Vlad established that the fangs had to be scared out of Dennis, but in this case it was a case of Incredible-Hulk-Like rage that prompted Dennis' transformation. Either way, the emotions of fear and anger being the catalysts towards a more monstrous self makes sense, since the tribe of monsters are othered by the humans.

Drac, Mavis, and Dennis team up to defeat Bela and all the other bat-minions that Vlad kept in his castle. The fight scenes signify their coming together as a monster tribe. Finally, when Bela attempts one last strike on Johnny by attempting to stake him through the heart, Vampa Vlad uses his supernatural magic to reduce the man-bat to the size of an actual bat. He flees the scene with Whinnie's hungry siblings following for a quick snack. Returning focus to the Dracula family, the inconsistencies of their character and ideology are revealed yet again as Vlad boldly changes direction asserting that no one is going to harm *his* family. Dennis wants affirmation that he is now "cool," reinforcing the earlier discussion of humans coded as wimps. Drac comforts Dennis by assuring him that no matter what he is, his grandpa will accept him. But ultimately, by the end of *HT2* does anyone actually believe the Count? With Dennis' fangs-coming-out party, the manipulation Drac has employed throughout the HTF has worked yet again. Mavis (surprisingly chipper) exclaims that now the family does not have to move and they can stay in the hotel. So Drac can exert his vampiric control on another generation. Will Mavis ever leave this hotel?

Sandler and Sony Animation will team up for a *Hotel Transylvania 3* in 2018; no surprise considering how profitable the franchise has become. They have reinvented the classic movie monsters into lovable, non-threatening entities that are accepted by their on-screen human companions as well as the viewing audience. It will be interesting to see where they take the franchise, and if some of the glaring cultural biases and racial/tribal demarcations continue. Knowing Sandler's body of work, they no doubt will. Will they fast-forward to Dennis' teen years, where he and Whinnie the Werewolf are dating? Will Drac have a problem with that because although a monster she is not a vampire? Will the complicated monster hierarchies break down? Perhaps Mavis and Johnny will be saddled with the burden of finding Drac a new mate. Of all the common vampire tropes, his predatory sexual deviance is replaced by patriarchal control over his daughter. Could a wife be his next "victim"? Imagine if this potential mate was a human. Imagine if after a family vacation to California, Drac meets her there. Imagine if she wants him to move to California. Will he go? Will he let Mavis and Johnny run the hotel, or will he insist that they ALL move to California? How will he perpetuate his exogamy in future scenarios? Obviously, this speculation merely begs the question of if anyone learns anything from these films, the characters or the audience.

Through Mavis and Johnny's courtship in *HT* we think that after centuries of distrust, humans and monsters are finally accepting and tolerant of each other's tribe. But with their marriage and pro-creation in *HT2* we learn that alas, no, it is not acceptable to merely "be yourself." Drac and Vlad are hell bent on Dennis becoming a monster, and Drac's reassurances that he would accept him no matter what never ring true. The message is always mixed and constantly convoluted. He is relieved that Dennis is a monster, and once again the vampire dominates the cultural climate of the Hotel Transylvania Universe. But realistically, perhaps this is a reflection on contemporary western society. Using the coding from the HTF as a hypothetical subtext, are all gentiles blindly accepting of their children if they marry a Jew? Is the reverse true? Do parents or grandparents of bi-racial children attempt to hijack or appropriate their cultural norms onto their children, whether overtly or subversively like Drac does? On some levels it is bound to occur. If we code Dennis' "wimpy" human characteristics as some form of gender identity questioning, do the fangs represent a phallic symbol of masculinity? Perhaps what the HTF is trying to relay is that it is not always a clear case of just accepting other cultures, but a process the protagonist in its films must endure. Much like the character of the vampire has changed throughout the centuries, so must Drac's long standing fears and doubts about the motives of humanity over his tribal dominance.

Notes

1. The original *Hotel Transylvania* film will be abbreviated as *HT*, the sequel *HT2*, and the franchise as HTF. All the films in this series are rated PG (Parental Guidance) which is classified as children aged eight years and older.

2. There is also a connection between the Jews and blood libel, which purported that Jews used the blood of Christian children in their Passover rituals, as a way to re-enact the crucifixion. Blood libel accusations began to increase in Europe around the 12th century: "Typically the unexplained death or the disappearance of a Christian child was followed by the accusation that the Jews murdered the child in a re-enactment of the crucifixion and collected the blood to be used as an essential component of the Passover matzoth or as a remedy for some mysterious ailment typical of the Jews" (Dan 4).

Works Cited

Carroll, Noel. "Nightmare and the Horror Film: The Symbolic Biology of Fantastic Beings." *Film Quarterly* 34.3 (1981): 16–25.
Dan, Peter. "How Vampires Became Jewish." *Academia.org*. http://www.academia.edu/4913745/How_Vampires_Became_Jewish. Accessed 14 April 2016.
Gill, Pat. "The Monstrous Years: Teens, Slasher Films, and the Family." *Journal of Film and Video* 54.4 (2002): 16–30.
Hollinger, Veronica. "The Vampire and the Alien: Variations on the Outsider." *Science Fiction Studies* 16.2 (1989): 145–160.
Hudson, Dale. "Of Course There Are Werewolves and Vampires: True Blood and the Right to Rights for Other Species." *American Quarterly* 65.3 (2013): 661–687.
Libby-Robinson, Sara. "Blood Will Tell: Anti-Semitism and Vampires in British Popular Culture, 1975–1914." *Golem: Journal of Religion and Monsters* 3.1 (2009): 16–27. http://lomibao.net/golem/admin/pdfs/7_GOLEM3-1-2009_Robinson.pdf. Accessed 14 April 2016.
Polidori, John. "The Vampyre." *The Penguin Book of Vampire Stories*. Ed. Alan Ryan. New York: Penguin Books, 1987. 7–24.
Rymer, James M. "Varney the Vampire (excerpt)." *The Penguin Book of Vampire Stories*. Ed. Alan Ryan. New York: Penguin, 1987. 25–35.
Stoker, Bram. *Dracula*. Ed. Glennis Bryson. Ontario, Canada: Broadview Editions, 1998.
Tenga, Angela, and Elizabeth Zimmerman. "Vampire Gentlemen and Zombie Beasts: A Rendering of True Monstrosity." *Gothic Studies* 15.1 (2013): 76–87.
Zornado, J. "Children's Film as Social Practice." *Comparative Literature and Culture* 10.2 (2008): 1–10. http://docs.lib.purdue.edu/cgi/viewcontent.cgi?article=1354&context=clcweb. Accessed 31 July 2016.

Filmography

Hotel Transylvania. Dir. Genddy Tartakovsky. Perf. Adam Sandler, Selena Gomez. Sony Animation Studios, 2012.
Hotel Transylvania 2. Dir. Genddy Tartakovsky. Perf. Adam Sandler, Selena Gomez. Sony Animation Studios, 2015.

Food for Thought

Vegetarian Vampires in Children's Reading Diets

JANE M. KUBIESA

The voracious vampire, and his or her bloodlust, has been at the heart of countless narratives for the adult audience for hundreds of years. When that character found its way into Anglo-American children's literature in the twentieth and twenty-first centuries it underwent a remarkable transformation that was in no way greater felt than with the unprecedented alteration to its vampiric appetites. It stands to reason that the same violent and often sexualized depictions of blood drinking as portrayed in adult vampire literature, or even the slightly more sanitized versions present in young adult fiction, are absent in texts intended for the under 12s audience. However, what these feedings are replaced with in terms of food sources, the manner of those feedings and the way in which authors approach these meal times is extremely significant in the children's market and in literary food studies.

These replacements speak volumes on the role of diet and nutrition for children in contemporary society and the ways in which vampire "food" is portrayed to children to promote differing messages from healthy eating and portion control, to exclusion diets and the environmental impact of certain food choices. According to Kara K. Keeling and Scott T. Pollard in *Critical Approaches to Food in Children's Literature* (2009), food has always been a recurring theme in children's fiction and is now an important field in literary criticism (10). In a literary environment where the increased focus upon food and eating as a central theme in children's vegetarian vampire narratives correlates with the heightened significance attributed to food in the cultural sphere, this essay offers an investigation into the concept of the "vegetarian" vampire, his or her feeding habits and food choices, and the ways in which these are reflective of real-world eating trends for the under 12s.

As the most well known "vegetarian" vampires in popular culture at present, *Twilight*'s (Meyer 2005) Edward Cullen and his family refuse to feed on humans and instead subsist on a diet of animal blood. This vegetarianism "by vampire standards" becomes something closer to real-world vegetarianism in children's literature, where non-blood drinking vampires abound (Kazez 25). They survive on a range of diets where animal products are eschewed in favor of conventional or unconventional food substitutes. *Twilight* contemporaries *Vampire Island* (2007–2009) by Adele Griffin, *Viktor the Vegetarian Vampire* (2012) by Rachel Adams, and Rebecca Blackhurst's *The Adventures of Count Grumpula* (2013) are prime examples of these blood or food replacement scenarios. However, the notion of the vegetarian vampire in modern children's stories predates *Twilight* by more than two decades thanks to pioneering authors from the late 1970s to the 1990s and their vampire characters like James and Deborah Howe's *Bunnicula* (1979–2006), Ann Jungman's *Vlad the Drac* (1981–1994) and Willis Hall's *Count Alucard* (1981–1999).

1980s and 1990s: Villainized Vegetarians, Dietary Acceptance and Size Discourse

Bunnicula: A Rabbit Tail of Mystery (1979)

James and Deborah Howe introduced the eponymous character of a vampire bunny intent on draining vegetables of their juices. The series contained food narratives indicative of period eating trends predominantly for the 1980s, but moving into the 1990s, which changed little over its publishing run. This groundbreaking novel set the scene for a vegetarian vampire story that would continue until the 1990s and be reprised for younger readers in the 2000s. The Howes create a liminal children's character who, as his name suggests, is both rabbit and vampire: a creature who appears to be a pet rabbit, but who is equally a fanged, red-eyed, nocturnal vampire being from the Carpathians who was found at a cinema showing of a Dracula movie. The nature of his vampirism revolves not around the contents of his diet, which comprises of normal leporine fare, but the manner in which he feeds upon those foods and the resultant corpse-like husks of vegetables left behind after feeding. As a vampire rabbit, Bunnicula eats by sinking his fangs into vegetables and draining them of their juices. While this rabbit exhibits vampire characteristics and is fearful of garlic, his adoptive family never discover his vampire nature and he is never anything more than a beloved family pet in their eyes. Bunnicula never harms anyone and is merely written as scary by Howe as a way to add drama and suspense to the plots of the many books he features in.

The Bunnicula series is food-centric and its eating-oriented narrative can be ascribed to some degree to the fact the narrator is a "meal-minded dog" (Howe, 1979 81). The frequent references to food and the concentration on the meat and candy elements of the family's diet may again be attributable to Harold the dog's position as narrator, which could skew the reader's perception of the family's eating habits. However, the dog narrator religiously remarks upon everything the family intends to consume and any food he comes into contact with, so one must assume he relates his own and his human family's dietary habits reliably. In comparison to the vampire's vegetable regime, the Monroe family and their pets are portrayed as having a diet which is largely made up of meat and sugary treats such as chocolate and fudge. The American white-collar parents lack knowledge about healthy eating and their inability to recognize Bunnicula's vampirism is indicative of the absence of awareness of vegetarianism. Their eight and ten-year-old sons are more aware but have no desire for a diet change.

A difference in dietary lifestyles creates a notable dichotomy between the vegetarian diet of Bunnicula and the sugary carnivorous fare of everyone else in the series. Therefore the vegetarian vampire "spinach-sucker," who is simply a foil for the plot and is never a fully realized central character, is created as a cypher for the non-meat eating individual and is villainized as a vampire stereotype to be exterminated (Howe, 1979 74). The active exclusion of meat from the diet was launched as the vegetarian movement in America with the publication of *Diet for a Small Planet* (1971) only eight years before the first *Bunnicula* book, so it was still a new societal concept and somewhat distrusted as revealed in the guise of Bunnicula (Bluejay n.p.). By the 1980s vegetarianism had moved into the mainstream consciousness and was increasing in popularity, although it was still a contested site for a child's diet. The controversy amongst the conventional medical establishment surrounding eminent child expert Dr. Benjamin Spock's 1998 recommendation that children over the age of two be fed on a vegetarian or vegan diet is further proof of this (Dworkin 69).

In such an environment, vegetarianism is villainized in the *Bunnicula* books. In one telling misunderstanding of the differences between the words "stake" and "steak," Bunnicula is comically attacked by a steak-wielding assailant, proving that meat is the ultimate weapon against the vegetarian. The *Bunnicula* version of the "Crew of Light" is even made up of carnivores: a cat and one or two dogs. The candy and meat diet of all of the other characters is normalized in the eyes of the reader, and the vegetarian is projected as something potentially dangerous. A vegetarian restaurant in town is called

"VICIOUSLY VEGGIE" and is described on its sign as "POWER FOOD FOR THE POWER HUNGRY," which speaks volumes for the positioning of vegetarianism in this literary universe (Howe, 1999 63). Thus the child audience is left in no doubt as to where their allegiance should lie and what eating habits are drawn as being most appropriate.

While food is a central theme in this series, there is remarkably little eating done within the bounds of the narrative. Bunnicula steals and hides food and is secretive about eating. The other pets eat, but the evidence of both the family's meals and those of Bunnicula are shown only through leftovers or potential meals. The family's leftovers are devoured by their pets, but Bunnicula's leftover "vegetable spectres" (Howe, 1983 73) represent the potential salad and vegetables the family could have eaten but are denied by Bunnicula's vegetarianism. Their food "spectres" instead become drained, lifeless, white specimens in a revelation of the true nature of vegetables as something unpalatable that even a vegetarian vampire does not fully consume. But much more than this, these vegetable victims are represented as something deleterious to health. The entirety of *The Celery Stalks at Midnight* (1983) is dedicated to this concept whereby Bunnicula's leftovers become "killer vegetables" and a danger to the townsfolk because of their potential to spread vampirism, although it is vague as to how this might happen (Howe, 1983 44). The increasing real-world popularity of vegetarianism creates the fictional notion that healthy eating is contagious and this is played upon through the use of the "children hate vegetables" stereotype to produce a rhetoric whereby the vegetable, and therefore vegetarianism, is harmful. Thoughts of "killer parsnips, blood-thirsty string beans, homicidal heads of lettuce" all lead back to Bunnicula (32). By the end of the under 12s series in 2006, the rabbit is welcomed as part of the family and his eating habits are grudgingly accepted, a move reflective of the real-world normalization of child vegetarianism of the period.

Vlad the Drac (1982–1994)

After finding a miniature baby vampire on holiday in Romania, the Stone children take him home to London and adventures ensue, largely centered upon his naughtiness and unusual food choices. Unlike Bunnicula, Vlad the Drac's "vegetarian" diet is immediately accepted. He explains to children Judy and Paul that he is a vegetarian because the sight of blood makes him faint. Instead he feeds on the literally sanitized blood substitutes of detergents and cleaning products of all kinds, in a comedic contravention of societal food rules as explained by Carolyn Daniel in her 2009 pre-eminent publication *Voracious Children: Who Eats Whom in Children's Literature* (15). The acceptance of differing dietary preferences is an important one to Ann Jungman's narrative and Vlad is allowed to freely explore his feeding requirements without intervention or castigation, especially following the vampire's admittance that his lack of blood-drinking meant he was a disappointment to his mother. Thus young readers are taught that difference, especially with regard to food choices, is acceptable and nothing to be ashamed of. Vlad, however, does not afford the same acceptance to human food and often says how disgusting it is, particularly with regard to meat. As he is babied by the children, they take this in their stride and develop into the roles of de facto parents, showing young readers that such closed-mindedness in relation to food is something attributable to babies and a behavior which should be ignored.

Unlike Bunnicula's forced secretiveness surrounding his feeding habits, Vlad's are celebrated and encouraged. Throughout the series Vlad's meal times are juxtaposed with those of his adopted family, middle-class British humans who enjoy a healthy and balanced diet. This begins in the first books with his family drinking cocoa, while he sips a thimbleful of medicine, or with his taking tea with a teacher by drinking bicycle oil. By the end of the series Vlad's diet is normalized to the point where he is sharing meal times with the family, extended family, and friends and his eating habits are fully integrated into theirs without compromising his unique feeding preferences. In the final books Vlad even finds himself having a barbecue with his human family and friends and gets his own bar of soap popped onto the grill and prepared for him to enjoy alongside their foods. The juxtaposition not only emphasizes the importance of inclusion within family meal times, it equally delineates human food and vegetarian vampire food to avoid child readers sampling any of the chemicals Vlad eats.

Jungman also promotes the virtues of accepting a range of foods into the dietary repertoire of children using her child vampire's ever expanding tastes as a conduit. At the beginning of the six-book series Vlad largely feeds on washing up liquid and likes nothing more than piercing the bottles with his fangs in a mock show of vampire aggression. He tries human food and dislikes it, apart from tastes of candy floss and garlic, but is treated to an ever increasing array of household chemicals, cleaning products, and non-traditional food stuffs including shoe polish, soap, dry cleaning fluid, and toothpaste, giving a whole new meaning to the modern term "eating clean." The importance of introducing new foods into the diets of the young is driven home alongside the message that trying new foods is part of a culinary adventure, a significant message in an era of increasing food availability and choice.

One point which almost derails these positive food messages is the lack of portion control in Vlad's meals. While this vampire is small enough to fit inside someone's pocket, he is frequently seen eating enormous portions which are half his size or greater. A meal might be a full tin of shoe polish or a carton of scouring powder, while on one occasion he consumes two tanks of petrol and on another he is given a buffet of "a tin of floor polish, a bottle of window cleaner, a bar of soap, a huge box of water softener and a packet of scouring powder" at a restaurant (Jungman, 1989 91). Gluttony or feasting has been a long-running theme in children's literature since the nineteenth century. When the vampire enters the equation the connotations of plenty become quite different, even if the vampire in question is "vegetarian." He may glut himself on non-traditional foodstuffs, but the underlying notion of a vampire over-eating still conjures images of human victims, even if the consumer is pocket-sized. Vlad's food "vampirizing" calls to mind period messages of eating excess and its human victims and 1990s anxiety surrounding child obesity, with the imaginary human victims found in the category of imagined reader. Despite consuming a vast amount of such an unusual diet, Vlad does not develop any medical side effects nor do his over-eating issues manifest as obesity, he simply grows. He is, however, more than willing to make unkind comments about the weight issues or eating habits of others. On a plane journey he tells a fellow passenger she has done nothing to work up an appetite and should not be eating such a large meal and later adds: "from the look of you, I would say you decide too often that you are hungry" (22). Vlad does not take his own dietary advice, nor does he offer others the same kind of food acceptance he is the beneficiary of. He does, however, provide proof that washing one's mouth out with soap, or any of the other detergents in his diet, does not work in his case.

Continuing the thread on vampire victims, Jules Zanger notes that the role of the vampire in the 1970s and 1980s is diminished by his socialization and humanization and the loss of a focus on human victims (21–22). No doubt he would see further diminishment in the domestication of the 1980s child vampire and his rejection of victims in favor of vegetarianism. What Zanger sees as a loss of a human focus in this period, I would argue is a gain within the sphere of this new kind of vampire because he or she is now more or less socialized and integrated in human society, while at the same time becoming a human focus in his own right by virtue of the humanization Zanger dismisses (21). Such humanization means this vampire is ideally suited as a vehicle for constructing social commentary. In this way the vampire becomes us, or in this case a child of the 80s/90s, which means Vlad is perfectly placed as a socially administered construction of childhood and its dietary mores.

Added to the trend for over-eating is the alarming way large portions of food are used as gifts or to console. For every birthday or Christmas Vlad receives large gifts of food; he is given food to cheer him up, and in one instance food is given as an apology. On several occasions he is seen comfort eating, with one notable occurrence where he eats many bars of soap while crying, admitting he is eating to comfort himself, a rather alarming development in the childhood construction of food borrowed from more adult texts. Interestingly, alcoholic drinks are given in appropriately scaled down receptacles such as thimbles or egg cups. Vlad may begin the series as a baby vampire, but over the relatively short narrative timeline he matures and has a family of his own, even though he still behaves in a very child-like way and is never described as being an adult. This goes some way to explain consumption of alcohol on his part and since the majority of his non-traditional meals would contain some form of alcohol for its astringent or detergent properties, the adult-generated fear surrounding the allowance of alcohol consumption within a children's narrative is a moot point. In Jungman's defense, she uses this sometimes excessive alcohol consumption and the resultant hangover as a cautionary tale to children to warn against the dangers of alcohol abuse.

Willis Hall's *Vampire Series* (1981–1999)

Hall's Count Alucard is for all intents and purposes, a traditional vampire. He lives in a castle in Transylvania, turns into a bat, has a garlic allergy, and descends from the Dracula line. He differs from his ancestors, both familial and canonical, in that he is a friendly vegetarian who, like his contemporary Vlad the Drac, is scared of blood. For most of the early books in the series Alucard is a fruitarian and adds other vegetarian food items to his diet as the series unfolds, some more healthy than others, until he can more precisely be termed an ovo-lacto vegetarian. Unlike Bunnicula or Vlad, Alucard does not glut himself with food; instead he eats healthy food in meager portions. His tall, thin appearance is often commented upon and his slimness becomes as much of a vampire trademark as the Count's opera cloak. His gentleness with food and his careful table manners also recommend him as a role model for the young reader.

By contrast the humans in the books are mostly described as being overweight in a realization of societal over-eating fears introduced into the narrative arena by Ann Jungman. The adult vampire is not overweight and by extension neither is the child reader, at this juncture in time. The majority of characters in Hall's series are referenced with a plethora of confirmatory adjectives like portly, stout, plump, fat, pudgy, and apple-cheeked. This is further affirmed with the accompanying illustrations initially by Babette Cole and then Tony Ross, whose British seaside postcard style caricatures reveal the humans in all their rotund glory. Hall does not make overt judgments about food choice or weight, but does create a whole cast of characters who enjoy junk foods, takeaways, and sugary treats to excess. These include the ice cream stall's "white-overalled fat lady" and the burger chef addicted to his own cooking, demonstrating a mimesis of eating trends leading to obesity in developing countries from the 1980s onwards, initially seen in adults and later in children (Hall, 1991 21, Popkin et al. 3). Hall's use of diet stereotyping moves from Britain to the USA in one book where the earlier mentioned carnivorous Crew of Light become obese, doughnut-eating cops pitted against the vegetarian Alucard in a direct confrontation between the contemporary rhetorics of healthy and unhealthy eating, and tellingly the vampire comes out on top.

The problem of the 1990s vampire has been said to lie in the blurring of boundaries between humanity and the monstrous, particularly as monsters have always been used to construct human identity (Auerbach 5). Because of Alucard's diet his status as vampire, and therefore monster, is transmuted further into the realm of humanity. He is often persecuted by humans unaware of his eating preferences. As such it is these predatory humans who become monsters. Their meat-eating ways are at odds with Alucard's meat-free lifestyle and this reveals a veiled lingering distrust of vegetarianism from earlier decades, but also a level of confusion in terms of monstrous and non-monstrous eating, translated as healthy or unhealthy diets for the young. The ambiguity surrounding this matter continues and increases into the 2000s in modern societal food debates.

While the Count's style of dining is characterized by his elegant table manners, dainty appetite, and the fact he is often denied access to food through various plot scenarios, his human counterparts are largely written as aggressive over-eaters "spearing" or "capturing" the food on their plates in a cautionary retelling of the vices of unhealthy eating, excessive food consumption, and poor table manners (Hall, 1994 114). What is more, they even try to convert him to their way of eating and create a discourse of unhealthiness or illness around his eating lifestyle and vegetarianism. Alucard's "chubby" landlady thinks he would benefit from a change of diet due to his pale and thin countenance and attempts to ply him with sausages and bacon (Hall, 1993a 2). His gluttonous human cousin unsuccessfully tries to tempt Alucard with breakfast kidney while "chewing on a gristly" kidney morsel, and the aptly named "Mr Hurtzburger" proffers barbecued meat (Hall, 1994 30, 1993b 26). All offers are refused and the vampire manages to avoid a carnivorous conversion not unlike those forced upon humans by his vampiric ancestors.

In truth, the healthy eating ideal probably falls somewhere between the limited rations on the vampire's diet, which in extreme cases might involve only a peach as a meal, and the "greasy" excesses of the human world and Hall goes some way to communicate that fact with the juxtaposition of these two food lifestyles (Hall, 1981 29). With this in mind "obesity discourse" as outlined in *Education, Disordered Eating and Obesity Discourse* (2008) instead becomes a discourse of size because the discussion in question centers upon a dialogue between the oppositional states of plumpness and slimness (Evans et al. 13). Hall does, however, champion the ideals of fresh, unadulterated foods through the Count's joy in sampling fruit. Alucard, who can transform into a fruit bat, adores fruit of all kinds, particularly oranges. Oranges have held much significance throughout history but have been read in recent children's literature as representing the joy and pain of growing up, an apt analogy here for the adult eating choices ahead of the child reader according to Hall's delineation of them (Everett 202).

By way of encouragement towards a healthy eating lifestyle, all of the fruit Alucard eats is described in mouth-watering terms and in terms of its juiciness and the reader cannot help but be desirous of the same fare. Carolyn Daniel notes the "visceral pleasure" of food descriptions in children's literature and likens it to the same emotional response gained from reading a restaurant menu or watching a television cooking show (2). The Count's joy for fruit falls into this category and turns the experience of eating it into something remarkable. Alucard's enthusiasm and love of fruit becomes something more with his manner of feeding because he sinks his fangs into it, in true vampire fashion, before eating it. Unlike Bunnicula's leftovers, Alucard's immediately leave the narrative and are never drawn as toxic. The Count's preference is for the juiciest, fleshiest fruits and in this way fruit juice becomes a substitute for blood, particularly when blood oranges or tomato juice are on the menu. The act of piercing the fruit skin is rendered in a similar way to the vampiric act of breaking through human flesh and one such fruit feast is described as follows: "He bit into … [a peach] with his long, sharp teeth. The golden juice spurted out and ran down his pale slim fingers" (Hall, 1981 123). The similarities between vampiric blood drinking and this fruit meal are obvious and this manner of feeding becomes slightly more dubious when plums are involved and when the vampire sinks his teeth into "the deep-purplish skin" reminiscent of the bruised flesh of a human neck. Of course, this goriness only serves to make fruit that much more alluring for the young reader.

2000s: Eco-Vegans, Vicious Carnivores and Vampiric Eating Disorders

Vampire Island (2007–2009)

Thirteen-year-old Lexie, eleven-year-old Maddie, and their brother Hudson, aged nine, are vampire fruit bat hybrids. They live with their parents in New York and are the child narrators of Adele Griffin's Vampire Island series. This nutritionally progressive text not only puts child vampires at the forefront of its narrative to reinforce the connection between vampire and the child reader, it also deals with a number of food trends only now finding widespread favor. These vampires avoid blood or meat because it is associated with the unspecified location of the "Old World" and persecution. In the Old World, as vampire fruit bats, this family survived on a diet of fruit and occasionally drank blood from small mammals because it was the source of their immortality. They moved to the New World for a better life where they would eventually transform into humans by giving up their bat abilities and immortality, and avoiding blood. Blood and meat are therefore linked to an outmoded way of life and to conflict. In its stead the family undertakes a vegan lifestyle whereby seeded-fruits make up the bulk of their diet and where they eat only raw food, do not partake in frozen foods to avoid preservatives, and are lactose intolerant as a species.

Modern processed foods with their hidden sugars, colorings, and additives are at odds with the pure food stuffs of the vegans, so much so that they can poison vampires, causing sickness and even death. The blatant attack on the food industry of the modern world eschews and cautions against foods with no natural ingredients. Instead a cure for the poisoning caused by processed Western food is offered in the plot and it is made from natural produce. The "clean eating" raw foodist regime adopted by these child vampires not only avoids the approximate 3,800 additives found in the typical daily Western diet, it also confirms an animal-friendly stance, goes some way to tackling the current obesity epidemic, and highlights the possibilities of a meat-free exclusion diet in the minds of the young (Atkins and Bowler 214). The kind of food thinking adopted by Griffin has proliferated in texts for children in the 2000s with titles including *V Is for Vegan: The ABCs of Being Kind* (2013) and *That's Why We Don't Eat Animals: A Book About Vegans, Vegetarians and All Living Things* (2009).

This variation of eating, as hinted at above, is also seen as being guilt-free. As vegans, the Livingstone family has a diet that is not harmful to animals. Even as blood-drinking vampire bats they found the practice of killing and drinking blood "distasteful" because by their very nature they were connected to the eco-system around them and to other creatures (Griffin, 2007 34). As vampire fruit bat hybrids they have green "fruit-fortified blood" proving that environmentalism and their "green" credentials are fundamentally ingrained within them, a metaphor used to attribute the same eco-characteristics to young readers. In this case the obvious connotation of cannibalism from fruit-based bats eating a fruit diet is overlooked in the narrative. As bats the Livingstones had the ability to communicate with other animals, they helped by offering food to creatures in need, and scattered fruit seeds from their diet to propagate them. While their new diet means they have largely lost their bat abilities, they still try to connect with nature and the eco-message is a powerful one across all three books in the series. The family now actively saves their fruit pips and seeds to scatter and these leftovers are viewed as having the potential for new life rather than the Bunnicula trope of being dangerous. The vegan discourse of innocence is upheld and the tenets of recycling, animal conservation, and eco-activism are lionized.

The idea of sharing food with animals in need links to the concept of the wholesomeness of sharing food generally, and the solidarity and buy-in this creates from participants (Anderson 172). The family is often depicted sharing vegan meals around the table, an important aspect of American life, and they share their food with friends and neighbors at gatherings, with no pseudo vampiric table manners to reveal their origins. The same trope is applied in the 2012 children's picture book *Vincent and the Vampires* by Jules Marriner, where the plot revolves around a vegetarian vampire bat child who leaves his blood-drinking family to find community and acceptance in a house of like-minded monster vegetarians. In this paradigm eating is transformed into the basis for community and the glue which bonds family, friends, and other loved ones. Vegetarianism is no longer something which happens in the shadows and the 1980s/1990s suspicion of vegetarianism which forces Bunnicula to eat alone at night is long gone. The children often share fruit-based smoothies with friends in a "popular health food restaurant" called Candlewick Café, something which is highly frequented and easily accessible on the high street and a far cry from the previously mentioned "VICIOUSLY VEGGIE" eatery (Griffin, 2007 6, Howe, 1999 63).

The moniker of viciousness has been transposed from the vegetarian to the carnivore by the 2000s, mirroring shifting opinions in real-world eating trends and also the meat-eater as monstrous trope seen in Hall's work. In the 2013 series *The Adventures of Count Grumpula*, author Rebecca Blackhurst creates a fictional world for younger readers where the eponymous boy vampire has left behind his blood-drinking ways to become vegetarian. In fact, since his diet mostly consists of mangoes his eating regime is closer to being labeled as fruitarian. Grumpula turns fruitarian because of his fondness for nature, and as a result this "sensitive soul" becomes a friend to nature and the environment and a better citizen (Blackhurst 2013, 1). In contrast blood-drinking vampires are written as destructive, actively damaging to the environment, and violent; they regularly "tear the branches off the trees and chase and beat the woodland folk" (15).

Vampire Island contains a dietary spectrum with vegans at one extreme and carnivores at the other and the concept of the vicious carnivore is somewhat more nuanced for older readers. Vegan vampires are written as peaceful, "kind-hearted," and a "pure link between the human and animal world" (Griffin, 2008 59, 2007 21). Their conversion to a purely vegetarian diet to ultimately become human reinforces the humane aspect of humanity and implies something much less complimentary with regard to meat-eaters. Unreformed pureblood vampires and meat-eaters occupy positions of cruelty, "heartlessness and vengefulness" (Griffin, 2007 94). "Following the notion that eating badly can have detrimental effects on the eater, the idea that eating healthy, natural food can produce natural, proper children seems logical," Daniel asserts of this traditional trope of children's literature modified for the modern age (Daniel 25). It also ties into the idea of contemporary eating as a balancing act between food categories and moral and social implications (Sutton 2).

Within these dietary and behavioral extremes lie vampires, and by extension young human carnivores, who have ventured from the vegetarian lifestyle to experiment with meat eating. According to the unwritten rules of the food spectrum, the more meat/blood one eats, the crueler one becomes. Natural predator Maddie, who is noted for her general meanness and who can often be found drinking blood from mosquitoes, tries steak tartare and then gorges herself on bugs. She goes from spying on her pureblood vampire neighbors to torturing them with garlic and eventually killing them. Afterwards her mom comments: "Too much protein in Maddie's diet isn't safe" (Griffin, 2007 102). This is surely an understatement for such an unpleasant and murderous child, but perhaps also a warning for young readers about the dangers of too much meat. In this case, meat certainly is murder.

To further drive home the anti-meat message confirmed vegan Lexie also begins to eat meat for the edge it gives her over her human classmates in a class election. She begins by snacking on bugs "just for the rush" and before she knows it is spending all of her allowance buying steak tartare in an addiction-like state (Griffin, 2008 70). As her meat consumption increases so does her cruelty and she resorts to dirty tricks to win the election. She paints herself as the ideal vegetarian candidate and alters a photograph of her running mate eating a sandwich until it looks like she's consuming "a greasy, dead-cow cheeseburger" (Griffin, 2009 72). The additions of a sweaty upper lip and a double chin that makes the girl look like "a pig and a slob" equate meat-eaters with greed, laziness, and obesity, qualities viewed as being anti-vegan (72).

The only thing worse than being a carnivore, according to the narrative, is being a failed vegetarian. A witch who comes to the New World and disavows her vegan diet, preferring instead to return to the Old World and its ways is described as being crueler and more powerful than before she attempted the vegan lifestyle. However, understanding and encouragement is offered to those new to a vegan lifestyle and those readers struggling to maintain it. When the Livingstone daughters deviate from their New World eating regime, their family accepts them and steers them in the right direction. When they are eating fruit and wishing it was blood or suffering the pangs of meat withdrawal and missing its taste, their family offers support. The ultimate reinforcement of the vegetarian lifestyle comes with the knowledge that it is possible to become a pureblood vampire by consuming meat/blood. Thus deviation from veganism, and the associated lapse in principles, resorts in turning into the very creatures who persecuted the Livingstones in the Old World, and therefore into the kind of being they would least like to be.

Rachel Adams' *Viktor the Vegetarian Vampire* (2012)

Child vampire Viktor is not like other vimps (vampire children); he is allergic to blood so vomits when he takes his morning transfusion. After hearing about vegetarians he believes he might be one, but the topic is silenced by his mother as something shameful. As vampires do not eat food, they cannot be vegetarian—only humans can. Viktor is marked by this difference and because his fangs have not developed he is further alienated from vampire society and bullied at school. The de-fanging trope is continued in Helen Wendy Cooper's 2013 book for the under sevens, *The Vegetarian Vampire: The Lost Fangs*, where fangs are overtly coded as a representation of the carnivorous nature of the vampire. When fangs fall out, if they are lost, new ones do not grow. As such care must be taken of one's dental health, no doubt to promote oral hygiene amongst children, but also to ensure successful feedings, and to physically signpost vampire identity. A lack of fangs acts as an outward sign of Viktor's vegetarian leanings, after all not only is he allergic to blood, but he also lacks the tools to obtain it from humans. He is mocked by other vimps, called names like "Rip," "Tear" and "Gash," synonyms for aggressive feeding (Adams 13).

A doctor believes Viktor's lack of development and his food allergy are caused by his supermarket-delivered frozen blood diet, in continuation of the "fresh is best" narrative established in Vampire Island. The effects of a processed food diet are called into question, alongside its health benefits and its ability to retard physical development. In criticism of processed blood the doctor comments: "You don't know where it comes from. It could be contaminated or contain additives" (14). This idea mirrors an earlier passage where a human child is espousing the benefits of growing vegetables on an allotment. The perceived correlation between processed foods and illness or lack of good health, particularly with vulnerable groups like children, is one which is increasingly common in the West and which helped spur the development of the organic food trade.

The act of vomiting after eating, although attributed to a food allergy, brings the concept of food into the realm of the eating disorder. Viktor's vomiting is noted for its exceptionalness and treatment is sought for the disorder. When this "allergy" is combined with the normal vampire practices surrounding food in this text, it produces something troubling for the young reader. Vimps take lessons at school on how to fit in with the human world so they can accomplish their first feeding on unsuspecting victims. Since they are prohibited from eating they must divine methods of discarding food without being detected. Instructions include carrying small plastic bags to dispose of food without notice and avoiding too obvious and frequent trips to the bathroom to throw away meals. It could be argued that these vampire lessons and the intention to maintain control of eating behavior actually sound like guidance on successfully hiding an eating disorder, not something to be promoted to the under 12s audience (Abraham 15). Considering Viktor manages to break away from this world, his escape is a victory for systems of eating wellness. He moves from a scenario where postprandial vomiting is his norm to one where he enjoys a healthy, balanced diet. Vegetarianism, in this sense, is utilized as a metaphor for normalcy and of physical well-being for the child.

Aid for Viktor's supposed developmental issues comes in the form of medical intervention sought by his mother: a doctor is tasked with preventing his vomiting and a dentist provides false fangs. For Addams the medicalization of food issues falls in line with the industrialization of food produce, as something suspicious and possibly deleterious. "Medicalization," where "nation-states have increasingly sought to exercise authority and control over potentially recalcitrant populations" particularly children, attempts to shift ownership of health and food intake away from the individual and to homogenize difference, marking the "medical conviction" of vegetarianism as uncooperative or transgressive (Evans et al. 15, Anderson 175). Addams rails against this threat and as a result the preparation of the medicine prescribed by the doctor is botched by an inept pharmacist and Viktor is instead given a treatment containing wild garlic. As garlic is anathema to vampires, Viktor's mother and his classmates are poisoned when he unknowingly breathes garlic fumes in their direction.

A similarly comedic incident occurs with Viktor's prosthetic fangs, which malfunction when he is about to bite the neck of his first victim in an important feeding-related rite of passage, which he is unable to complete. Medical treatment is viewed as a joke, as an unnecessary intervention into non-medical issues and as another example of food-related subjects being tampered with by science, government, or industry. Just two years later the medicalization of "food" is praised by author Artemis Greenleaf in *Carl, The Vegetarian Vampire* (2015) because it allows his vampire family to exist without feeding on humans by imbibing a blood substitute called "The Synth" (Greenleaf n.p.). Synthetic blood comes in four "flavors": "Regular," "Hi-Cholesterol," "Lo-Sugar," and "Extra-Iron" to mimic processed food varieties and also human medical conditions affecting the blood (Greenleaf n.p.). The successful scientific intervention is tempered by a scientific failure. The maker of "The Synth" tries to produce a sun block powerful enough to allow nocturnal vampires to go out in daylight, but it only succeeds in turning their skin orange. Hence scientific advancements and interventions are still treated with caution within the vegetarian narrative to some degree.

Viktor dreams of eating (human) food; he wishes his morning blood transfusion was made of raspberries and is punished at school for admiring a picture of ice cream, in a reversal of the vegan Livingstone children's fantasies about meat. This common trope of food fantasy or desire is a traditional one in children's literature and even has an entire book for younger children dedicated to it; in J. Otto Seibold's *Wunce Upon a Time* (2008) vegetarian vampire Dagmar goes on an adventure to get candy (Daniel 2). Dagmar may have parental permission to eat candy as part of his balanced diet of home-grown fruit and vegetables and the accompanying awareness of food sources this brings, but Viktor's food choices are much more complex in his society. Authority figures like his teacher and mother try to quell his deviant behavior, which may be metaphorized for any unexpected or unwelcome traits exhibited by children that fall outside of the norm. Here the represented desire for becoming a vegetarian from the position of living in a carnivorous hegemony is made more stark because Viktor wants to move from drinking blood, to eating human vegetarian food. This is so serious because a vampire who eats food transforms into a human with just one bite. The unexpected plot twist of a postprandial vampire becoming human further locates this text within the food sphere and proves that eating is transformative, provides agency, equals self-creation, and has an effect on all aspects of one's being. Food also provides community, echoing the sentiments in Vampire Island. Once Viktor becomes human by eating food, he is able to join his human relatives where he finally achieves acceptance.

Conclusion

As a multi-faceted, complex, and infinitely transformable being, the vampire has been transmuted into a vegetarian children's character, a great leap from the animated corpse of folklore "lurking in far-off boneyards" (Schillace 267). His or her genre appropriate literal vegetarianism, as opposed to the carnivorous vegetarianism of young adult fiction, represents an understandable sanitation and domestication of the vampire to mediate his or her passage into literature for young children. But much more than this, the vampire's vegetarian conversion has brought about new opportunities for interpretation and reinterpretation for this age-old creature of folklore and firmly installed him as a staple of children's reading diets and a salient vessel for the refraction of coeval societal eating trends for the under 12s.

David Sutton has reasoned that the current preoccupation with vampires coming about at the same time veganism and vegetarianism are mushrooming in popularity and legitimacy, registers a sublimated concern for the ethics of contemporary eating, something clearly evidenced in the character and construction of the children's vegetarian vampire (6). The 1980s and 1990s saw the villainization of vegetarianism and the later resigned acceptance of it in the Bunnicula series, which in turn gave way to a universal acceptance of difference in the stories of Vlad the Drac. Vlad's depicted over-eating and the associated anxieties surrounding the potential for obesity were realized in Willis Hall's writing and metamorphosed into a debate on the rightness of diet and a discourse on size. By the 2000s these societal eating debates evolved into the championing of "clean eating" veganism in the Vampire Island series and the newly developed concept of food responsibility and its related eco-messages. In turn vegetarianism was pointedly normalized in Rachel Adams' vampire tale as a representation of physical wellness and an antidote to the eating controls of the State. As the embodiment of modern social eating practices and a vehicle for the discussion of the problematization of food for children, the vegetarian vampire covers the gamut of issues and has successfully negotiated and challenged each new discourse.

In writing about constructions of childhood through food, critic Jean Webb examines cooking in children's vampire tale *Monster Chef* (2014) by Peter Bently; she notes the ways in which it raises food awareness for the reader by parodying UK food culture (20). The same awareness of food is raised through the identification of the vampire as vegetarian, because eating and diet are brought to the fore. This produces an ongoing construction and reconstruction of childhood that queries eating and the place of meat in Western diets for the young reader, using his or her contemporary cultural discourse, whichever time period it may relate to. Webb further likens the habit of deconstructing restaurant dishes to the practice of literary critics reinterpreting texts (21). I would posit that it is the vampire that is being deconstructed and reimagined for the pre-teen audience, both in Bently's book and the sample texts here. If a creature known for his or her blood-thirsty nature can become a convert to vegetarianism, then becoming a staple in children's reading diets is a piece of cake.

WORKS CITED

Abraham, Suzanne. *Eating Disorders*. 6th ed. Oxford: Oxford University Press, 2008.
Adams, Rachel. *Viktor the Vegetarian Vampire*. London: CreateSpace, 2010.
Anderson, E.N. *Everyone Eats: Understanding Food and Culture*. 2nd ed. New York: New York University Press, 2014.
Atkins, Peter, and Ian Bowler. *Food in Society: Economy, Culture, Geography*. London: Arnold, 2001.
Auerbach, Nina. "My Vampire, My Friend: The Intimacy Dracula Destroyed." *Blood Read:*

The Vampire as Metaphor in Contemporary Culture. Ed. Joan Gordon and Veronica Hollinger. Philadelphia: University of Pennsylvania Press, 1997. 11–16.
Blackhurst, Rebecca. *Count Grumpula and the Wood Witch.* New Zealand: Cobble Creep Creations, 2013.
Bluejay, Michael. "A Short History of Vegetarianism." *Vegetarian Guide.* 1998. http://michael bluejay.com/veg/history.html. Accessed 25 July 2016.
Daniel, Carolyn. *Voracious Children: Who Eats Whom in Children's Literature.* London: Routledge, 2006.
Dworkin, Norine. "Into the Mouths of Babes." *Vegetarian Times,* 253, September 1998, p. 69.
Evans, John, Emma Rich, Brian Davies, and Rachel Allwood. *Education, Disordered Eating and Obesity Discourse.* London: Routledge, 2008.
Everett, James. "Oranges of Paradise: The Orange as Symbol of Escape and Loss in Children's Literature." *Critical Approaches to Food in Children's Literature.* Ed. Kara K. Keeling and Scott T. Pollard. London: Routledge, 2009. 193–206.
Griffin, Adele. *The Knaveheart's Curse.* London: Puffin Books, 2008.
_____. *V is for ... Vampire.* London: Puffin Books, 2009.
_____. *Vampire Island.* London: Puffin Books, 2007.
Hall, Willis. *The Last Vampire.* London: Young Lions, 1981.
_____. *The Vampire's Christmas.* London: Red Fox, 1994.
_____. *The Vampire's Holiday.* London: Young Lions, 1993a.
_____. *The Vampire's Revenge.* London: The Bodley Head, 1993b.
Howe, James, and Deborah Howe. *Bunnicula: A Rabbit-Tale of Mystery.* London: Hodder Children's Books, 1979.
_____. *Bunnicula Strikes Again!* London: Hodder Children's Books, 1999.
_____. *The Celery Stalks at Midnight.* London: Hodder Children's Books, 1983.
Jungman, Ann. *Vlad the Drac.* London: Barn Owl Books, 1982.
_____. *Vlad the Drac Down Under.* London: Young Lions, 1989.
Kazez, Jean. "Dying to Eat: The Vegetarian Ethics of *Twilight*." *Twilight and Philosophy: Vampires, Vegetarians, and the Pursuit of Immortaility.* Ed. Bridget Carrington and Jennifer Harding. New Jersey: John Wiley & Sons, Inc., 2009. 25–37.
Keeling, Kara K., and Scott T. Pollard. "Introduction: Food in Children's Literature." *Critical Approaches to Food in Children's Literature.* Ed. Bridget Carrington and Jennifer Harding. London: Routledge, 2009. 3–20.
Popkin, Barry M., Linda S. Adair, and Shu Wen Ng. "Global Nutrition Transition and the Pandemic of Obesity in Developing Countries." *Nutrition Review* 70.1(2012): 3–21.
Schillace, Brandy. "Children of the Night." *Unnatural Reproductions and Monstrosity: The Birth of the Monster in Literature, Film, and Media.* Ed. Andrea Wood and Brandy Schillace. New York: Cambria Press, 2004. 267–294.
Sutton, David. "Comment: Reflections on Meat-Eaters, Vegetarians, and Vampires." *Ethnos: Journal of Anthropology* (27 January 2016): 1–10.
Webb, Jean. "Constructions of Childhood Through Food in Children's Literature." *Feast or Famine? Food and Children's Literature.* Ed. Bridget Carrington and Jennifer Harding. Newcastle upon Tyne: Cambridge Scholars Publishing, 2014. 8–21.
Zanger, Jules. "Metaphor into Metonymy: The Vampire Next Door." *Blood Read: The Vampire as Metaphor in Contemporary Culture.* Ed. Joan Gordon and Veronica Hollinger. Philadelphia: University of Pennsylvania Press, 1997. 17–26.

Every Generation Gets the Vampire It Needs

What Can Vampire Narratives in Children's Films Tell Us About Childhood in the Twenty-First Century?

ALLISON MOORE

Children's cultural worlds and those of adults are not separate and distinct. If we accept the arguments advanced by sociologists of childhood that the categories of "adult" and "child" are fictions, social constructions that change across time and place,[1] then it follows that any attempt to delineate between the cultural activities and social practices of adults and children are arbitrary. Adults frequently enter children's cultural worlds and derive nostalgic and/or regressive pleasure (Kramer) from doing so and children draw on adults' cultural worlds, incorporating them into their own in a process that William Corsaro calls "interpretive reproduction" (18).[2] It is, therefore, more appropriate to consider the cultural worlds of adults and children as overlapping and interacting.

Given this interplay, it should come as no surprise that the proliferation of the figure of the monster, and, in particular, the vampire, in contemporary adult cultures has coincided with a concomitant increase in representations of monsters in children's literature, films and narratives. Nina Auerbach famously stated that each age gets the vampire it needs (145), illustrating the metaphorical nature of the vampire; an empty vessel into which the anxieties and fears of the epoch can be placed, examined and addressed. While this is certainly the case, it can be further argued that within every era that the vampire emerges, different generations get the vampire they need. So, the vampire in children's film and literature fulfills different functions to the vampire of teenage and young adult fiction, which, in turn, is different to the vampire that reflects the fears and anxieties of adults. The vampire that appears in children's film and literature can be seen as a re-imagining of existing cultural constructions. Discussing horror in children's animated films, Erin Hawley suggests that "horror tropes, narratives, conventions and characters have been reshaped ... with a child's perspective in mind" (2015).

This essay will focus on vampire narratives in children's films, identify recurrent themes and critically examine what they tell us about constructions of childhood in the twenty-first century. It will argue that it is possible to identify continuities and discontinuities with earlier children's stories and traditional fairy tales. On the one hand, as the vast majority of children's literature is written by adults for children it continues to reflect adult perceptions of who children are and who they should become. In this sense, contemporary vampire narratives perpetuate constructions of childhood predicated on futurity and represent the norms and moral values adults want children to develop in order to become responsible adult citizens of the future. On the other hand, the vampires in these narratives or the child protagonists' relationships with them open up space in which children can resist adult demands and exercise agency and choice. Rather than being passively molded and shaped into the adults of the future, these vampire narratives in children's films allow us to view children, not as "members-in-the-making" but as social actors who co-construct their social worlds. They present children as human beings and "locate children within the real world of norms, values, expectations and responsibilities" (Wyness 180) rather than human becomings who need adults to guide and teach them these norms, values and responsibilities.

What Is a "Children's Film"?

Although they are worthy of study in their own right, children's films should be understood in the broader context of children's literature. Children's literature defies easy definition. It is usually limited to books, and frequently understood to be those books that are deemed high quality. However, in a multi-media age it would be a gross omission to exclude other story telling formats that contribute to children's literary practices from the category of children's literature. Hall provides a broader definition of children's literature which "encompasses popular culture as well as high cultural or classic texts … literature in this broader sense could include a range of print genres as well as oral literature, theatre, film, television" (136). Of course, online literacy practices could also be added to this definition of children's literature with specific sites dedicated to the promotion of films, wikis providing additional and/or background stories to the film plot and fanfiction providing children opportunities to reinterpret and reimagine the original narrative.

Identifying what *is* and what *is not* a children's film is not as easy as it may at first appear. According to Ian Wojcik-Andrews, "Not all children's films are just about children and not all films children see are children's films. Defining a children's film, and thus the child viewer said films presuppose, is something of an impossibility" (7). Definitions of children's films are never neutral and are shaped by a number of factors including personal opinions about what constitutes an "appropriate" film for children, institutional classifications and age-rating of films and cultural context, where the categorization of a film as a children's film is influenced, if not determined, by culturally specific constructions of childhood and, by extension, assumptions about what is deemed suitable for a child audience. In determining whether a film can be classified as a children's film, one might also take account of the presence (or not) of child protagonists, the content and the medium, with animation, for example, generally seen as a children's medium in the Global North. Given this definitional complexity, the essay will draw on an institutional definition, while still cognizant that this definition is not unproblematic as it reflects dominant constructions of childhood and is based on adults' assumptions about what children want to watch and, more importantly, what children *should* and *should not* watch. Notwithstanding these limitations, it will focus on films released between 2000 and 2015 that have been classified by the British Board of Film Classification as the categories "Universal" and "Parental Guidance." Six films formed the basis of the analysis for this study—*The Little Vampire* (Edel 2000), *Scooby Doo and the Legend of the Vampire* (Jeralds 2003), *Vampire Dog* (Anderson 2011), *My Babysitter's a Vampire* (McDonald 2012), *Hotel Transylvania* (Tartakovsky 2012) *and Hotel Transylvania 2* (Tartakovsky 2015).

Retold Stories: Continuing Metanarratives in Vampire Stories for Children

The figure of the vampire that appears in children's films draws on and reflects pre-existing conventions and characteristics of the vampire narrative. This is, of course, true of all vampire cinema with Ken Gelder suggesting that "all vampire films are self-citational [because it] is almost impossible for one vampire film not to cite or invoke another vampire film or vampire novel" (3). What is interesting about the children's films analyzed for this essay is that, not only did they cite the general tropes of the vampire genre, some of them explicitly cited another vampire film in the form of Stephenie Meyer's *The Twilight Saga*. In *Hotel Transylvania*, when Dracula catches sight of a scene from one of the *Twilight* films he sighs "This is how we're represented? Unbelievable!" The most explicit citations of *Twilight* appear in *My Babysitter's a Vampire*. Set in the town of Whitechapel, much of the action takes place in the high school, not unlike its *Twilight* counterpart. Further, central to the storyline is the advance screening in the town of the film *Dusk III: Unbitten*, a story about Rochelle and Jakeward,[3] who is a vampire. Although it is not possible to say why the writers chose to make such explicit references to The Twilight Saga—a sign of respect at its success, an attempt to link their film with *Twilight* and in so doing enjoy/exploit some of its popularity or simply as parody?—what is evident is that the children's films in question are all re-telling and re-framing existing stories.

According to Stephens and McCallum, existing stories "are always dealt with in relation to or in dialogue with an overarching cultural and moral perspective, or assumed bundles of values" (x). They refer to this "bundle of values" as the Western metaethic, which in children's literature is largely underpinned by literary humanism emphasizing individual freedom, personal choice and growth and development of one's personality or humanity. This humanistic informed metaethic produces a limited number of meta-narratives which serve to reinforce and reproduce a society's status quo and, therefore, inculcate children into the norms and values they will be expected to hold as responsible adult citizens of the future. Perhaps one of the most enduring metanarratives in children's stories is the binaries of good and evil or right and wrong; a metanarrative that was clearly evident in all of the films analyzed. In films rated as "U" or "PG" and therefore intended for a younger audience, the evil character is easily identifiable because of the way they look, talk or dress. In this way, moral complexity is eradicated and young viewers are left in no doubt as to whom they should sympathize with and who should be feared.

In *The Little Vampire*, Tony, who has just moved from San Diego to a small and remote rural village in Scotland, befriends a vampire called Rudolph. All Rudolph and his family desire is to lift the vampire curse that plagues them and become human beings again: "We want to become humans, not eat them for dinner." The main obstacle in their way comes in the form of Rookery, the Vampire Hunter. His evil intent is inscribed on his body, or what Bourdieu called "bodily hexis" (69–70). He is unwashed and unshaven, has dirty nails and bad teeth and he wears what appears to be vampire fangs on a chain around his neck. In *Vampire Dog* Fang, the eponymous hero is hunted by "mad scientist" Dr. Warhol and her hapless assistant, Frank, who want the dog's vampire DNA to develop a formula for an anti-ageing cream. Dr. Warhol shares none of the physical markers of Rookery the Vampire Hunter but her evil machinations are also evident in how she presents herself. She is perfectly made up, wears stilettos even on a heist at the local dog pound and is rarely seen without her headscarf and sunglasses, even indoors and at night. Dr. Warhol belongs to the long tradition of the female villain as femme fatale characterized by excess, sexual potency,[4] inability to control their actions or emotions, "their aggressive, often hysterical, actions and by their conceiving of acts of extreme physical or emotional cruelty" (Mallan 6). The realization of her plan depends on the closure of the local high school which she intends to turn into her laboratory. She convinces the school's headmaster, Mr. Hickman, to help her with the devious plot but when there is a risk of failure, she tells him "This school will close and if you let me down I will carve you up like a Thanksgiving turkey."

Even when the villain is not represented in such explicit ways, evil forces are still an ever-present danger in many of the films. However, this time because the evil characters are less obvious, they are potentially more dangerous. In *My Babysitter's a Vampire*, the vampire group is headed by Jesse, who is actually Reverend Horace Black, leader of an evil cult from the time of the first settlement of the town of Whitechapel. When the townspeople found out about the cult they trapped all 219 members in their place of worship and burned them alive. Jesse/Reverend Horace Black has returned to steal 219 souls from the living to resurrect the dead cult members. However, at school Jesse and his friends are seen as the "cool kids" by their fellow pupils who look at them with a mixture of admiration, envy and fear. Desperate to be like the "cool kids" they are only too quick to attend a party at Jesse's house or attend the advance screening of *Dusk III: Unbitten*, providing him with the ideal opportunity to capture the souls he needs. The evil characters in these films trick, lure or tempt the "good kids" to make "bad" choices and behave in "morally dubious" ways. In other films it is the binary of right and wrong that must be addressed. Children learn that they must not tell lies (*Hotel Transylvania*), they should not put their needs before those of others (*Hotel Transylvania 2*), they should not be mean to others (*Vampire Dog*; *My Babysitter's a Vampire*) and the importance of loyalty, friendship (*Scooby Doo and the Legend of the Vampire*) and family is emphasized. In children's vampire films, the fate that awaits evil villains, both male and female, is presented as just deserts for their treachery and cruelty; good triumphs over evil; those who make the "right" moral judgments are rewarded, while those deemed to be lacking in moral fiber are punished.

A number of scholars have argued that the vampire in contemporary narratives for an adult audience has been domesticated.[5] This domesticated vampire evokes sympathy or at the very least empathy and blurs the boundary between human and monster. In so doing, the binaries of good and evil are challenged and social relationships are seen as morally complex and even morally ambiguous. However, the vampire in children's narratives, while certainly domesticated, has much in common with the traditional fairy story or folktale and functions as a pedagogical tool in the transmission of dominant cultural norms and values.

And They All Lived Happily Ever After...

Another metanarrative of children's literature and film is the normalcy of heterosexuality. If we accept the argument advanced by Stephens and McCallum that the Western metaethic produces a limited number of metanarratives which function to perpetuate societal norms and values, then the representation of romantic love and relationships in children's literature and film can be seen to reinforce and reproduce compulsory heterosexuality and heteronormativity. In 1980, in her famous essay *Compulsory Heterosexuality and Lesbian Existence*, Adrienne Rich claimed that heterosexuality is a sociopolitical institution that is maintained by force. Rather than an inevitable and natural choice, heterosexuality should be understood as "something that has to be imposed, managed, organised [and] propagandized" (Rich 648). It becomes compulsory because it is institutionalized in the very fabric of a heteropatriarchal society and same-sex possibilities are silenced, trivialized and/or pathologized. The term "heteronormativity" refers to the ways in which sex, gender and sexuality are constructed as causally connected and conflated to such as extent that it is assumed that there is, or there should be, congruence between them in what Judith Butler called the "heterosexual matrix." So, a normatively masculine man expresses his gender identity and sexuality through his attraction to and desire for his opposite but complementary other—a feminine woman. Institutionalized and taken for granted, heteronormativity is predicated on the belief that "Het[erosexual] culture thinks of itself as the element form of human association, as the very model of intergender relations, as the indivisible basis of all community and as the means of reproduction without which society wouldn't exist" (Warner xxi).

Karin Martin and Emily Kazyak identify two distinct but related representations of heterosexuality in children's G-rated films[6]: "First, heterosexuality is constructed through hetero-romantic love relationships as exceptional, powerful, magical and transformative. Second, heterosexuality outside of relationships is constructed through portrayals of men gazing desirously as women's bodies" (Martin and Kazyak 1). Both representational forms were clearly evident in the children's vampire films that were analyzed. However, it was also possible to identify a third representation of heterosexuality. In keeping with the heterosexual matrix based on assumed congruity between biological sex, cultural gender and sexual identity, characters who transgressed societal expectations of their sex/gender were often positioned outside the heterosexual matrix.

The notion of hetero-romantic love as powerful, magical and transformative is a major narrative in *Hotel Transylvania*. After his wife (and mother of his child), Martha, was killed by humans, Dracula commissions the construction of a hotel in the remote Transylvanian countryside, where he can take his daughter Mavis to keep her from harm's way and where other monsters can take their vacations safe in the knowledge that there are no humans on site. The hotel is like a fortress, set in 400 acres of haunted forest that is surrounded by a graveyard of the undead, all designed to keep humans at bay. However, on the eve of Mavis' 118th birthday a human backpacker named Jonathan (Johnny) does traverse the scary forest, arrives at the forest and is met by Dracula himself. Desperate to prevent Mavis from meeting Johnny and to maintain the myth he has constructed about humans as dangerous Dracula attempts to disguise him as monster called Johnny Stein, a distant relative of Frankenstein on his right arm's side. However, Mavis and Johnny do eventually meet and when they do there is a moment of magic. Their eyes lock, both of their eyes widen, sparkle and flash pink. Still convinced that any relationship between a human and vampire will be harmful Dracula convinces Jonathan to leave the hotel. However, he realizes that he has made a terrible mistake when Mavis opens the gift that her mother had left for 118th birthday. It is a book about how she met Dracula:

> Two lonely bats crashed in the night
> They felt a Zing. Love at first sight
> They knew right then they would be husband and wife
> For a Zing only happens once in your life.
> Your Zing will come my love. Cherish it [Tartakovsky 2012].

A Zing is love at first sight and is based on the notions that individuals only experience true love once in their lives and that true love conquers all (see also Cokely) Mavis looks at her father with sadness in her eyes and says "I thought we Zinged, Dad.... But I guess it was only me." Thinking that her Zing is not reciprocated she tells Dracula that she has no more dreams. Because true love happens only once in a lifetime, a missed opportunity means a future without love. Realizing he has made a terrible mistake, Dracula is determined to bring Johnny back to the hotel. When he attempts to recruit his monster friends to find Johnny they protest that, as a human, he might have killed them, but Dracula tells them, "I think they Zinged." With eyes filled with tears Frankenstein says, "You only Zing once in your life," and all the monster friends rush out in search of Johnny. Such is the transformative power of the "Zing," or true love, that it can overcome centuries of mistrust and conflict between humans and monsters.

In a less dramatic, but still transformative way, heteronormativity is central to the plot in *Vampire Dog*. The "Zing" that Mavis and Johnny experienced was evident in the first meeting of Ace and Skylar, the central protagonists in the film. Ace and his mother have moved to the town of Lugosi and are starting a new life in a new neighborhood, school and job. Ace first sees Skylar on moving day. He is sitting on the porch at the front of their house with his mother and Skylar rides past on her bicycle. Not unlike Mavis and Johnny, their eyes lock, the scene moves into slow motion and suddenly music begins to play. It is as though Ace has been transfixed, even hypnotized, by Skylar but this scene is abruptly broken when he falls backwards into a pile of empty boxes. Their hetero-romantic relationship, implied rather than explicitly stated, transforms both of their lives. For Skylar, it allows her to accept herself for who she is rather than making compromises to belong to a group of "cool" girls. For Ace, it gives him confidence, in particular the confidence to play his drums in public, something he has never been able to do because of his debilitating shyness. Although ridiculed by other kids in the high school throughout the film, Ace and Skylar are oblivious to it and are emboldened by their newfound relationship.

Outside of these life-changing and all conquering hetero-romantic love relationships, heterosexuality is portrayed as "frivolous, entertaining and crude ... [based on] the heterosexiness of feminine characters, and the heterosexual gaze of the masculine ones" (Martin and Kazyak 15). Laura Mulvey has argued that in a society predicated on sexual inequality, such as heteropatriarchy, men are always positioned as the active subject who looks and women as the passive object who is looked at, and further, "[T]he determining male gaze projects its phantasy on the female figure, which is styled accordingly" (Mulvey 837).

The desirous male gaze was a recurrent feature in children's vampire films. However, where the hetero-romantic representation of heterosexuality is frequently constructed as a major or even driving storyline, the heterosexual gaze of male characters towards females is never central to the plot, and is in fact usually irrelevant to the development of the narrative. Rather, it would appear that these scenes are there purely for entertainment or comedic value. For example, when Dracula's new hotel is being built, four male zombies working on the construction site set down their tools and stare at a female zombie as she walks past. They make no attempt to communicate with her but do share their thoughts with each other through hand gestures, including thumbs up and placing thumb and index finger together to create a circle, which signifies "okay."

Similarly, in *Scooby Doo and the Legend of the Vampire* Daphne becomes the object of male gaze. Set in Australia, the gang (Daphne, Freddie, Velma, Shaggy and Scooby) is taking a tour of the country in their Mystery Van and decide to make Bondi Beach one of their first stops. Daphne, who is drawn in such a way as to reflect normative standards of beauty—long hair, slim waist, long legs, red lips and large eyes—is standing on the beach, wearing a bikini and applying sun cream. Two men stop, stare at her, and one says to the other, "What a Sheila!" to which the other replies, "I'll say." She is later shown sitting on her beach towel with four men stood, towering over her. The men smile but do not talk to Daphne. Instead, it would appear that she is simply the object of their projected phantasies. It is noteworthy that Velma, who has a fuller figure, a shorter stature, wears glasses and a high necked sweater is neither bikini clad, being dressed in a t-shirt instead, nor is she the object of the male gaze reflecting the fact that it is only certain types of bodies that are normatively constructed as desirable.

Martin and Kazyak suggest that the objectification of women and their bodies does not stop at the gaze; it is "often translated into objectifying, sexist language" (18). *My Babysitter's a Vampire* is littered with such language and comes principally from Benny, Ethan's best friend. Although he is cast as a "geek" and positioned outside the "cool" group of kids at school, he is portrayed as a "good guy" fighting the evil vampires. Yet he uses sexist language indiscriminately, for example, referring to "primo high school babes," saying "Hey, hot stuff" as a young girl walks past him in the corridor and "That is one babetastic tower of babe-ylon" about Sarah, the babysitter in the film's title. Referring to young girls as "babes" may be intended to be humorous and highlight Benny's awkwardness around girls. After all, the girls on the receiving end of his comments usually ignore him or roll their eyes in exasperation. However, in a climate where fears about the sexualization of young girls is commonplace and there is increasing evidence of girls' experiences of everyday sexism Benny's quips seem far less humorous. Notwithstanding the contestation over the causes, scope and consequences of sexualization, if it is taken to mean that a person's value is equated only or primarily with physical attractiveness defined by narrowly defined normative standards (APA) then the desirous male gaze and objectifying, sexist language in children's films becomes deeply problematic.

The Little Vampire is the only film that did not explicitly represent heterosexuality through either hetero-romantic love or the desirous male gaze although heterosexuality is not entirely absent. After Tony saves the Sackville-Bagg family from Rookery, the vampire hunter, Rudolph's sister Anna proclaims, "The age of chivalry is not yet dead." She becomes smitten with Tony. She writes him a love poem and gives him a gift of a dead mouse "from the old country" for luck but Tony is oblivious to her affections. There was, however, an example of characters being positioned outside of the heterosexual matrix. Tony tells Rudolph that he is being bullied by two boys in his class. Determined to put an end to this the two friends visit the tormentors' bedroom in the middle of the night. Awakened in their beds and absolutely terrified, the brothers scream, loudly and Rudolph issues them with a warning to leave Tony alone. The following morning Tony is waiting for them at school and asks "Sleep well last night girls?" This "insult" is also used in *My Babysitter's a Vampire* when Ethan and Benny try to leave after crashing the vampires' party to rescue their friend Rory. They are stopped by one of the vampires who says "Whoa, where are you girls going?" In these examples, the term "girl" is being used to signify "weakness, incompetency, lack, inferiority" (Renold 84) and in so doing the boys' masculinity is challenged because, particularly for young boys, being masculine means not being feminine. Consequently, any hint of femininity must be quashed, as must the suggestion of homosexuality. Now a vampire, Rory appears at Ethan's bedroom window and, in keeping with vampire folklore, he needs an invitation before he can enter.

> RORY: So can I come in?
> ETHAN: Yes but just as long as you promise no bloodsucking.
> RORY: Dude! My mouth on your neck? [Rory shivers] [McDonald 2012].

Where boys are feminized to indicate weakness, female characters are often masculinized to indicate their transgression of societal gender expectations. Female villains in Western animation are frequently drawn, if not to reflect stereotypical masculine characteristics, then certainly as androgynous—tall, slim, angular facial features. In *Vampire Dog*, when Dr. Warhol barks an order to her assistant, Frank, he quickly replies "Yes Sir. Er madam. Er, Doctor," addressing her first as male, then female and finally with the non-gendered title of "Doctor." Her evil scheming and hatred of children and animals are not compatible with socially constructed notions of femininity and, therefore, represents a challenge to the heterosexual matrix based on congruity between biological sex and cultural gender. For Butler the "knowability of the human" (Butler 183) requires coherence with the cultural assumptions underpinning the heterosexual matrix so Dr. Warhol incoherence renders her, and specifically her gender, unknowable.

As Jeffrey Weinstock notes "Vampire narratives are always, inevitably, about sex—although what each has to say obviously will vary depending upon time and place" (4). As a result the figure of the vampire has always presented fertile ground for theorists of sexuality and numerous analyses have been presented including, the bite as metaphor for phallic penetration; the vampire as libidinal creature unencumbered by sexual anxieties and repression; breaking of taboos and engaging in sexual excess; transgression of sexual mores; with the emergence of HIV, the vampire and its bite signified the transmission of the virus; and the list goes on. However, the vampire in these children's films is firmly entrenched in heteronormativity and heterosexuality is normalized. The hetero-romantic love relationships, desirous male gaze and the positioning of some characters outside the heterosexual matrix can be seen as a continuation of traditional fairy tales and, in particular, their adaptation as Disney Princess films in which everyone lives happily ever after.

It Is Great to Be a Vampire!

So far, the recurring themes identified and discussed have reflected adult concerns about what is "appropriate" with regards to children's films and adult expectations about the moral codes and social norms that children need to acquire to fulfill their responsibilities as adults of the future. However, children are not passive consumers of popular culture. Regardless of the messages adults want children to take from these films, children exercise agency and choice in the way they interact with them, "bringing to bear their own interpretations, adapting and shaping them to their own ends" (Kehily and Swann xi). The figure of the vampire or the vampire's relationship with the child protagonists in these films opens up a world for children beyond their own and provides them with opportunities to imagine themselves without the limitations imposed on them by adults.

Writing about the appeal of Harry Potter, Roni Natov (310) suggests that it is both his ordinariness and his extraordinariness that children are drawn to. Orphaned and treated appallingly by his adoptive family, the Dursleys, Harry is forced to sleep in a cupboard under the stairs, is denied information about the death of his parents and is generally treated with disdain. Although his circumstances are extreme, Natov argues that Harry Potter can be seen as "a kind of Everychild ... [because] ... he embodies this state of injustice frequently experienced by children" (311–312). Thankfully, relatively few children experience the level of emotional abuse and physical deprivation that Harry does, but young children's lives *are* characterized by hardships simply because of their position as children in an adult-centric world. It is what Frances Waksler refers to as "the hard times of childhood" (216); the everyday and ordinary difficulties that children experience at the hands of adults. These are not times that adults would define as hard, nor are they the result of adults' intentional cruelty. Indeed, many of the hard times children experience are the result of adults acting in, what they think, is children's best interests. However, Waksler suggested that the hard times that children experience are the result of a lack control over many aspects of their lives and she identified three main areas—lack of control over the physical world, lack of control over the world of emotions and lack of control over the moral world.

These ordinary and everyday difficulties were clearly evident in the films. Both Ace in *Vampire Dog* and Tony in *The Little Vampire* lack control over their physical world where they are required to leave their homes and the friends they have because their parents have got new jobs. Their relocation results in more hardships due to being the new kid in school. At the start of both films Ace and Tony are subjected to torment and ridicule by their fellow pupils. Children's lack of control over the emotional world is often a product of adults' belief that they are incapable of complex emotions. Two examples of complex emotions that Waksler identifies are fear and embarrassment, especially embarrassment over the way adults behave in public. In *My Babysitter's a Vampire*, Benny's grandmother explains to her grandson and his friend, Ethan, that they have special powers that will help them in their fight against Jesse/Reverend Horace Black and his vampire cult. She tells Ethan that he is a Seer and says that he should have started having visions as they emerge during puberty. Much to Ethan's embarrassment and in front of his best friend, eight-year-old sister Jane and babysitter, Sarah, she adds, "You have got your big boy hair haven't you?" When Tony has yet another of his dreams about vampires, which actually turn out to be visions, feeling distressed and upset, he goes to his parents' room and joins them in their bed. Desperate to return to sleep, his parents try to reassure Tony that vampires are not real. From her research, Waksler found that such reassurances are not always interpreted as such by children. In the words of one of her participants whose mother said monsters did not exist, "I would wonder to myself about how she could be so stupid. I knew they were there and she didn't care" (217). Lack of control over the moral world is concerned with truth telling; in particular, children not being believed and different standards and expectations of truth telling for children and adults. When Tony discusses vampires and his dreams/visions he is not believed by his parents, his teacher or the other children in his class. When Ace tells his mother that Fang is a special dog and needs special care, she dismisses this by saying "All kids think their pet is special." In *Hotel Transylvania* and *Hotel Transylvania 2* Dracula constructs numerous and elaborate lies to stop Mavis from venturing out into the human world and to prevent her and his grandson Dennis from leaving Transylvania for California. Child viewers recognize and are able to identify with these hard times and, just like Harry Potter, the child protagonists in these films do represent a kind of Everychild.

Although the child protagonists reflect the hard times of childhood they also demonstrate strategies of resistance and subvert adult demands and expectations of them. This is usually most clearly evident in their relationships with the vampire characters. When Dracula first meets Johnny at the hotel he attempts to hypnotize him by erasing his memory and forcing him to leave the hotel. The hypnosis does not work however due to Johnny's contact lenses and Johnny retains control over his mind and body. Dracula also has the ability to freeze time which he uses to hatch secrets plans. In *Vampire Dog* Fang uses hypnosis on a number of occasions to make Frank act like a chicken and later a dog, Dr. Warhol behave like a cat and one of the boys bullying Ace is hypnotized to pour a cold drink over himself. Natov suggests that "supernatural powers invite children to imagine beyond the boundaries of their limitations; what if I could see and hear without being seen or heard; what if I could fly; what if I could read minds" (316). In *The Little Vampire*, Tony resists his parents' and babysitter's instruction to go to bed and, instead, goes flying with Rudolph. On one occasion, Tony even engages in a quid pro quo arrangement with him insisting that he will only help him in his quest to become human again if he takes him flying. Enforced bedtimes and naps were recurrent themes in Waksler's research into the hard times of childhood and the idea of resisting this control over one's physical body is an attractive one for children.

Resistance to adult control is also evident when child protagonists ignore the demands that have been made of them. In *My Babysitter's a Vampire* Ethan's parents hire a babysitter, principally for his sister following Ethan and Benny's less than attentive supervision of her. They instruct him to stay indoors and be on his best behavior when the babysitter arrives. Similarly, Ace is grounded by his mother following Fang's very public visit to his high school, leaving a path of destruction in his wake. However, if both boys are to save the day, they must defy their parents' wishes. Ace has to get Fang, who has been taken to the local dog pound, and get to the school if Lugosi High School is to win the Battle of the Bands competition, which they must do if the school is to remain open. Ethan must leave his house to attend the nighttime advance screening of *Dusk III: Unbitten* if Jesse/Reverend Black's plan to steal human souls is to be stopped. The boys' decision to go against their parents' instructions should not be seen simply as an act of willful defiance. Rather, they know that they have to be defiant if they are to be successful in their goals. According to Chappell, "An adult rhetoric of safety and control exists in ... contemporary society, suggesting that if children submit to established [adult defined] limits they will remain safe from outside threats" (291).

However, acts of resistance such as those demonstrated by Ace and Ethan introduce complexity and choice to children. Instead of discrete binaries, good/evil, right/wrong, safety/danger are more contingent and best thought as continua against which children "may choose to accept or challenge the limits they are given depending on their own subject position and context of real or perceived threat to their safety and wellbeing" (291). Faced with the threat posed by Jesse/Reverend Black Ethan decides that the right thing to do for his safety and the safety of others is to defy his parents' wishes. Although she does not say so explicitly, Ace's mother does acknowledge the complexity of moral decision-making. After Ace's school has won Battle of the Bands due to Ace overcoming his nerves and demonstrating his drumming skills it is no longer at risk of being closed. She tells him, "Ace, I'm not happy about you sneaking out, okay. Even if it was for Fang. But I'm also very, very proud of you for drumming tonight."

Conclusion

The domesticated vampire of adult literature, who evokes sympathy, empathy or even pity and seems to have more in common with their human counterparts than previously presented, has blurred the boundaries between human and monster. If the vampire is capable of experiencing the same range of emotions as humans, including those not hitherto associated with them such as love, regret and shame, then the binaries of good/evil, right/wrong begin to disintegrate. To some extent, it should come as no surprise that this manifestation of the vampire is so prevalent in contemporary popular culture because it reflects the uncertainty, change and concomitant anxieties thought to characterize the twenty-first century (Levina and Bui 1–2). What does seem surprising, at least at first sight, is that the vampire narratives in children's literature and film remain so firmly rooted in the fairy stories and folklore of the past where "baddies" wear their evil intent in their sleeve and the way they are depicted makes it very difficult, if not impossible, to sympathize with them. Similarly, sexual diversity is absent from these re-tellings of traditional stories. It can be argued that vampires in adult literature represent all that is feared and all that is desired about sexuality, they are "pure id, libidinal energy incarnate, and this makes them both dangerous and dangerously attractive" (Weinstock 4) and the more recent domesticated vampires present sexuality in complex and ambiguous ways. Yet, the vampire narratives in children's films continue to be perpetuate heteronormativity. If every age gets the vampire it needs, it seems that the vampire in children's films needs children to conform to compulsory heterosexuality.

It is important to remember, though, that it is largely adults who write children's fiction. So, the representation of simple and unambiguous moral tales can be seen as adults' attempts to protect children from the harsh realities of adult life in the twenty-first century; an attempt to maintain childhood innocence for as long as possible or, more accurately, an attempt to maintain the construction and façade of childhood innocence. The naturalization of heterosexuality and the reification of heteronormativity in these films contribute to the myriad ways in which children are schooled into heterosexuality.

However, children do not live in a separate world and innocence is not a natural condition of childhood; it is something that is imposed on them by adults and contributes to the perpetuation of the adult/child dichotomy. If we accept the argument that children are human beings and not human becomings, they are social actors in a world characterized by uncertainty and ambiguity, interpreting and incorporating this uncertainty into their own social and cultural worlds. Although adults may want to project certain expectations on to children about who they are and who they should become, evident in the traditional narratives identified in this essay, children have ways to circumvent these demands; something that the vampires and child protagonists in these films allow children to imagine.

Notes

1. See, for example, Chris Jenks 1996, Allison James and Alan Prout 1997, Allison James, Chris Jenks, and Alan Prout 1998, Allison James and Adrian, L., James 2004, Roger Shipley Smith 2010.
2. See also William Corsaro 2003.
3. Jakeward is a conflation of the names Jacob and Edward, two male protagonists and Bella's love interests in the *Twilight* series.
4. See, for example, Bell 1995, Sells 1995, Craven, 2002.
5. See, for example, Gordon and Hollinger 1997, Zanger 1997.
6. G-rating is the classification awarded by the Motion Picture Association of America for films considered appropriate for General Audiences, meaning all ages can be admitted. It is the equivalent of a film classified as "U" by the British Board of Film Classification.

Works Cited

American Psychological Association Task Force. *Report of the APA Task Force on the Sexualization of Girls*. American Psychological Association 2007 http://www.apa.org/pi/wpo/sexualization.html. Accessed 1 July 2016.
Auerbach, Nina. *Our Vampires, Ourselves*. London: University of Chicago Press, 1995.
Bell, Elizabeth. "Somatexts at the Disney Shop: Constructing the Pentimentos of Women's Animated Bodies." *From Mouse to Mermaid: The Politics of Film, Gender, and Culture*. Ed. Elizabeth Bell, Lynn Haas, and Laura Sells. Bloomington: Indiana University Press, 1995. 107–124.
Bourdieu, Pierre *The Logic of Practice*. California: Stanford University Press, 1980.
Butler, Judith. *Bodies that Matter: On the Discursive Limits of Sex*. London: Routledge, 2000.
_____. "Doing Justice to Someone: Sex-Reassignment and Allegories of Transsexuality." *The Transgender Studies Reader*. Ed. Susan Stryker, and Stephen Whittle. London: Routledge. 2006.
_____. *Gender Trouble: Feminism and the Subversion of Identity*. London: Routledge, 1990.
Chappell, Drew. "Sneaking Out After Dark: Resistance, Agency, and the Postmodern Child in JK Rowling's Harry Potter Series." *Children's Literature in Education* 39 (2008): 281–293.
Cokely, Carrie, L. "'Someday My Prince Will Come': Disney, the Heterosexual Imaginary and Animated Film." *Thinking Straight: The Power, Promise and Paradox of Heterosexuality*. Ed. Chrys Ingraham. London: Routledge, 2005. 167–182.
Corsaro, William, A. "Interpretive Reproduction in Children's Peer Cultures." *Social Psychology Quarterly* 55.2 (1992): 160–177.
_____. *The Sociology of Childhood* (4th edition). Thousand Oaks, CA: SAGE, 2014.
_____. *We're Friends Right? Inside Kids' Culture*. Washington: Joseph Henry Press, 2003.
Craven, Allison "Beauty and the Belles: Discourses of Feminism and Femininity in Disneyland." *The European Journal of Women's Studies* 9.2 (2002): 123–142.
Gelder, Ken. *New Vampire Cinema*. London: Palgrave Macmillan, 2012.
Gordon, John, and Veronica Hollinger. "Introduction: The Shape of Vampires." *Blood Read: The Vampire as Metaphor in Contemporary Culture*. Ed. John Gordon and Veronica Hollinger. Philadelphia: University of Pennsylvania Press, 1997. 1–7.

Hall, Christine. "Children's Literature." *Children's Cultural Worlds*. Ed. Mary Jane Kehily and Joan Swann. New York: Open University Press, 2003. 133–182.
Hawley, E. "Re-Imagining Horror in Children's Animated Film." *M/C Journal: A Journal of Media and Culture* 18.6 (2015). http://journal.media-culture.org.au/index.php/mcjournal/article/view/1033. Accessed 12 July 2016.
James, Allison, and Adrian. L. James. *Constructing Childhood: Theory, Policy and Social Practice*. London: Palgrave Macmillan, 2004.
James, Allison, and Alan Prout, eds. *Constructing and Reconstructing Childhood*. London: Falmer Press, 2004.
James, Allison, Chris Jenks, and Alan Prout. *Theorizing Childhood*. Cambridge: Polity Press, 1998.
Jenks, Chris. *Childhood*. London: Routledge, 1996.
Kehily, Mary Jane, and Joan Swaan. "Introduction." *Children's Cultural Worlds*. Ed. Mary Jane Kehily and Jane Swann. New York: Open University Press, 2003. ix–xiii.
Kramer, Peter. "Would You Take Your Child to See This Film? The Cultural and Social Work of the Family-Adventure Movie." *Contemporary Hollywood Cinema*. Ed. Steve Neale and Murray Smith. London: Routledge, 1998. 294–311.
Levina, Marina, and Diem-My T. Bui. "Introduction: Toward a Comprehensive Monster Theory of the 21st Century." *Monster Culture in the 21st Century: A Reader*. Ed. Marina Levina and Diem-My T. Bui. New York: Bloomsbury Academic, 2013. 1–13.
Mallan, Kerry M. "Witches, Bitches and Femmes Fatales: Viewing the Female Grotesque in Children's Film." *Papers: Explorations into Children's Literature* 10.1 (2000): 26–35.
Martin, Karen, A., and Emily Kazyak. "Hetero-Romantic Love and Heterosexiness in Children's G-rated Flms." *Gender & Society* 23.3 (2009): 315–336.
Mulvey, L. "Visual Pleasure and Narrative Cinema." *Film Theory and Criticism: Introductory Readings*. Ed. Leo Braudy and Marshall Cohen. Oxford: Oxford University Press, 1999. 833–844.
Natov, R. "Harry Potter and the Extraordinariness of the Ordinary." *The Lion and the Unicorn*, 25.2 (2001): 310–327.
Renold. E. *Girls, Boys and Junior Sexualities: Exploring Children's Gender and Sexual Relations in the Primary School*. London: Routledge, 2005.
Rich, Adrienne. "Compulsory Heterosexuality and Lesbian Existence." *Signs: Journal of Women in Culture and Society* 5.4 (1980): 631–660.
Sells, Lynn. "'Where Do the Mermaids Stand?': Voice and Body in *The Little Mermaid*." From *Mouse to Mermaid: The Politics of Film, Gender, and Culture*. Ed. Elizabeth Bell, Lynn Haas, and Laura Sells. Bloomington: Indiana University Press, 1995. 175–192.
Smith, Roger. *A Universal Child?* London: Palgrave Macmillan, 2010.
Stephens, John, and Robyn McCallum. *Retelling Stories, Framing Culture Traditional Story and Metanarratives in Children's Literature*. New York: Garland Publishing, 1998.
Waksler, Frances Chaput. "The Hard Times of Childhood and Children's Strategies for Dealing with Them." *Studying the Social Worlds of Children: Sociological Readings*. Ed. Frances Chaput Waksler. London: Falmer Press,1998. 216–238.
Warner, Michael. "Introduction." *Fear of a Queer Planet: Queer Politics and Social Theory*. Ed. Michael Warner. Minneapolis: University of Minnesota Press, 1993. vii–xxxi.
Weinstock, Jeffrey Andrew. "Vampires, Vampires, Everywhere!" *Phi Kappa Phi Forum* 90.3 (2010): 4–5.
Wojcik-Andrews, Ian. *Children's Films: History, Ideology. Pedagogy, Theory*. London: Routledge, 2000.
Wyness, Michael. *Childhood and Society* (2nd edition). London: Palgrave Macmillan, 2012.
Zanger, Jules. "Metaphor into Metonymy: The Vampire Next Door." *Blood Read: The Vampire as Metaphor in Contemporary Culture*. Ed. John Gordon and Veronica Hollinger. Philadelphia: University of Pennsylvania Press, 1997. 17–26.

Filmography

Hotel Transylvania. Dir. Genndy Tartakovsky. Columbia Pictures, 2012.
Hotel Transylvania 2. Dir. Genndy Tartakovsky Columbia Pictures, 2015.

The Little Vampire. Dir. Uli Edel. Cornerstone Pictures, 2000.
My Babysitter's a Vampire. Dir. Bruce MacDonald. Fresh TV, 2011.
Scooby Doo and the Legend of the Vampire. Dir. Scott Jeralds. Hanna-Barbera, 2003.
Twilight. Dir. Catherine Hardwicke. Summit Entertainment, 2008.
Vampire Dog. Dir. Geoff Anderson. Joker Films, 2011.

Looking Back and Seeing the Future

Adult Nostalgia and Negotiating the Future in Children's Books and Films Featuring Vampires

SIMON BACON *and* KATARZYNA BRONK

Introduction

Logically nostalgia, children's literature and cinema would seem an incongruous conjunction, an oxymoron almost, as the youngest members of society—children 12 years old and younger—have not experienced enough popular culture or are even far enough away from their past to be nostalgic about either. And yet a yearning for days past and an idealized vision of childhood itself form the basis of many narratives created for children to read/watch/engage with. As observed by many theorists on the subject, this is due mainly to the adults that write said narratives and project their own desires in regard to childhood, though not necessarily their own, onto the characters and scenarios created. In contrast, vampires often have too much past, not just in relation to their own individual histories, but within the vampire genre itself which, as noted by critics such as Ken Gelder and Jeffrey Weinstock, is exceptionally self-referential and citational, meaning that each new literary or cinematic vampire is constructed with one eye firmly on the past. This inevitable referencing of earlier vampires more often than not contains a degree of nostalgia, particularly that of seminal figures such Count Dracula and his younger relation, Count Orlok. Nostalgia is then an important factor, not just in bringing the past into the present, but also negotiating ways into the future, both in texts for children and those featuring vampires.

Subsequently, this study aims to consider the intersections between these two threads within children's literature and film since the 1970s to see if and how they might reinforce each other; or whether congruities between them offer readings that do not just look backwards but forwards into ways of negotiating what is not always a rose-tinted future.

Ideal, Idealized and Idealistic

Nostalgia, while originally used in the eighteenth century to describe the intense melancholia felt by the Swiss Royal Guard stationed in the Vatican who missed their homes and family back in Switzerland (Illbrock 105), is now used to describe many forms of real or imagined loss or even the desire to suture the wounds and traumas of the past. Childhood in particular is an idealized, imagined time/place delineated by the perceived inadequacies of the present. Much of this can be seen to come from the Golden Era of children's literature, the Victorian period, but nostalgia here seems to be almost endemic quality where, as noted by Catherine Robson, adult writers created a "retrospective imagining of the early years of life as a paradise of innocence and purity" (Robson 8). This idealization, while hinting at a prelapsarian innocence (Gillis xx), equally speaks of a retrospective "wiping the slate," a chance to reimagine what one's childhood might have been, as further explained by Valerie Krips, "few adults would want to return to childhood as it was actually lived, with all its unremembered difficulties, humiliations, and problems, but returning to a past in which the problems of adulthood are by and large unknown is a different and much more enticing prospect" (16). Texts meant for consumption by children can often be seen to exemplify this idyllic vision of childhood—an outplaying of the idealized childhood that the texts' author/s wished they had then being imposed on children now.

This nostalgic view of childhood, then, views literature and film for children as "going back to fight the ghosts of the past in order to move forward rather than a staying behind" (Jagodzinski 120). Obviously, this is not always as positive a move as it sounds for it imposes a very particular view on children whose environment/expectations are very different to those experienced by older generations. However, the use of nostalgia as a corrective tool to change the past and, consequently, the present, also requires that the child partakes of adult nostalgia, or as Nodelman observes "[i]n a sense the text invites child readers to develop a double consciousness—to be both delightfully childlike and separate from that childlikeness, viewing and understanding it from an adult perspective" (Nodelman 46). In this way texts will contain scenarios that are constructed by the authors' nostalgic view of what childhood should be, while also referencing elements that invoke a remembrance of the writers own youth. The first kind of nostalgia (the imagined one) is then reinforced by the second one—the actual remembrance of real things. Texts which work in this way are constructed from material that the child is meant to view as nostalgic, even though they will have no foreknowledge of it, while other parts will have referents within the child's own past—however brief that might be—and so might indeed invoke a remembrance of times past.

Fictional vampires operate very much in this kind of environment constructed from the remembrance of the past. As mentioned above the vampire genre is possibly one of the most self-referential, due in part to the dominance of one particular text in its canon, that of Bram Stoker's *Dracula*. Of course, it is not the only seminal text within the genre but *Dracula* is arguably the first to grip the popular imagination, not just as a novel, but as a play, and, more importantly, as a film. Tod Browning's *Dracula* is often cited as the first sound horror movie. It stamped the Transylvanian Count indelibly into the popular consciousness, or rather the use of Bela Lugosi as the vampire did. The actor's aristocratic manner, greased back widows peak hair, high-collared cape and thick, almost impenetrable, Hungarian drawl have been ready signifiers of all things vampiric ever since. Equally, the unofficial cinematic adaptation of Stoker's novel by F. W. Murnau, *Nosferatu: A Symphony of Horror* (1922), created the feral vampire that has become the dark cousin of the romantic vampire and remains integral to the genre. Resultantly, a large amount of contemporary vampire narratives, including those intended for children, can be seen to reference, often nostalgically, these earlier vampires. As Nina Auerbach notes, "there are many Draculas—and still more vampires who refuse to be Dracula or play him" (1), intimating that even those not like Stoker's vampire are very *knowingly* not like him.

Vampires in texts meant for children particularly can be seen to take a nostalgic direction, with *Sesame Street's* Count Von Count possibly being the most obvious example, with its blatant referencing of Bela Lugosi's performance as the vampire—oddly though Count Von Count has fangs, whereas Lugosi did not. Coming forty years after Browning's film, The Count first appeared in Sesame Street in 1972, and was clearly the product of adult nostalgia rather than based on that of its intended audience—although the by the 1970s vampire would have been familiar to the young as a popular Halloween costume (*True Ghost Tales* 2012).

However, while vampires were relatively new to children's books and films in the 1970s, by the early twenty-first century the situation has changed considerably and the foreknowledge expected of the younger audience has greatly increased. For example, television series/franchises such as *Monster High* (meant for audiences of 11+) reference the highly popular young adult series The Twilight Saga (*Monster High-Fright On*, 2011). Searching for other examples, the present study will subsequently look at a selection of texts and characters ranging from the 1970s up to the present day—Count Von Count, *Bunnicula, Mona the Vampire, Dick and Jane* and *Monster High*—to examine the levels of adult nostalgia and idealization involved. This is in order to discuss whether they are intended to fulfill the authors' desire for an idealized vision of childhood, or offer ways of negotiating with one's past to better cope with the future.

Counting Backwards

Although already mentioned above it is worth taking a closer look at Count Von Count from *Sesame Street* as he exemplifies much of how one kind of adult nostalgia works in this study. *Sesame Street* can certainly be said to present something of a nostalgic idyllic vision of childhood—and even more so the first DVDs released of the early shows in 2006 (Skenazy 68-69). However, the Count himself is almost totally a creation of (and for) adult remembrance. The muppet/puppet created for the part is directly taken from Bela Lugosi's performance from the 1931 film and has a widows peak, long-hooked nose and arched eyebrows as well as a high collared cape, though there is an added monocle, pointed ears and two large fangs, neither of which were seen in the Universal original.[1] He lives in a large castle full of cobwebs, possibly, in the Carpathian Mountains, as did Dracula. Unlike Lugosi's vampire though he has bats as pets and is obsessed with numbers and counting. While this obsession is something of a pun on his name, in Eastern European folklore vampires were often deterred or detained by their compulsion to count either grains of millet or seeds, or with untying knots (Dundes 114)—nets were put in the coffins of people suspected of being undead so that they would undo all the knots first before leaving their graves. One suspects the show's creators were not aware of the latter, but the other vampiric signifiers would have been used to trigger adult remembrance rather than any foreknowledge that the young audience of the show might have had.

That said, although the majority of vampires on film at that time were mainly intended for adults (the Hammer series of Dracula films starring Christopher Lee and which began with *Dracula* [Fisher: 1958] were highly popular at the end of the 1960s/start 1970s), some children might have seen *The Munsters* (Burns 1964-1966) which was a family show featuring Yvonne De Carlo as Lily Munster and Al Lewis as Grandpa, who were both vampires—Grandpa in particular shared many features with Lugosi's Count. Also interestingly, when Count Von Count actually counted numbers, after each one a crack of thunder was heard, something which was never part of Browning's film—which is actually noted for its lack of sound in the scenes set in

Transylvania, apart for the howling of the wolves outside (the "music" of the creatures of the night)—and is associated more with mad scientist horror films such as *Frankenstein* (Whale 1931).[2]

This, like the details of Lugosi's Dracula, would have been learnt by the adult audience from their own, many viewings of the films which were shown on late night television in America from the late 1950s (*The Creeping Bride* 2010). Consequently, the thunder and lightning can be seen as playing to adult expectations and, effectively, teaching children to respond to the same signifiers as those used to trigger grown-up nostalgia. Count Von Count is literally made from adult nostalgia which in turn will be utilized nostalgically by the children of the 1970s when they grow up—an obvious example of this would be the episode "Smile Time" in the television series *Angel* from 2004 where the hero of the program, a vampire detective, is turned into a muppet/puppet just like the Count from *Sesame Street*. While the counting Count cannot be seen to have produced any later imitators it did, arguably, opened the way for more vampires to appear in texts, etc., meant for children.

Bunnies, Ducks and Other Animals

Bunnicula: A Rabbit-Tale of Mystery by James and Deborah Howe was published in 1979 and it is one of the earliest examples of a friendly vampire in young children's books. It establishes a few important features that became central to the rules of how vampires can be used in works for the very young. Firstly, it uses an animal as the main character, which has a similar effect to The Count being a muppet/puppet. It immediately makes it safer and less scary—this will be carried on into examples such as the television series *Count Duckula* (Cosgrove and Hall 1988–1993), the film *Vampire Dog* (Anderson 2012) and, arguably, the vampire storyline in the television series *My Little Pony: Friendship Is Magic* (Faust 2012–present). Secondly, the vampire character is vegetarian, and although it is a rabbit, this feature still looks forward to the early twenty-first century where various kinds of "veggie" vampires exist.[3]

Bunnicula was written at the time when the idea of the "sympathetic" vampire was being explored with authors such as Anne Rice (*Interview with the Vampire*, 1976) and Chelsea Quinn Yarboro (*Hotel Transylvania*, 1978), allowing their undead protagonists to speak for themselves and not only exploring their own motivations but often choosing to control or sublimate their need for human blood. Bunnicula himself though, while exhibiting these "modern" traits, very much looks backwards and like Dracula before him is not allowed to speak for himself. The audience has to depend on the unreliable narrator Harold, a dog owned by the Munroe family, to discover the unfolding events. Actually, the shadow of Dracula looms large at the start of the book, as does adult nostalgia, for the rabbit is found by the Munroes—Mr. and Mrs. Munroe and their two sons, Toby, aged eight, and Pete, aged ten—on a family excursion to the cinema to see *Dracula*. This must have been a screening of Browning's original as the children would not have been allowed in to see any of the Dracula films released during that period. Once there they discover a baby rabbit in a blanket left by their seats with a note that none of them can decipher, though as it happens a worldly Harold is able to translate it for the reader—"Because my family got around a lot, I was able to recognize the language as an onscreen dialect of the Carpathian Mountain region. Roughly translated it read, 'Take good care of my baby'" (Howe and Howe 9). And when the Munroes with the as yet unnamed bunny open the front door retuning to Harold and their cat Chester, their entrance is greeted with a flash of lightening framing them all in the doorway.

These opening scenes contain many levels of remembrance and nostalgia. The excitement of the children seeing their first "grown up" film and the intimated "birthing" point of the bunny from Browning's film. The translation of the documents by the narrator, as in Stoker's novel, and the lightening flash utilize the same nostalgia for old horror films, as mentioned earlier. In honor of the film where he was found, the rabbit is named Bunnicula (a combination of the words bunny and Dracula). The further remembrance of Lugosi's Dracula is reinforced by the white rabbit's black marking which resembles a widow's peak on its head and a bat-winged cape over its body.

As the story develops Harold takes on the role of a self-taught Van Helsing as he tries to prove to Chester and the Munroes that Bunnicula is up to no good. However, unlike in Stoker's text, the lead vampire hunter is unable to sway the minds of those around him and the Transylvanian rabbit is accepted into the family in spite of his difference—he sucks the juices out of fruit and vegetables leaving them pale and empty and sleeps all day. The story goes on to create an idyllic view of family life with the various pets fully integrated into the household with all its members devoted to each other. The idea of the "perfect" family is itself something of a nostalgic construct and one often leveled at texts from the 1980s where, as noted by Ben Furnish "conservative politicians and polemicists sounded the call to a return to 'family values'" (Furnish 4), which was itself based on nostalgia for the imagined model family from the 1950s. This layered remembrance of remembrance is not completely backwards looking as its open acceptance of outsiders suggests a proactive response to the ever widening world of globalization and immigration. However, it is worth remembering that Bunnicula's inclusion into the family is predicated on the fact that the overall dynamics of the family unit remains the same—his difference becomes part of the nostalgic construct but is not allowed to change it. *Bunnicula* then works on adult nostalgia but also begins to be affected by a growing genre and the notion that its reading audience will have more base knowledge about vampires—hence the inclusion of a veggie vampire that confounds that expectation. The next text to be considered plays on these expectations further, not least in that it does not feature a real vampire at all.

Performing the Vampire

Mona the Vampire by Sonia Holleyman was first published as a book in 1990, and then turned into an animated series that ran from 1999 until 2003. It then produced subsequent books which, together with the series, utilize various forms of nostalgia although the original story, meant as a one-off tale is slightly different. Therefore, it is worth briefly looking at that before considering the later series. The book, meant for 4–9 year olds, features Mona Parker, a little girl with a vivid imagination. The story begins with her and her cat Fang listening to a spooky bedtime story read by her father. The following day, because of the story, Mona is obsessed with vampires and talks nonstop about them to her parents and everyone at school, causing them to think she is a little strange. Cycling home from a shop with Fang she takes a shortcut through a graveyard just as a storm starts. Mona gets frightened and extremely wet. Arriving home both feel ill so Mona's mother puts them to bed with hot chocolate. But that night Mona has nightmares, which puts her off the idea of vampires, and the next morning she puts away her costume and returns to her normal self. However, that night her father reads her a story about aliens with the inference that this will be her next obsession.

The story is founded on a nostalgic view of childhood where obsessions come and go, and parents protect their children through their "phases" until they grow into responsible young adults. A review of the time reinforces this idea and describes Mona as "impressionable" and as looking like "Dracula's daughter" (*Publishers Weekly* 1991), though the cape she wears is covered in flowers and her hair is tied into long black ponytails each held with a small black bow. It is possibly only the plastic fangs she wears that truly identify her as a vampire. As such, her costume is very much based on the costume-box idea where the child's imagination makes ordinary items signify the garb of Princesses, soldiers or whatever—fancies that are worn once and then cast off.

However, by the time the animated series appeared this had significantly changed. Mona's fascination with vampires is no passing whim but a profound part of her developing personality, and her costume is equally important as transitional objects that facilitate her phantasy but also her personal transformation into something other. Claire Rabin notes how transitional objects are used by children to gain a sense of self in the world (98), and Joseph Newirth further explains how such objects, experiences "describe the development of the individual's capacity to use symbolic thought, to infuse objective experience with personal meaning" (150). Mona finds her place in the world and becomes her own person because of these objects. In the series Mona experiences something of a sixth sense in regard to certain people and situations, and her costume allows her to see these for what they really are, be it attacks by robots, aliens or zombies, but also rescue her family, friends or town. Her friends, Lily and Charley, are equally part of her phantasy world and dress as their own versions of superheroes, Princess Giant and Zapman respectively, to help Mona in her adventures.

The three children are picked on or bullied at school for being different, and so their solidarity and costumed alter egos provides them all with agency and positive reinforcement. This rather subverts the cozy nostalgia of the original book turning Mona's brief fancy into a full blown obsession, but one which is constructed as a vital part of her developing personality—without it she could not realize her true abilities or true self. Nostalgia, then, becomes not so much a recreation of the idealized past but a vision of a possible future, and one where parents/adults have little control over what, or how, their children will develop and grow. Interestingly though, many of the scenarios enacted by Mona and her friends are those taken from films, television series or books, and so are based on various forms of remembrance of the characters themselves, and more than likely, of the intended audience as well.

The signifiers of vampirism are particularly interesting in Mona as they reduce them to an almost purely symbolic function, the cape could be any of pattern as long as it is a cape and indeed, it is only given its vampiric connection because of the fangs that she wears. As such, Mona partakes of a very modern vampire nostalgia that sees its power focused around its fangs. Lorna Piatti-Farnell observes how pre–*Dracula* a vampire's teeth were not important, even Stoker only briefly mentions them, but in contemporary texts "fangs are part of 'being a vampire' as a fighting unit, a separate bodily entity divorced from human physiological structures" (70). It is Mona's fangs then which demarcate her as something other than those around her but also forms links with the kind of outsider status seen in The Count—they create a nostalgic connection to the past, while creating individuality in the present. The vampire in Mona is turned into a symbolic entity, which is something that the next text continues to do, but in more directly combating the idea of adult nostalgia, so much so that it is not totally certain who the intended audience is—children or their parents.

208   Section Three: Symbolism, Meanings and Interpretations

Nostalgia with Dick and Jane

The *Dick and Jane* early readers were used in American schools from the 1930s right up to the 1970s, and, as such, form the backdrop for many adults' often nostalgic view of their childhood. The brother and sister duo and their mother and father firmed a very particular view of the American family, and indeed the American Dream itself (Schaie 373). Their extreme whiteness became something of a manual not only on how to speak but how to be American as well. As noted by Dominic Pulera, "The Dick-and-Jane stories provided those out of the mainstream—minorities, white ethnics and the poor—with a model of the majority culture's acceptable value system, and prepared them for participation in civil society" (44). However, the increasing recognition of the multicultural nature of American society saw them fall out of favor, particularly in schools, but this did not end their publication. As commented by Catherine Compton-Lilly, "the books were reissued in 2003 for the sake of nostalgia and with warnings from the publisher that they were not needed for reading instruction" (71).

Dick and Jane and Vampires (2010) falls into this latter category, though it was not a reissue but rather a new work, as the earlier volumes would never feature such risqué subject matter. The book, written by Laura Marchesani, follows the same style of the originals using the whole word and repetition methods. It sees the children involved in everyday situations but the plot slowly begins to develop a sense of menace. It can be seen in the passage below, where Dick and Jane are playing near their mother's ironing board that is draped in a large housecoat:

> Look, Dick.
> Look, look.
> Look at the red ball.
> Look, Jane.
> I will get the red ball.
> Oh, Jane.
> Look, look.
> That is not a red ball [38–40].

The images accompanying the text show the red ball changing into a man's shoe and just as Dick is about to touch it a bat flies out from the ironing board. The bat, and later the figure of a male vampire, appears in the illustrations but is not seen by the children, configuring something of an invisible threat. In fact, in a text that is 144 pages long, the word vampire does not appear until page 96, and at that point, once the "threat" has been named, it is no longer a menace.

The next tableau sees Dick and Jane and their younger sister Sally dress up in bags to play a game chasing the vampire; and in the next one it helps them find a ball. By page 106 the vampire is totally accepted and happily plays with the family:

> Oh, Vampire.
> See funny Dick.
> Dick can play.
> Oh, Mother.
> Oh, Father.
> Jane can play.
> Sally can play.
> Oh, Father.
> See Vampire.
> Funny, funny Vampire.
> Vampire can play [106-108].

The vampire itself is very traditionally dressed in the style of Lugosi, evening dress and high collared cape, and has the distinctive widow's peak and fangs. While remembering the classic 1931 film, the vampire itself appears younger, more the age of the children's parents, making it seem more like an uncle or close friend of the adults. As the story continues, the vampire dresses up in the Mother's clothes to amuse the children, and they then wear his, seeing his identity as performative and interchangeable—it is only the costume that creates one's identity, not unlike with Mona mentioned earlier. It is also interesting as it has the effect of queering the vampire, and seeing him wear his cape over a blue dress and a child's pink bonnet, recalls homosexual readings of *Dracula* and that otherness to the All American family is his sexuality. But the book goes to great lengths to dispel that and has Dick and Jane finding a female vampire for him to be friends with. Consequently, the narrative arc of the tale sees the vampire change from a predator—a "stranger danger" type character—to a figure that is recognized for its difference, potentially defined by its sexuality, but is accepted into the family and ends up following their heteronormative example.

This would seem to show a nostalgic view of the original books but explicitly example the otherness that they purposely avoided, yet also revealing the didactic nature of their ideological message. As Pulera noted, this is "preparing them for entry into civil society." And yet one scene in the tale disavows such a reading—the children look at their reflections in a pond and the vampire does not have one (again a remembrance from Browning's film), revealing him to being innately different to them no matter how much he might look like them. This dissonance is also seen in the way the vampire is drawn in the illustrations which is slightly different to the rest of the characters—the family seem wholly of the American past and are drawn in the same style as the original Dick and Jane books from the 1950s (this includes the clothes that they wear), while the vampire looks slightly more modern—

in fact very reminiscent of Dracula from *Love at First Bite* from 1979—and is also painted and drawn in a much freer way which often gives the impression of him floating above the surface of the image. This visual out-of-stepness disrupts the nostalgic view, highlighting the unreality of the world depicted as well the unbridgeable difference between the majority culture and those perceived as other.

As mentioned earlier, it is questionable just how much *Dick and Jane and Vampires* is actually meant for young children and its level of engagement would seem aimed at those already familiar with the characters, those who would equally recognize the dissonance it creates in relation to the originals.[4] The book is actually one of dissonance and separation, and even one of layers where the world of the children hovers below that of their parents, but that of the vampire seems to be able to move through both yet, ghostlike, remains untouched, Consequently, *Dick and Jane and Vampires* feels separate from the world of twenty-first-century children, and also from the other kinds of vampires depicted in contemporaneous books which are specifically created to appeal to a younger audience, and particularly the kinds shown in series such as *Monster High*, which appeared the same year as Marchesani's book and is designed to be as familiar as possible to its preteen audience.

I Monster

Monster High is a franchise developed by Mattel, and unlike the previous examples it was designed as a multimedia concept from the start, appearing as films, television series, webisodes, books, dolls and other merchandise.[5] As a franchise, it is aimed at 'tweens, which nominally covers the 8–12 year old range, but various parts of the franchise go as low as 6 years in their recommended age. It is based on the idea of a typical American high school— in the way that *High School Musical* by the Disney Channel is typical—except that all the students are children of famous monsters. And so the main characters are Frankie Stein, Clawdeen Wolf, Cleo De Nile, Lagoona Blue and Draculaura daughters of Frankenstein's Monster, The Wolf Man, The Mummy, The Creature from the Black Lagoon and Dracula respectively. While their parents, who are rarely seen, are very much constructed using adult nostalgia for the classic monsters from films from the 30s, 40s and 50s, the children are very much about contemporary representations of school, though a forward looking idealization of what it will be like once they are teenagers.

Draculaura is actually 1,599 years old and only came to school to make "age adjacent" friends. As described by the Monster High website, she is "bright, ambitious and scary-optimistic" and even though her father is "totes strict" with her she maintains a "cheerful outlook on life ... not just for a vampire ... for any monster" (play.monsterhigh.com). The character herself has long brown hair tied into two ponytails, wears high pink lace up boots with a heart stamped on each one, matching the heart shaped beauty mark on her left cheek. She has large golden colored eyes and very red lips to highlight her two bright white fangs. Whether intentional or not, her look is highly reminiscent of Dracula's brides from Stoker's novel where "All three had brilliant white teeth, that shone like pearls against the ruby of their voluptuous lips" (Stoker 41). This, consequently, gives the girl something of an overtly sexualized signification, a point that has been noted not just in relation to Draculaura but the other main female characters (Ghouls) as well. According to a Monster High fansite, The Sun Herald and Fox News ran stories accusing the show of presenting "impossible bodily shapes" (Ife 2011), encouraging young girls "to feel ashamed of their bodies, to focus on being sexually appealing and sexually attractive from a pre-pubescent age" (McKay 2011). As with Barbie, also owned by Mattel, before them, the Monster High girls conform to a (nostalgic) heteronormative ideal of the female body, and one which is based around the overt sexualization of the body, which is similarly used in Stoker's novel but to denote the monstrous, out of control women/girls, that have become vampires.

Monstrosity, at least the normalization of it, is one of the main ideas of Monster High—in a place where everyone is different, or monstrous, no one is a monster. Yet all the characters have a "monster quirk" which marks them out as other. For Draculaura thus is the fact that she cannot see herself in a mirror, with the main consequence being she might look a "little batty," though fortunately she is "scary-good at applying lip gloss" (play.monsterhigh.com). Her hereditary need for blood is elided by being a vegan, or as she says herself "No icky blood for me, so it's fruits, vegetables and a lot of iron supplements" (play.monsterhigh.com) As such, the uniqueness of each character is the part that needs to be sublimated or discretely dealt with so that their public persona matches that of everyone else. This again feeds into the idea of an idealized future of never-ending youth (a projected nostalgia) as the "Ghouls" in the franchise are all configured as 15-year-olds—no matter how many hundreds of years they might have existed for—and so they become role models for their 'tween audience. The nostalgic future for 6–12 year olds is not so much taken from their experience of their own lives but rather seen in material (books, films etc.) meant for young adults. As mentioned, the format of the show itself cites *High School Musical* (Ortega: 2006), *Camp Rock* (Diamond: 2008), *Glee* (Brennon: 2009–2015) and even young adult texts like the Twilight Saga—the television movie *Monster High: Fright On* (Dal Chele; 2011) cites the films as *Twihard* and sees the vampires and werewolves as warring factions complicating the relationship between Draculaura and

Clawdeen's brother, Clawd. Following on from that, the majority of the plots of the various films, books, etc., center around friendship and boyfriends but in largely normative ways seeing the monsters as not that much different to the "normies" (normals), except for their more imaginative dress sense. The result of this is that *Monster High* becomes a vehicle for projecting the past (heteronormative adult idealization/nostalgia) into the future, maybe not so surprising for a series that was created as a franchise to sell merchandise.

The Past and the Present into the Future

Nostalgia and remembrance are an inherent part of cultural production—the present is inevitably built on the foundations of the past, whether affirmatively or negatively, with fondness or antagonism. Texts for children, whether films, books, etc., are often even more so, not only being produced by people other than those within that age category but by those that can equally see it as their duty to offer an idealized representation of childhood as both a didactic and aspirational tool. Here, the past is as much a product of the present as it is the other way round. As noted by Svetlana Boym:

> There should be a special warning on the side view mirror: The object of nostalgia is further away then it appears. Nostalgia is never literal, but lateral. It looks sideways. It is dangerous to take it on face value. Nostalgic reconstructions are based on mimicry; the past is remade in the image of the present or a desired future, collective designs are made to resemble personal aspirations and vice versa [354].

More so, as intimated by Boym, nostalgia and remembrance are multidirectional and even layered so that various kinds intersect and resonate with others, making the outcome extremely difficult to quantify or control. As discussed above vampires in children's texts operate in three distinct areas, the vampire genre, adult/author nostalgia and children's/audience remembrance and each text/example exemplified the ways in which these intersect.

Count Von Count is predominantly based on adult nostalgia in its construction as children in the 1970s, at least that of the target audience for Sesame Street, would have little foreknowledge of the vampire genre and the world constructed around him is largely idealized. That said, the otherness of the remembered vampire is changed from a dangerous outsider—as seen in Browning's Count Dracula—to a quirky foreigner. *Bunnicula* continues this, though the increasing visibility of the vampire in popular culture, not least because of Count Von Count himself, would increase the possible foreknowledge of the audience.

The children's home life is equally idyllic as that of the world created in *Sesame Street*, but the nostalgic otherness of the vampire is so removed from its source that it is fully embraced into the American family. These first two texts partially accomplished their nostalgic work by making their vampires not only non-human but non-threatening, by picturing them as a felt puppet and a small rabbit. *Mona* strips away the adult nostalgia re past vampires and relies on the most basic of vampire signifiers that its intended audience would know and recognize. Her family is idealized but her relationship to them changes subtly between the first book and the later texts (books and series). In the original Mona herself is the nostalgic creation of a fickle child that changes its obsessions frequently, while the later narratives see her as an active agent in her own phantasy worlds. Here, while her parents and friends remain constants, she negotiates her evolving identity in relation to the outside world via the touchstone of her "vampire" senses, which because they are a costume that can be worn or removed at will, remain under her own control. *Dick and Jane and Vampires* seems entirely a work of adult nostalgia as its meaning can only be discovered through comparing it to earlier texts—and this is not just from a year or so in the past, but 30 or 40 years.

As such, although the story can be read as a tale of acceptance of difference, the subversive nature of the vampiric outsider is only really seen in comparison to the strict adherence to ideological normativity of the originals. *Monster High* combines something of all of these, seeing a remembrance of the classic monsters, but modernizing them through the vehicle of their children. A vision of a possible future is offered by setting the stories in a High School, the next step in most of its young readers academic development, and dealing with such themes as long term friendships and romantic, if exclusively heteronormative, partnerships. However, much of the creative side of this evolution is guided by adult consumerist idealization, which directs its audience of future teenagers into looking, wearing and buying a fixed set of consumables. *Monster High* equally shows the growing sophistication of its target audience, in that younger children are increasingly familiar with texts about vampires, and particularly those meant for teenagers and young adults.[6]

Children are then seen as active participants in the creation and consumption of nostalgia and are able to respond to embedded remembrance or intertextuality, but an intertextuality that does not just work backwards or sideways but forwards into works that delineate possible futures for the intended audience. This somewhat changes the direction of nostalgia, or idealized remembrance, with it no longer seeing the past shaped by the longings of the present but a present being potentialized by aspirations for the future. Such visions are not solely the remit of narratives featuring vampires, but the undead do seem to uniquely carry the weight of the past into the future, while offering the possibility of transformation and agency as they move into the world of tomorrow. Consequently, they can be seen to form a bridge between adult nostalgia and youthful aspirational remembrance that does not forget where we have come from but embraces where we might be going, and, importantly for those coming to grips with who they are or might be, provides a space of phantasy where these possibilities can be explored.

Notes

1. Somewhat curiously, the vampire figure used for Count Chocula, a breakfast cereal produced by General Mills and which came out in March 1971, had pointed ears, along with a pointed nose but its fangs are its two front teeth (like Murnau's vampire Nosferatu) and its widows peak is enhanced with two bouffant spines on top.

2. The film *Young Frankenstein* (Brooks 1974) spoofs many of the conventions of early/classic horror films and uses lightning strikes to add a dramatic effect each time an important or portentous line is spoken.

3. This is equally true for some YA narratives, such as the Twilight Saga, which twists it slightly to more free-range or organic blood supplies, while *True Blood* (Ball: 2008–2014)/*The Southern Vampire Mysteries* (Harris: 2001–2013) use a synthetic blood substitute.

4. The book is sold alongside the other *Dick and Jane* books in the young children's category on Amazon and in bookshops.

5. The official Monster High website lists the many branches of the franchise and merchandise options.

6. Recent texts which feature increasing levels of intertextuality are *Scream Street* (Donvaband 2015–present), Marceline the Vampire Queen from *Adventure Time* (Ward 2010–present) and *My Sister the Vampire* (Mercer 2007–present).

Works Cited

Auerbach, Nina. *Our Vampires, Ourselves*. Chicago: University of Chicago, 1996.
Boym, Svetlana. *The Future of Nostalgia*. New York: Basic Books, 2001.
Compton-Lilly, Catherine. *Reading Time: The Literate Lives of Urban Secondary Families and Their Families*. New York: Teachers College Press, 2012.
The Creeping Bride. "Dracula (1931)." *Shock*, October 29, 2010. http://shocktheater1.blogspot.com/2010/10/dracula-1931.html. Accessed 11 September 2016.
"Draculaura." play.monsterhighwww. n.d. http://play.monsterhigh.com/en-us/characters/draculaura. Accessed 24 September 2016.
Dundes, Alan. *The Vampire: A Casebook*. Madison: University of Wisconsin Press, 1998.
Furnish, Ben. *Nostalgia in Jewish-American Theatre and Film 1979–2004*. New York: Peter Lang, 2005.
Gelder, Ken. *New Vampire Cinema*. London: Palgrave Macmillan, 2012.
Gillis, John R. "The Birth of the Virtual Child." *Beyond the Century of the Child*. Ed. Willem Koops and Michal Zuckerman. Philadelphia: University of Pennsylvania Press, 2003. 82–95.
Hollyman, Sonia. *Mona the Vampire*. London: Orchard Books, 1990.
Ife, Holly. "Doll a Hairy Problem." *Herald Sun*, 14 March 2011. http://www.heraldsun.com.au/archive/news/doll-a-hairy-problem/story-e6frf7l6-1226020730745. Accessed 11 September 2016.
Illbrock, Helmut. *Nostalgia: Origins and Ends of an Unenlightened Disease*. Evanston: Northwestern University Press, 2012.
Jagodzinski, Jan. *Youth Fantasies: The Perverse Landscape of the Media*. London: Palgrave Macmillan, 2004.
Kincaid, James R. *Child-Loving: The Erotic Child and Victorian Culture*. London: Routledge, 1992.
Krips, Valerie. *The Presence of the Past: Memory, Heritage, and Childhood in Postwar Britain*. New York: Garland Publishing, 2000.
Marchesani, Laura. *Dick and Jane and Vampires*. New York: Grosset and Dunlap, 2010.
McKay, Hollie. "Mattel's Waxing and Shaving Monster High Doll Sparks Outrage." *Fox News Entertainment*, 16 March 2011. http://www.foxnews.com/entertainment/2011/03/16/

mattels-waxing-shaving-monster-high-doll-sparks-outrage.html. Accessed 23 August 2016.
"Mona the Vampire." *Publishers Weekly*, 1 November 1991: 80. Biography in Context. http://ic.galegroup.com/ic/bic1/MagazinesDetailsPage/MagazinesDetailsWindow?failOverType=&query=&prodId=BIC1&windowstate=normal&contentModules=&displayquery=&mode=view&displayGroupName=Magazines&limiter=&currPage=&disableHighlighting=false&displayGroups=&sortBy=&search_within_results=&p=BIC1&action=e&catId=&activityType=&scanId=&documentId=GALE%7CA11519823&source=Bookmark&u=scschools&jsid=c55c9c1237a6b105170928974f38cdef. Accessed 24 September 2016.
Newirth, Joseph. *Between Emotion and Cognition: The Generative Unconscious*. New York: Other Press, 2003.
Nodelman, Perry. *The Hidden Adult: Defining Children's Literature*. Baltimore: Johns Hopkins University Press, 2008.
Piatti-Farnell, Lorna. *The Vampire in Contemporary Popular Literature*. London: Routledge, 2014.
Pulera, Dominic. *Visible Differences: Why Race Will Matter to Americans in the Twenty-First Century*. New York: Continuum, 2002.
Rabin, Claire. *Winnicott and "Good Enough" Couple Therapy: Reflections of a Couples Therapist*. London: Routledge, 2014.
Robson, Catherine. *Men in Wonderland: The Lost Girlhood of the Victorian Gentleman*. Princeton: Princeton University Press, 2011.
Schaie, K. Warner. "Historical Processes and Patterns of Cognitive Aging." Ed. Scott M. Hofer and Duane F. Alwin. *Handbook of Cognitive Aging: Interdisciplinary Perspectives*. Los Angeles: SAGE, 2008. 368–383.
Skenazy, Lenore. *Free Range Kids: Giving Our Children the Freedom We Had Without Going Nuts with Worry*. San Francisco: Jossey Bass, 2009.
Stoker, Bram. *Dracula* [1897]. London: Signet Classics, 1996.
True Ghost Tales. *Halloween. Costumes History and Origins*. 2012. http://www.trueghosttales.com/history-halloween-costumes.php. Accessed 24 September 2016.
Weinstock, Jeffrey. *The Vampire Film: Undead Cinema*. London: Wallflower, 2012.
Wong, Shelley. "Transgression as Poesis in The Bluest Eye." *Toni Morrison's The Bluest Eye: Bloom's Modern Critical Interpretations*. Ed. Harold Bloom. New York: Infobase Publishing, 2007. 53–66.

FILMOGRAPHY

Dracula. Dir. Tod Browning. Universal City, CA: Universal Pictures, 1931.
Mona the Vampire. Created by Sonia Hollyman. Halifax, Nova Scotia: DHX Media, 1999–2003.
Nosferatu: A Symphony of Horror [Nosferatu, eine Symphonie des Grauens] Dir. F. W. Murnau. Fine Arts Guild, 1922.
Sesame Street. Created by Joan Ganz Cooney, and Lloyd Morriset. New York City: Children's Television Workshop, 1969–present.
"Smile Time," *Angel* (5:14). Created by Joss Whedon and David Greenwalt. Los Angeles: 20th Television, 2004.

About the Contributors

Simon **Bacon** is an independent scholar who has coedited numerous books, including *Undead Memory, Little Horrors* and *To Boldly Go*. His monograph, *Becoming Vampire*, came out in 2016. He is currently editing *The Gothic* and writing his second monograph, *Dracula and Identity*.

Jen **Baker** received her doctorate from the University of Bristol (UK). Her thesis examined negative and Gothic manifestations of child death in Anglo-American literature and culture. She is cofounder and chief editor of *HARTS & Minds*, and has published on evil children and unsettled childhoods in literature and film.

Jacquelyn E. **Bent** has a Ph.D. in forensic research psychology and works as a professor of managerial analytics in New York. Her writing focuses on the intersection of psychology and pop culture.

Andrew M. **Boylan** has written both fiction and nonfiction within the vampire genre. He is the creator of the long-running blog *Taliesin Meets the Vampires*, which includes a comprehensive review list of vampire-related films and TV shows.

Katarzyna **Bronk** is an assistant professor of English at Adam Mickiewicz University (Poznan, Poland). She was awarded a research grant to study old age and ageing in English theatre and drama. Her research interests include the nature, dynamics and mechanisms of intergenerational contract and conflict.

Mark **Chekares** is an English instructor at Bristol-Plymouth Regional Technical School (Taunton, Massachusetts). He has written about Puritan zombies in *Paranorman* and reanimation of a deceased canine in Tim Burton's *Frankenweenie*. His research interests include animated feature films and sequential art narratives.

Jack **Fennell** teaches English literature at the University of Limerick and is a visiting fellow at the National University of Ireland Galway. He has published on dystopian literature and comic books. He wrote *Irish Science Fiction* and was a translator for *The Short Fiction of Flann O'Brien*. His research interests are science fiction, the Gothic and gender.

Phil **Fitzsimmons** is assistant dean of research in education, business and science at Avondale College of Higher Education (Cooranbong, Australia). He is the author of *Teaching Children's Literature Through the Mayhem of Myth* as well as numerous articles and book chapters.

Chloé **Germaine Buckley** is a senior lecturer at Manchester Metropolitan University (UK). She has published on children's Gothic, weird fiction and witches in media. She is coeditor of *Telling It Slant* and the author of *Twenty-First-Century Children's Gothic*. Her research examines Gothic resistance to imperialism, racism and nationalism.

Jane M. **Kubiesa** is a Ph.D. candidate at the University of Worcester (UK). She researches the Gothic body in contemporary young adult serial vampire fiction. She has published on the vampire maiden, the fin de siècle fallen woman, and the physical fascination of the Victorian era, as well as the cross-generational appeal of *Twilight*.

Allison **Moore** is a senior lecturer in social sciences at Edge Hill University (UK). She has taught across the disciplines of sociology, early childhood studies and childhood and youth. Her research interests include the sociology of sexuality and representations of childhood and youth in popular culture.

Leslie J. **Ormandy** is a composition and English instructor at Clackamas Community College (Oregon) where she teaches about vampires in literature. Her research interests include monsters in children's literature. She has written book chapters on vampires, and she is editor of *The Morals of Monster Stories*.

Sharon **Pajka** is a professor of English at Gallaudet University (Washington, D.C.). She earned her Ph.D. in English education from the University of Virginia. She has published on portrayals of deaf characters in adolescent literature and teaches interdisciplinary courses in the general studies program.

Index

Abbott, Stacey 3, 136, 137, 143
adolescence 50, 54, 55, 85, 110, 135, 147; pre-adolescence 85, 106, 113, 116, 117
adult: absenteeism 33, 54, 66, 113–115; control 3, 12, 33, 54, 74, 102, 127, 141, 163, 166, 185, 193, 195; culture 10, 17–18, 23, 26, 36, 44, 48, 85, 106, 117, 102, 183, 184–5, 187, 196; nostalgia 13, 131, 133, 172, 201–5, 207–8, 210, 213; young 25, 83, 115, 124, 157, 180, 184, 211, 218
agency 3, 5, 6, 8–11, 13, 101–5, 107, 109, 111, 114, 126–8, 139, 142, 180, 184, 193, 197, 207, 213
anti-hero 2, 7, 21, 25, 26
archetype 18, 25, 26, 38, 101, 135, 138, 140, 154
Asma, Stephen 112, 114, 228
Auerbach, Nina 3, 31, 127, 173, 183, 202
authenticity 137, 138, 141
authority 4, 55, 73–5, 99, 104, 105, 108, 114, 127, 133, 155, 179, 180

babies 34, 88, 159, 160, 172, 205
babysitter 112, 186–7, 191–2, 194–5
bat 31, 35, 38, 39, 43, 67, 89, 91, 122, 123, 140, 141, 152, 157, 159, 176, 189, 208; morphing 38, 56, 89, 117, 157, 162, 163, 175; vampire 20, 89, 118, 119
becoming 9, 14, 99, 110, 119, 120, 137, 164, 171, 180, 184, 197
blood 4, 18, 20, 25, 34, 40, 41, 52, 53, 59, 63, 82, 97, 101, 103–9, 110, 121, 140, 156, 166, 181; allergy 5, 12, 172; substitute 23, 25, 56, 84, 160, 167, 174–9, 211, 214
Blood of Dracula 17, 27
bloodlines 103, 153, 159, 211
Bunnicula 22, 27, 167–70, 172, 174, 176, 181, 203, 204–5, 212

Carmilla 4, 6, 14, 96, 97–99, 103–4, 107
Carroll, Noel 115, 155, 165
childhood 8, 12, 45, 50, 59, 63, 124, 132, 139, 141, 144, 157, 161, 171, 172, 181, 183–5, 193, 194, 195–6, 198, 200–1, 203, 206, 208, 212
contagion 38, 95, 96–9, 101, 102, 103, 104–7, 136, 153
costume 1, 58, 59, 206–7, 209, 213
Count Von Count 2, 20–21, 25, 202–3, 204, 212
cruelty 50, 51, 134, 155, 177, 187, 193
culture 1, 2, 4, 5, 6–7, 12, 51, 55, 57, 66, 77, 78, 55, 134, 139, 141, 142, 150, 161, 164, 167, 181, 183, 184, 188, 193, 196, 200, 208, 210, 212; American 67, 68, 138; monster 151–2, 156, 158; youth 17

death 23, 85, 99, 100–101, 121, 122, 123–5, 127, 132, 142, 161, 163, 164, 175, 193
Dhampir 161–2
diet 5, 12, 59, 83, 85, 92, 117, 118, 159, 166–71, 173, 175–8, 180–1
domestic 2, 48, 69, 71, 97, 102, 148, 150, 154, 171, 180, 187, 196
Dracula 1–2, 4, 8, 13–4, 21–4, 30, 31–44, 53, 56, 66–7, 69, 70, 76, 99, 101–5, 106, 107, 139, 142, 153–7, 159–61, 167, 189, 194, 200, 202–5, 209–11
Draculass 57–60
Draculaura 84, 91–2, 211
dream 52, 53, 54, 88, 101, 137, 180, 189, 194; American 132, 208
Duckula 23, 83, 136, 204

evil 24, 29, 43, 51, 78, 83, 84, 85, 116, 123, 128, 139, 143, 155, 186–7, 191, 196; vampire 43, 191

family 4, 5, 17, 19, 24, 34, 39, 56, 77, 85, 88, 97, 116–21, 125, 126–7, 132, 138, 140, 152, 159, 161, 163, 167–70, 172, 175–7, 179, 186, 187, 191, 193, 205, 209, 213; -friendly 2, 6, 12, 20, 22, 203
fangs 10, 13, 24, 56–8, 86, 89, 90, 91, 92, 152, 156, 160–4, 167, 170, 174, 178–9, 202, 203, 209, 211, 214; fake 1, 3, 20, 82, 206–7

220 Index

femininity 7, 8, 9, 43, 57–9, 75, 95–102, 110, 111, 142–3, 146, 190, 192; non-normative 5, 74, 86; vampiric/monstrous 10, 74, 96, 98, 104, 110
feminism 54, 60, 101, 103, 105–7, 109, 132
Frankenstein 34, 104, 189; Monster 4, 9, 19, 20, 21, 23, 152, 204, 210
Freud, Sigmund 45, 83, 112
faze 75, 137, 138, 140, 190–2
fhost 6, 20, 30, 32, 52, 54, 55, 67, 69, 70, 201, 210
fothic 2, 4–12, 29–31, 32, 33, 34, 36, 38–9, 40, 41, 43–5, 5, 63, 65, 66, 76, 81, 82, 85, 91, 95, 103–4, 105, 106–7, 108, 109–110, 134

heteronormative 4, 12, 13, 39, 55, 75, 98, 141, 188–92, 196, 211, 212, 213
homophobia 4, 12, 86, 192, 209
horror 1, 8, 18, 19, 20, 23, 27, 29, 30, 44, 48, 49, 51, 55, 57, 59, 60, 100, 106, 112–3, 115, 135, 151, 156, 184, 202, 204, 205, 214
Hotel Transylvania 12, 25, 150, 163, 164, 185, 187, 189, 194, 204

identity 3, 5, 7, 8, 10, 11, 30, 35, 58, 65, 67, 73, 75, 76, 81, 96, 108, 110, 123, 124, 129, 139, 141, 143, 152, 159, 161, 164, 173, 178, 188, 209, 213
immigrant 9, 64, 65, 66, 68, 76–9, 118, 119, 153

Jung, Karl 9, 10, 83–4, 90

Le Fanu, Sheridan 4, 6, 18, 96, 97, 98, 100
The Little Vampire 6, 22, 26, 56, 115, 185, 186, 191, 195

magic 9, 87, 88, 89, 158, 163, 188, 189
masculinity 43, 64, 65, 96, 97, 98, 110, 164, 188, 190, 192
memory 42, 49, 114, 131, 133, 140, 194
Mona the Vampire 6, 24, 203, 206–207, 209, 213
monster 4, 12, 19, 26, 29–30, 32–3, 37, 39–40, 45, 52, 63, 67, 68, 74–5, 78, 79, 90, 112, 114–6, 128, 134, 138–9, 142, 151–2, 156–64, 173, 176, 181, 183, 189, 194, 194, 198; high 9, 60, 83–7, 91, 92, 203, 210–3; Universal classic 1, 12, 14, 19, 20–1, 23, 210
monstrous 2, 4, 5, 10, 30, 31, 58, 63, 74, 85, 86, 92, 133, 134, 136, 138, 139, 143, 151, 152, 154, 156, 158, 163, 173, 176, 211
Mummy 1, 9, 210
The Munsters 2, 14, 19, 203

nightmare 90, 93, 96, 129, 132, 206
Nosferatu (film) 41, 142, 155, 202
Nosferatu/Orlok 143, 200, 214
nostalgia 13, 88, 131, 133, 140, 141, 146, 200–8, 210–3

orphan 123, 124–5, 126, 193
otherness 2, 4, 6, 9, 10, 58, 79, 106, 134, 160, 209, 212
outsider 5, 6, 9, 7, 125, 152, 205, 207, 212, 213

parents 10, 22, 34, 61, 84, 102, 112–21, 123–5, 127–8, 152, 156–7, 161, 164, 168, 194–5, 206–7, 209, 210, 213; absent 10, 33, 115, 119; dead 115, 116, 123–4, 127; stand-in 113, 125, 128, 170
phallic 164, 192
Polidori, John 6, 154
psyche 82, 83, 89, 90, 112, 143
psychology 41, 50, 97, 109, 119, 132, 135
pureblood 118, 177, 178

racism/anti-Semitism 4, 12, 77, 153–4, 164
resurrection 23, 136, 187
Rice, Anne 2, 100, 204
romance 49, 51, 55, 86, 154, 188
Romania 71, 74, 75, 78, 79, 81, 82, 169
romanticism 2, 14, 25, 42, 50, 85, 161, 190, 192, 202, 213

Scooby Doo 20, 26, 185, 187, 190
Sesame Street 2, 18, 20, 21, 22, 25, 83, 136, 202–3, 204, 212
sexism 12, 57, 88, 191
sexuality 4, 13, 55, 58, 60, 75, 82, 86, 95–9, 101–2, 106, 108, 139, 141, 142, 151, 156, 157, 166, 187–8, 190–2, 196, 209, 211
Stephanou, Aspasia 95, 96, 99, 101, 103, 104, 106, 108, 110, 136, 137, 139, 140, 142
Stoker, Bram 2, 4, 14, 18, 29, 34–6, 37, 38–42, 44, 66, 69, 76, 78, 96, 97, 98–100, 102, 153–5, 202, 205, 207, 211
suburbia 19, 141
supernatural 6, 24, 35, 47, 52, 54, 78, 85, 89, 92, 103, 104, 106, 107, 112, 114, 115, 118, 122, 155, 160, 162, 162, 195
superstition 96, 104
symbolism 1, 7, 13, 17, 18, 25, 31, 83, 136–7, 138, 139–41, 150, 153, 154, 161, 164, 182, 207

teacher 9, 10, 58, 59, 63–9, 71–9, 101, 113, 114, 121, 170, 180, 194
transformation 34, 39, 82, 89, 90, 91, 96, 100, 105, 108, 110, 118, 137, 142, 146, 153, 157, 163, 174, 175, 180, 188, 189, 190, 213
Transylvania 20, 38, 42, 56, 61, 63, 66, 67, 71, 74, 77–8, 80, 161, 202
trauma 10, 113, 124, 160, 201
tweens 10, 84, 112–7, 118, 119, 121–3, 210
Twilight saga 6, 12, 44, 88, 167, 182, 185, 186, 197, 202, 211, 214

undead 1,2, 4, 6, 8, 9, 11, 12, 13, 24, 41, 82, 83, 119, 142, 189, 203, 204, 213
urban legend 60, 85

vampire: bats 89, 117–9, 122, 141, 159, 174–6; child 13, 43, 56, 113, 162, 170, 178, 186; female 4, 5, 8, 10, 18, 24, 47, 52, 57–9, 63, 76, 91–2, 95–100, 106–10, 150, 161, 209; rabbit 22, 167–8, 203; slayer 2, 3, 21, 24, 42, 44, 60, 102, 104, 191, 205; teenager 4, 7, 106, 113, 120
Vampire Dog (film) 25, 185, 186, 187, 189, 192, 193, 194, 204
Vampyre 6, 18, 28, 154, 155
vegetarian 6, 12, 20, 21, 22–3, 63, 84, 166–9, 170, 171–3, 176–81, 204, 205, 211
Victorian 4, 39, 42, 79, 98, 111, 153, 156, 201

Vlad 24, 25, 152, 153, 154, 158, 162–4, 169–72, 181

werewolf 19, 21, 30, 34, 55, 85, 107, 109, 119, 151, 163, 210, 211
Whitby 41, 100, 101
The Wolf Man 1, 19, 20, 23, 210

young adult 83, 107, 115, 116, 125, 157, 166, 180, 184, 202, 206, 211, 213

zombie 14, 45, 151, 157, 161, 190, 207